contents

C
BA
Tec
Tac

HUMAN KINETICS

Library of Congress Cataloging-in-Publication Data

Coaching basketball technical and tactical skills / American Sport Education Program.
  p. cm.
  Includes index.
  ISBN-13: 978-0-7360-4705-0 (soft cover)
  ISBN-10: 0-7360-4705-0 (soft cover)
  1. Basketball--Coaching.   2. School sports--Coaching.   I. American Sport Education
Program.
  GV885.3.C594 2007
  796.3307'7--dc22

                                    2006012162

ISBN-10: 0-7360-4705-0
ISBN-13: 978-0-7360-4705-0

Acquisitions Editor: Amy Tocco; **Project Writer:** Kathy McGee; **Project Consultant:** Don Showalter; **Developmental Editor:** Laura Floch; **Assistant Editors:** Cory Weber and Christine Horger; **Copyeditor:** Patrick Connolly; **Proofreader:** Sarah Wiseman; **Indexers:** Robert and Cynthia Swanson; **Permission Manager:** Carly Breeding; **Graphic Designers:** Bob Reuther and Nancy Rasmus; **Graphic Artists:** Francine Hamerski and Tara Welsch; **Photo Managers:** Dan Wendt and Laura Fitch; **Cover Designer:** Keith Blomberg; **Photographer (cover):** Dan Wendt; **Photographer (interior):** Dan Wendt; **Art Manager:** Kelly Hendren; **Illustrator:** Craig Newsom; **Printer:** Sheridan Books

We thank Flint Powers Catholic High School in Flint, Michigan, for assistance in providing the location for the photo shoot for this book.

Copies of this book are available at special discounts for bulk purchase for sales promotions, premiums, fund-raising, or educational use. Special editions or book excerpts can also be created to specifications. For details, contact the Special Sales Manager at Human Kinetics.

Printed in the United States of America   10 9 8 7 6 5 4 3 2 1

Human Kinetics
Web site: www.HumanKinetics.com

United States: Human Kinetics
P.O. Box 5076
Champaign, IL 61825-5076
800-747-4457
e-mail: humank@hkusa.com

Canada: Human Kinetics
475 Devonshire Road Unit 100
Windsor, ON N8Y 2L5
800-465-7301 (in Canada only)
e-mail: orders@hkcanada.com

Europe: Human Kinetics
107 Bradford Road
Stanningley
Leeds LS28 6AT, United Kingdom
+44 (0) 113 255 5665
e-mail: hk@hkeurope.com

Australia: Human Kinetics
57A Price Avenue
Lower Mitcham, South Australia 5062
08 8372 0999
e-mail: liaw@hkaustralia.com

New Zealand: Human Kinetics
Division of Sports Distributors NZ Ltd.
P.O. Box 300 226 Albany
North Shore City
Auckland
0064 9 448 1207
e-mail: info@humankinetics.co.nz

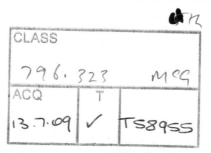

preface

If you are a seasoned basketball coach, you have probably experienced the frustration of watching your players perform well in practice and then seeing them underperform in games. In your playing days, you likely saw the same events unfold. Teammates, or perhaps even you, could shoot 7 out of 10 three-point shots in a shooting drill but could not transfer that kind of performance to games. Although this book will not provide you with a magical quick fix for all your team's problems, it will help you prepare your players for game day. Whether you are a veteran coach or are new to coaching, *Coaching Basketball Technical and Tactical Skills* will help you take your team's game to the next level by providing you with the tools you need to teach your players the game of basketball.

Every basketball coach knows the importance of technical skills. The ability of a player to make effective cuts, make a good outlet pass, shoot a jump shot, or make a good post move can significantly affect the outcome of the game. This book discusses the basic and intermediate technical skills necessary for your team's success. You will learn how to detect and correct errors in your athletes' performance of those skills and how to help them transfer the knowledge and ability that they gain in practice to execution in games.

Besides covering technical skills, the book also focuses on tactical skills, including offensive skills such as the skip pass, the give-and-go, and the backdoor cut, as well as defensive skills such as on-the-ball and off-the-ball defense, switching on the screen, and double teaming the post. The book discusses the tactical triangle, an approach that teaches players to read a situation, acquire the knowledge that they need to make a tactical decision, and apply decision-making skills to the problem. To advance this method, the book covers important cues that help athletes respond appropriately when they see a play developing, including rules, game strategies, and the strengths and weaknesses of opponents.

The book also covers planning at several levels by offering sample practice and season plans based on the games approach. The season plan lays out a season based on developing the skills in this book. The practice plans include a description of eight practice sessions, covering elements such as the length of the practice session, the objective of the practice, the equipment needed, the warm-up, practice of previously taught skills, teaching and practicing new skills, the cool-down, and evaluation.

Of course, playing the games is what your practices eventually lead to. The book shows you how to prepare long before the first game, including issues such as communicating with players, parents, officials, and the media; scouting your opponent; and motivating your players. You will learn how to control your team's performance on game day by managing such elements as the pregame routine, the warm-up, substitutions, time-outs, and end-of-game situations.

PART I

Teaching and Evaluating

Being a good coach takes more than knowing the sport of basketball. You have to go beyond that and find a way to teach your athletes how to be better players. To find effective ways to improve your players' performance, you must know how to teach and evaluate them.

In chapter 1, we go over the fundamentals of teaching sport skills. We first provide a general overview of the sport of basketball and talk about the importance of being an effective teacher. Next, we define some important skills, helping you gain a better understanding of technical and tactical skills, and we discuss the traditional and games approaches to coaching.

In chapter 2, we build on the knowledge of how to teach sport skills by covering the evaluation of technical and tactical skills. We discuss the importance of evaluating athletes, and we review the core skills that you should assess and how you can best do so. This chapter stresses the importance of preseason, inseason, and postseason evaluation, and it provides you with sample tools that you can use to evaluate your players.

By learning how to teach and evaluate your players, you will be better prepared to help them improve their performance.

chapter 1

Teaching Sport Skills

In 1891, Dr. James Naismith, a faculty member at the International YMCA Training School in Springfield, Massachusetts (now known as Springfield College), invented basketball as a competitive game that could be played indoors during the winter months. The game has changed and evolved a great deal since its inception. Today, basketball is played at all levels from youth to professional, and basketball at the high school level is one of the most popular sports in America for both men and women. Basketball has become a game of skill, teamwork, and strategy.

Effective Teaching

It is one thing to understand basketball skills, but being able to teach those skills is an entirely different thing. To be able to change your athletes' ability to perform basketball skills in both practice and games, you must be a master teacher and an excellent coach.

Many people think that a person who excelled in basketball as a player would make an excellent coach. But, being a good player does not always equate to being a good coach. To effectively coach, a person must be an effective teacher, because teaching is the essence of good coaching. As a coach, you must teach the skills that are essential to playing basketball successfully, but you also need to recognize the impact and influence that you have on your players' lives. With this comes a tremendous responsibility.

Good coaches, then, not only teach the mechanics of the game but also understand the way that athletes learn. Rather than tell players how to play, good coaches teach them how to learn the game for themselves. This approach demands that you do more than just work with the Xs and Os. The great player is the sum of many parts: technical skill, tactical skill, physical ability, mental acuity, communication proficiency, and strength of character (Rainer Martens, *Successful Coaching, Third Edition*, Champaign, IL: Human Kinetics, 2004, pp. 186-188). Although all of these skills are important, this book focuses on the technical and tactical skills that you need to be aware of in coaching basketball. To learn more about other skills that should be part of the makeup of a great athlete, refer to Rainer Martens' *Successful Coaching, Third Edition*.

As you are well aware, once your players take the court, they are in control. That's what you want as a coach—for your athletes to be able to perform the skills you have taught them. Your job as a coach is to prepare them to perform to their potential. Teaching your players the most essential tactical skills in basketball will help them to be prepared. It will help them make the most of game situations. It will also help you feel comfortable when your players take the court, because you will know that you have prepared them for the situations they are about to face.

Technical and Tactical Skills

As a coach, you have the responsibility of patiently and systematically explaining and drilling the athletes on the basic skills, position by position, that make up the game. These skills, called *technical skills*, are the fundamentals that provide each player with the tools to execute the physical requirements of the game. Each day at practice, you must also create scenarios on the court that require players to use their technical skills in a gamelike situation, forcing them to make decisions that simulate the choices that they will have to make in a game. These skills, called *tactical skills*, are the bridge between practice performance and game performance. Although the proper execution of technical skills is necessary for success, the tactical skills (i.e., the ability of the athletes to make the appropriate decisions) are the key to having everything come together when it counts—in the game.

The game of basketball involves a tremendous number of technical and tactical skills. Volumes have been written about basketball skills through the years, and it would be impossible to discuss all of these skills in this book. Consequently, we focus on the basic to intermediate technical and tactical skills that are essential in basketball. These skills were compiled with the help of the Women's Basketball Coaches Association (WBCA). The goal is to provide a resource that will help you improve your understanding and your instructional methods as you strive to teach your players the great game of basketball.

Technical Skills

We all know the importance of acquiring the technical skills in basketball. The proper execution of these technical skills by your athletes greatly affects the game. Technical skills may be defined as "the specific procedures to move one's body to perform the task that needs to be accomplished" (Martens, *Successful Coaching, Third Edition*, p. 169). You probably know many if not all of the technical skills that are necessary to succeed in basketball. For instance, when you think of technical skills in basketball, you may think of dribbling, passing, and shooting. However, your knowledge of the proper execution of those technical skills, your ability to effectively teach players how to perform those skills, your ability to detect errors and correct those errors, and your ability to recognize when those skills come into play within a game situation are all things that you will further develop over time, as you gain experience. We want to help you get there sooner. We want to take you from your current level of knowledge and help you go beyond this by learning how to

- focus on the key points of each skill,
- detect errors in an athlete's performance of those skills,
- correct the errors that athletes make, and
- help athletes transfer the knowledge and ability that they gain in practice to execution in games.

Tactical Skills

Although mastering the technical skills of basketball is very important, it is not enough to succeed in the sport. In addition to knowing how to technically play the game, your athletes also need to know how to play the game tactically. Resources on basketball have often overlooked the tactical aspect of the game, and even you may tend to leave tactics out of many of your practices. Sometimes, coaches can get so focused on the technical skills that they lose sight of the tactics.

Tactical skills can best be defined as "the decisions and actions of players in the contest to gain an advantage over the opposing team or players" (Martens, *Successful Coaching, Third Edition*, p. 170). One way that coaches can approach teaching tactical skills is by focusing on three critical aspects known as the *tactical triangle*:*

- Reading the play or situation
- Acquiring the knowledge needed to make an appropriate tactical decision
- Applying decision-making skills to the problem

This book provides you with the knowledge you need to teach players how to use the tactical triangle. Part III covers important cues that help athletes respond appropriately when they see a play developing—including rules, game strategies, and strengths and weaknesses of opponents that affect game situations—as well as ways to teach athletes how to acquire and use this knowledge. Part III will help you teach athletes how to make appropriate choices in a given situation and will show you how to empower players to recognize emerging situations on their own and make sound judgments.

Anyone who has observed basketball for any length of time has witnessed players making errors in games on plays that they have practiced many times in training sessions. Such situations can cause tremendous frustration, for both players and coaches. As you will see, however, these errors can be prevented!

---

*Reprinted, by permission, from R. Martens, 2004, *Successful coaching*, 3rd ed. (Champaign, IL: Human Kinetics), 215.

Traditional Versus Games Approach to Coaching

As mentioned previously, transferring skills from practice to games can be difficult. A sound background of technical and tactical training prepares athletes for game situations. But by incorporating gamelike situations into daily training, you can further enhance the likelihood that players will transfer skills from practices to games. To understand how to accomplish this, you must be aware of two approaches to coaching: the traditional approach and the games approach.

Part IV of this book provides examples of both the traditional approach and the games approach to coaching. Although each style has its particular advantages, the concept favored in this book is the games approach. The games approach provides athletes with a competitive situation governed by clear objectives and focused on specific individuals and concepts. The games approach creates a productive and meaningful learning environment in which athletes are motivated by both the structure of the drills and the improvement that they make. Finally, the games approach prepares athletes for competition because they have experienced settings that closely resemble the tactical situations that they will see in the game.

Traditional Approach

Most coaches are comfortable with the traditional approach to coaching. This method often begins with a warm-up period followed by a set of drills, a scrimmage, and finally a cool-down period. This approach can be useful in teaching the technical skills of basketball; however, unless coaches shape, focus, and enhance the scrimmages or drills, the athletes may not successfully translate the skills to game situations, leaving coaches to ponder why their team practices better than it plays.

Games Approach

Have you ever noticed how some athletes are great practice players, but when it comes to the game, they choke? When this happens, it is frustrating for the coach as well as the player. The best way to prevent this from happening is to provide your athletes with gamelike situations to practice the skills that you are teaching them. The games approach to coaching does just that.

The games approach is a coaching philosophy that stresses the importance of putting the skills that you teach your athletes into practice. You can drill your players on those skills over and over again. However, if the players do not get the opportunity to practice the skills in a gamelike situation, they won't be able to perform them in the actual game, when it really counts. You probably incorporate scrimmages into your practice sessions. Although scrimmages are beneficial because they provide gamelike situations, you need to do more. As a coach and an educator, you need to carefully plan and execute your practices in order for your players to get the most out of each practice experience. The games approach to coaching helps you do this.

The games approach emphasizes the use of games and minigames to help coaches provide their athletes with situations that are as close to a real game as possible (Launder, Alan G., *Play Practice*. Champaign, IL: Human Kinetics, 2001). But this method requires more than just putting the players on the court, throwing out a ball, and letting them play. You should use the following three components any time you use the games approach:

1. Shaping
2. Focusing
3. Enhancing

Shaping play allows you to modify the game in a way that is conducive to learning particular skills or concepts. You can shape play by modifying the rules, the environment (playing area), the objectives of the game, and the number of players (Launder, p. 56). In scrimmage situations, the stronger players often dominate, while the weaker players merely get through the scrimmage without playing a strong, active role. If you shape play by reducing the playing area or the number of players, every athlete will have the opportunity to learn and practice the skills for his or her position.

However, you cannot just shape the play and expect miracles. Rather, you need to be sure to focus your athletes on the specific objectives that you are trying to achieve in the game. Players are more apt to learn, or at least be more open to learning, if they know why they are trying to grasp the new information. They need to see how it fits into the bigger picture. You can help your players with this by providing them with clear objectives to achieve and by explaining how accomplishing these objectives will enhance their ability to play basketball.

Shaping play and focusing your athletes on specific objectives will not do them any good unless you play an active role and work on enhancing the play. By carefully watching your athletes play, you can stop the game when you recognize an opportunity to teach your athletes something that will enhance their play even further. For example, let's take a look at a game called "Switch on Screens." In this game, two minutes are set on the clock, and players play four on four. Players on defense must switch on all screens, and offensive players are given very specific rules to use down screens (toward the baseline) on all passes. The modifications made for this game allow players to focus only on the switch and on the skills used when switching on screens.

You have probably used the games approach in some way or another in your practices. Although you may have an understanding of how to use this approach, this book will take you a step further by showing you specific games that you can use to create great learning experiences for your athletes. In addition, as you gain a better understanding of this approach, you will be able to create additional games on your own.

Coaching basketball is a tough yet rewarding job. Basketball coaches are responsible not only for the development of good players, but also for the development of young men and women who know right from wrong and know how to make good behavioral decisions. The emphasis of this book is on the concepts and strategies of teaching the basic to intermediate technical and tactical skills of basketball, using both the traditional and games approaches. This book will provide you with a foundation for effective teaching. It will help you master the art of helping your athletes refine and improve the array of skills and techniques that make up the diverse, fascinating, and great game of basketball.

chapter 2

Evaluating Technical and Tactical Skills

Basketball is a team sport. In building your team, you should use specific evaluation tools to assess the development of the individual parts that make up the whole of the team. You must remember that basic physical skills contribute to the performance of the technical and tactical skills. In addition, a vast array of nonphysical skills—such as mental, communication, and character skills—overlay athletic performance and affect its development (Rainer Martens, *Successful Coaching, Third Edition*). In this chapter, we examine evaluation guidelines, exploring specific skills that should be evaluated and the tools to evaluate them. Evaluations as described in this chapter will help you produce more objective critiques of your players, something that you should continually reach for.

Guidelines for Evaluation

Regardless of the skill that you are measuring and the evaluation tool that you are using, you should observe the basic guidelines that govern the testing and evaluation process.

Understanding the Purpose

The athletes need to know and understand the purpose of the test and its relationship to the sport. If you are evaluating a technical skill, the correlation should be easy. But when you are evaluating physical, mental, communication, or character skills, you must explain the correlation between the skill and the aspect of the game that it will benefit.

Creating Motivation for Improvement

You must motivate the athletes to improve. Understanding the correlation between the skill and the game will help, but sometimes the games seem a long way off during practices and training. In the physical skills area, elevating the status of the testing process can help inspire the athletes. If you can create a game day atmosphere with many players present and watching as you conduct the testing, the athletes will compete with more energy and enthusiasm than they would if you ran the tests in a more clinical fashion. Goal boards and record boards that list all-time best performances can also motivate the athletes. These boards are most effective when they have several categories (e.g., separating guards from forwards and post players, so that guards can compete against each other in speed and agility and post players can compete with each other in strength) and when they list several places, such as the top 5 or top 10 performances, to give more athletes a reasonable chance to compete for a spot on the board.

The best motivation, though, is the concept of striving for a personal best effort in physical skills testing, or striving for an improved score compared to the athlete's last evaluation on measurements of technical, tactical, communication, and mental skills. When the athletes compare themselves today to themselves yesterday, they can always succeed and make progress, regardless of the achievements of their teammates. And when the athletes see themselves making progress, they will be motivated to continue to practice and train. This concept, while focusing on the individual, is not antithetical to the team concept. You simply need to remind the team that if every player gets better every day, the team must be getting better every day!

Providing Objective Measurement

All testing must be unbiased, formal, and consistent. Athletes will easily recognize flaws in the testing process, and when this occurs, they will lose confidence in the results. For the test to have any integrity, you must be systematic and accurate and must treat every athlete the same way. No athlete can be credited with a test result on a physical skill if he or she does not execute the test regimen perfectly. You must mandate good form and attention to the details of the test. The same is true of evaluation tools that do not involve quantitative measures. A coach who wants to evaluate technical skills must use the same tool for all athletes and must score them fairly and consistently in order for the athletes to trust the conclusions reached.

Providing Effective Feedback

You must convey the feedback to the athletes professionally and, if possible, personally. No athlete wants to fail, and all are self-conscious to a certain extent when they don't perform to their expectations or the expectations of their coach. At the same time, all athletes have areas that they need to improve, and you must communicate those needs to the athletes, especially if the athletes do not see or understand the need to make the improvement! Personal, private meetings with athletes are crucial to the exchange of this information. Factual results, comparative charts ranking the athlete, historical records of previous test results, and even reviews of videotape of the athlete's performances can be used to communicate both the positive areas of improvement and the areas where progress needs to be made. If you have a large number of athletes, you can accomplish these individual meetings in occasional and subtle ways—by asking the athlete to stay for a few minutes in the office after a position group meeting, by finding the athlete in the locker room after practice or a workout, by going out to practice early and creating an opportunity to talk to the player individually, or by calling the player into the office at random times just to talk. These in-person, one-on-one meetings are by far the best method to communicate to athletes the areas in which they need to improve.

Being Credible

You must apply the principles that you are asking your players to live by to the process of evaluating them. You must have expert knowledge of the technical and tactical skills for your sport so that you can accurately and consistently evaluate the skills that you see your players perform. You must understand the value of the physical skills (perhaps even in your personal lifestyle and health habits!) in order to convey the importance of these skills to the game. You must exhibit outstanding communication skills to be effective in your teaching, and you must exhibit those same skills in your dealings with other staff members, especially when you are visible to the players, so that you can establish credibility with the players regarding communication.

Evaluating Skills

Clearly, players must know the technical skills demanded by their sport, and they must know how to apply those skills in tactical situations when they compete. You must remember, however, that basic physical skills contribute to the performance of the technical and tactical skills and must be incorporated into the athlete's training plan. In addition, many nonphysical skills (such as mental capacity, communication skills, and character skills) are important to athletic performance and affect its development.

As you evaluate your athletes, one concept is crucial: Athletes should focus on trying to improve their own previous performance, as opposed to comparing their performance to those of teammates. Certainly, comparative data can help athletes see where they rank on the team and perhaps among other players at their position, and this kind of information may motivate players or help them set goals. But all rankings place some athletes on the team below others, and the danger of focusing on this type of system is that athletes can easily become discouraged if they consistently rank in the bottom part of the team. Conversely, if the focus of the evaluation is on every player improving compared with his or her own performance at the last testing, then every player on the team can be successful every time tests are conducted. Whether you are looking at physical skills or nonphysical skills, you should encourage your athletes to achieve their own personal best.

Evaluating Physical Skills

The essential physical skills for basketball are strength, speed, flexibility, and agility. The training and evaluation of those four physical skills are especially important in the off-season and preseason periods, when athletes are concentrating on overall improvement. In-season evaluation, however, is also important to ensure that any off-season gains, especially in strength, do not deteriorate because the players and coaches are devoting much of their time and attention to preparing game plans and practicing.

Testing should occur at least three times a year—once immediately before the basketball season begins to gauge the athlete's readiness for the season, once after the season to measure the retention of physical skills during competition, and once in the spring to evaluate the athlete's progress and development in the off-season program. In addition, you will constantly be evaluating your athletes throughout the season to make slight adjustments.

Of course, training programs can positively affect several skills. For example, improvements in leg strength and flexibility will almost certainly improve speed and jumping ability. Furthermore, no specific workout program will ensure gains for every athlete in each of the four skill areas. Consequently, testing and measurement of gains in these areas are critical in showing you and the athletes where they are making gains and where to place the emphasis of subsequent training programs.

Strength

Strength testing can be done safely and efficiently using multiple-rep projections of an athlete's maximum performance. The risk of injury for the athletes is minimal because they are working with a weight that is less than their maximum load. After a proper warm-up, the athletes should select a weight that they believe they can lift at least three but no more than seven repetitions. Using a chart of projected totals, the number of reps that each athlete accomplishes will yield his or her maximum load. This type of test is slightly less accurate than a one-repetition max test, in which athletes continue to work with heavier weights until they find the highest load that they can lift for one repetition. But the one-repetition max test takes much longer to administer and is not as safe because the athletes are working with peak loads. Furthermore, the accuracy of the test would be critical only if the athletes were competing with each other. Because the focus of the off-season training program is the development and improvement of each athlete, the multiple-rep projection is adequate for allowing each athlete to compare the test result with his or her own previous performances.

Speed

Speed training in the off-season can improve a basketball player's overall performance. Although strength exercises will help overall performance, if you want your players to improve their speed, the focus should be on resistance exercises that are more specific to the act of running, such as running uphill or using running parachutes or harnesses. Testing the players on sprint times before and after the resistance training will help motivate them throughout the off-season.

Flexibility

Flexibility is the most neglected physical skill but one of the most important. Increases in flexibility will help athletes improve their performance in just about every other physical skill. Off-season programs should stress stretching, and you should encourage (or mandate) athletes to stretch for at least 15 minutes each day. In addition, the training program should include exercises that require the athlete to bend and move—such as lunges, step-ups, and so on—so that the athlete

CORE STRENGTH

Like the proverbial chain that is only as strong as its weakest link, the core ultimately determines whether athletes can put it all together and translate their strength, speed, or agility into successful basketball performance. The *core* refers to the midsection of the body—the abdominal muscles, the lower back muscles, and the muscles of the hip girdle. These muscles connect lower body strength and functions with upper body strength and functions. Core strength, then, is essential for basketball, but at the same time, it is extremely difficult to isolate and test.

Basketball coaches repeatedly use the phrase "stay down" to emphasize the importance of keeping the legs bent and the center of gravity close to the ground for improved balance and quickness. Without a strong core, a basketball player will experience great difficulty in staying down while playing the game. The core also must be strong for a basketball player to be able to play with great explosiveness—combining strength, power, and speed into pulling rebounds down or taking the ball to the basket in traffic. Therefore, every physical training program for basketball must include exercises that strengthen and develop the core. This training program must go beyond sit-ups and crunches, which are important but not comprehensive enough to develop true core strength. Basketball players must incorporate active exercises such as lunges, step-ups, and jump squats to focus on development of the core.

As mentioned before, isolating core strength is difficult because it is involved in the performance of every physical skill. But any exercise that recruits one or more large muscle areas and two or more primary joints (such as the bench press) can be used to test core strength (NSCA, *Essentials of Personal Training*). The ultimate evaluation of core strength, however, is the athlete's performance of basketball skills in practices and games.

is stretching and training the hip girdle and lower back area while working on strength and power. While an individual's level of flexibility is difficult to measure, the classic sit-and-reach test provides a reasonable indication of the athlete's range and gives the athlete a standard to improve on.

Agility

The sport of basketball requires the athlete to change direction quickly; therefore, agility (balance and footwork) is a prerequisite for executing the fundamentals of the game and is a physical skill that must be continually trained and measured. The most common agility test for basketball is a 20-yard lateral shuttle run. In this test, the athlete starts on a designated line and runs 5 yards to the left or right, returns through the starting point to a spot 5 yards on the other side of that starting point, and then moves back to finish at the point where the athlete started (the yardage run is 5, 10, and 5). This test measures the athlete's ability to plant and change directions, and it requires the athlete to keep the core of the body low (in the athletic body position mentioned frequently throughout this book). The time on the lateral shuttle run should be about two-tenths of a second less than the athlete's 40-yard dash time. If the margin is greater, the athlete should emphasize speed development in his or her training program; if the margin is less, the athlete should emphasize agility drills in his or her training program.

Evaluating Nonphysical Skills

Athletic performance is not purely physical. A number of other factors influence it. You must recognize and emphasize mental skills, communication skills, and character skills to enable your athletes to reach peak athletic performance.

Despite the importance of the physical, mental, communication, and character skills, the emphasis in this book is on the coaching of essential technical and tactical skills. For an in-depth discussion of how to teach and develop both physical and nonphysical skills, refer to chapters 9 through 12 in Rainer Martens' *Successful Coaching, Third Edition*.

Mental Skills

Basketball is a fast moving game where players move from offense to defense in a split second and teams play multiple defenses and run complex offensive patterns. Successful basketball players must have the mental ability to sort out and isolate the cues that allow them to execute those offenses and defenses properly in a game. Guards have to see their teammates coming off screens—and see the defenders reacting—so that they can read what the play is and where it is going. Post players have to anticipate the skip pass so they can seal their defender before making a flash cut across the lane. A defender on the weak side has to be in good help position to be able to anticipate the pass and help on the pass to the post. The performance of these skills takes study, discipline, focus, and a belief that the system of cues will produce the desired results. The term *mental toughness* might be the best and simplest way to describe the concentration and determination required to perform these skills in the fast paced, high-intensity game of basketball.

Communication Skills

Basketball also requires strong communication skills at several levels—for example, among the players on the court and between the coaches and the players in classrooms, in practices, and on the sidelines during games. Basketball players need to be able to adjust to changing offenses and defenses, and clear communication is critical for all players to be on the same page during a game. You, as a coach, also have to convey adjustments to the game plan and strategy during time-outs and halftime talks. All these communication skills are essential to the sport of basketball, and you must spend considerable time coordinating your system of communication.

Character Skills

Finally, character skills help shape the performance of the team. Although the game is physical and fast paced, officials regulate it so that it remains fair and safe. Basketball players must play hard and aggressively, but within the rules of the game. They must show respect for the opponents as well as the officials. They must avoid any trash talk, unnecessary roughness, and displays of inappropriate behavior. Failure to follow these rules results in technical fouls or disqualification, and both outcomes clearly affect the team's performance. In all these cases, the team that has the most character among its players will have the best chance for success.

Evaluation Tools

Coaches have many tools to aid them in the evaluation process. As always, player and team statistics are readily available and, in addition to video, remain the main source of comparison and evaluation in the day-to-day workings of the game. However, new methods may provide a more well-rounded way of assessing skills. In recent years, many innovative charts have been developed to help coaches assess performance beyond what standard statistics may reveal.

Coaches sometimes read too much into statistics. The stats called in to the media are somewhat misleading because they do not truly capture the performance of your players. Many players play a role that cannot be seen in the stat sheet. For example, let's say that 10 made shots came off of perfectly set screens by player A. If player B, C, and D get all the credit for the 20 points in your evaluation, then player A probably won't be so interested in setting that outstanding screen. Therefore, much more than just statistics needs to go into your evaluation of players' performance. If only statistics are used, a fair evaluation of a player's tactical and technical skill development cannot be completed. Instead, coaches need a system to evaluate the technical and tactical skills required for basketball on a more detailed "skill-by-skill" basis. They need an instrument that allows them to look not only at the end result (e.g., scoring average) but also at the key elements, whether mechanical or strategically related, that determine the basketball player's ability to complete a task well.

Figures 2.1, *a* and *b*, are examples of an evaluation tool that allows you to isolate technical and tactical skills. By breaking down the skill into its component parts, this tool provides a more objective assessment of an athlete's performance of a skill than can be produced by statistics. You can use these figures (along with the information in parts II and III of this book) as a guide to create an evaluation tool for each of the technical and tactical skills that you want to evaluate during your season. For example, in figure 2.1*a*, we have broken down the technical skill of the bounce pass by pulling out each of the key points for the skill as described in chapter 3. This enables you to rate your players' execution of the skill in specific targeted areas.

As you may know, evaluating tactical skills is more difficult because there are many outside influences that factor into how and when the skill comes into play. However, as a coach, you can use a similar format to evaluate your players' execution of tactical skills. You will need to do the legwork in breaking down the skill into targeted areas, but in figure 2.1*b*, we have used a generic format to show you how you can break tactical skills down using the information found in chapters 5 and 6 as a guideline.

This evaluation tool, and the process of scoring that it advocates, may help you avoid the common pitfall of becoming preoccupied with the result of the skill and coaching and evaluating only the final outcome. This tool will help you pinpoint where errors are occurring and will enable you to focus on correcting those errors with your athletes.

This tool, by its very nature, however, is rather subjective. It asks the evaluator to rate on a 1 to 5 scale how well the player executes the basic elements of each technical or tactical skill, and those ratings would simply be the coaching staff's opinions based on their observations. However, the coach could add some statistical weight to the process by scoring the player on each play where the skill comes into use. For example, during a game, the coach could keep track of the number of shots taken off the pass and could score the player on his or her quickness getting to the ball, coming off a screen, or elevating with the shot. In this way, the coach could come up with a "new" statistic. Shooting percentage simply "grades" players on whether or not they are making the shots, but by tweaking the stat this way, the coach can better evaluate the shooter by pinpointing the area where the skill breaks down and analyzing each of the component parts. Knowing the exact part where the skill erodes can help the coach modify practices, enabling the player to work on overcoming the problem with the skill.

This evaluation tool enables you to go beyond the end result of a skill (e.g., points scored or assists) and focus your teaching on the cues and knowledge needed to execute a specific skill, giving the athletes an evaluation that alerts them to the

Figure 2.1a   Bounce Pass Evaluation

| Key Focal Points | SKILL RATING | | | | | Notes |
	Weak 1	2	3	4	Strong 5	
Proper stance	1	2	3	4	5	
Hand and arm positioning	1	2	3	4	5	
Stepping into the pass	1	2	3	4	5	
Accuracy on the bounce	1	2	3	4	5	

From ASEP, 2007, *Coaching Basketball Technical and Tactical Skills,* (Champaign, IL: Human Kinetics).

Figure 2.1b   Switching on a Screen Evaluation

| Player's Ability | SKILL RATING | | | | | Notes |
	Weak 1	2	3	4	Strong 5	
Avoids distractions as discussed in "Watch Out!"	1	2	3	4	5	
Reads the situation	1	2	3	4	5	
Uses the appropriate knowledge about the rules	1	2	3	4	5	
Uses the appropriate knowledge about the opponent's strengths and weaknesses	1	2	3	4	5	
Uses the appropriate self-knowledge	1	2	3	4	5	

From ASEP, 2007, *Coaching Basketball Technical and Tactical Skills,* (Champaign, IL: Human Kinetics).

key elements of the skill that need improvement. An important corollary to this teaching and evaluation strategy, then, is that sometimes when the result is positive, the evaluation of the athlete's technique might be substantially critical. The University of Michigan recently conducted a study of high school athletes and the expectations they had of their coaches. The top three expectations discovered were (1) that the coach not show favoritism; (2) that the coach be concerned with the individual, not just winning; and (3) that the coach have a positive attitude. This shows that coaches shouldn't neglect their interpersonal skills when dealing with their players.

For example, let's assume that the opposing team just put on a full-court press and that your team turned the ball over two consecutive times, so you call a time-out to make adjustments. The point guard may already know that he or she should keep good spacing on the court and not dribble into the trap. To merely tell the guard to stop dribbling into the trap without giving him or her some positive feedback would be counterproductive. Instead of just stating the obvious, you should talk to the guard about where the skill is breaking down—for example, you may have noticed that the guard was using the dribble too soon (and thus limiting the available options) and that a quick pass before the trap is started would be more effective.

Of course, the coach is powerless to help athletes in this way unless the coach knows and understands the key elements of each skill. Thus, the following chapters in this book are designed to provide that information to the coach. And by using the information on the technical and tactical skills outlined in parts II and III as a guide, coaches will be able to create evaluation tools like the one shown in figure 2.1 for each of the skills as they see fit during the course of the season.

The sample evaluation tool shown in figure 2.1, *a* and *b*, constitutes a simple way to use the details of each technical and tactical skill. It provides an outline for both you and the players to review as well as a mechanism for understanding the areas in which improvement is needed. The tool can also be used as a summary exercise. After a game, a week of practice, or a preseason or spring practice segment, the athletes can each score themselves on all their essential technical and tactical skills (including all the cues and focal points) and on as many of the corollary skills as desired. You can also score each athlete and then compare the two score sheets. The ensuing discussion will provide both you and the players with a direction for future practices and drills, helping you decide where the immediate focus of attention needs to be for the athletes to improve their performance. You can repeat this process later so that the athletes can look for improvement in the areas where they have been concentrating their workouts. As the process unfolds, a better consensus between the athlete's score sheet and your score sheet should also occur.

You must display the same mental skills that you ask your athletes to display—skills such as emotional control, self-confidence, and motivation to achieve—because the players will mirror your mental outlook. Likewise, players will model your character in terms of your trustworthiness, fairness, and ability to earn respect. You are a role model, whether you want to be or not, and the athletes will develop the proper mental and character skills only if you display those skills.

You must evaluate athletes in many areas and in many ways. This process of teaching, evaluating, and motivating athletes to improve their performance defines the job of the coach: "taking the athletes somewhere they could not get to by themselves." Without you, the athletes would not have a clear picture of the steps that they need to take, or how they should proceed, to become better players. You provide the expertise, guidance, and incentive for the athletes to make progress.

One final rule, however, caps the discussion of evaluating athletes. Athletes in every sport want to know how much you care before they care how much you know. You need to keep in mind that at times you must suspend the process of teaching and evaluating in order to deal with the athlete as a person. You must spend time with your athletes discussing topics other than their sport and their performance. You must show each athlete that you have an interest in and a concern for him or her as a person. Your athletes should know that you are willing to listen to their issues and that you are willing to assist them (if doing so is legal and they wish to be helped). Events in the athletes' personal life can overshadow their athletic quests, and you must be sensitive to that reality.

Now, it is time to start gaining a better understanding of the basic to intermediate technical and tactical skills of basketball. Becoming an expert on these skills will enable you to evaluate your athletes on the skills, help the athletes master the skills, and take your team to an even higher level.

PART II

Teaching Technical Skills

Now that you know how to teach and evaluate sport skills, you are ready to dive into the specific skills necessary for success in basketball. This part focuses on the basic and intermediate skills necessary for your team's success, including offensive technical skills related to passing, dribbling, offensive rebounding, and shooting, as well as defensive skills such as defensive positioning, blocking shots, defensive rebounding, and defending cuts and screens.

For each skill, we first present the "key points" for the particular skill. These points highlight the most important aspects of the skill, providing you and your players with a road map to proper execution of the skill. The remainder of the information for the skill is a detailed explanation of these essential components, including instructional photos and diagrams to guide you along the way.

For each skill, we also include a table that identifies common errors and describes how you can help your athletes correct those errors. To close the discussion of each skill, we include a useful "At a Glance" section to guide you to other tools in the book that will help you teach your athletes this particular skill—whether it is another technical skill that the players need to be able to perform to be successful, a tactical skill that uses this technical skill, or a practice plan or drill that can help you teach the skill.

chapter 3

Offensive Technical Skills

This chapter covers the offensive technical skills that you and your players must know to be successful. In this chapter, you will find the following skills:

Offensive Footwork

KEY POINTS

The most important components of offensive footwork are

○ proper stance,

○ starts and stops,

○ pivots, and

○ change of pace and direction.

Quickness and balance are fundamental to all skills in basketball. Simply put, balance is body control and readiness to make sudden movements. Without proper balance, your players will never be quick. And, in order for your players to develop proper balance and quickness, they must first develop proper footwork.

PROPER STANCE

To properly move and control their body, players must understand the role of the basic athletic stance (see figure 3.1). Players must be in a well-balanced athletic stance at all times. This stance will allow them to move quickly, change direction, jump, and stop under control.

Figure 3.1   Basic athletic stance for offense.

This athletic stance starts with the player getting low by bending the knees. The head is key to balance and should be positioned over the support base, slightly behind the knees and over the waist, with the back straight. The player should always keep the arms and hands above the waist, close to the body, with the elbows flexed.

When in the athletic stance, the player's feet should always be at least shoulder-width apart, with the weight evenly distributed on the balls of the feet. A staggered stance, where the lead foot (shooting foot) instep is on the same horizontal line as the toe of the other foot, allows a player to move quickly in any direction (see figure 3.2a). A parallel stance, where both feet are parallel to one another, is effective in jump stopping with or without the basketball (see figure 3.2b).

STARTS AND STOPS

The ability to move with and without the ball is essential to any individual offensive move. Starting and stopping are extremely important aspects of these movements. To start quickly, players must be in an athletic stance and shift their weight in the direction they intend to move, taking the first step with the nearest foot. For example, if a player is going to move left, the player will lead with the left foot.

Stopping quickly is just as important as starting quickly. Two types of stops are commonly used by offensive players: the two-step stop and the jump stop.

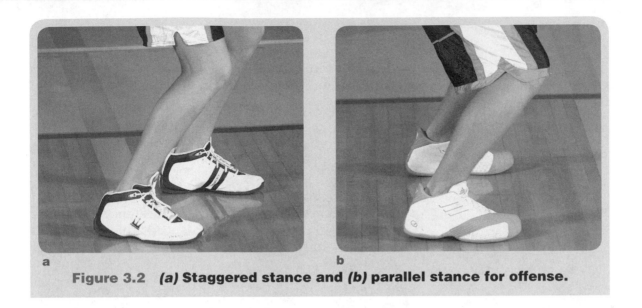

Figure 3.2   *(a)* **Staggered stance and *(b)* parallel stance for offense.**

Two-Step Stop

A two-step stop is executed by landing on the back foot first (see figure 3.3*a*); the front foot lands immediately after the back foot (see figure 3.3*b*). When a player uses this stop after catching a pass or ending a dribble, the player's back foot becomes the pivot foot. For example, when catching a pass on the perimeter, a player can use this stop effectively by landing on the inside foot first and then pivoting for the shot.

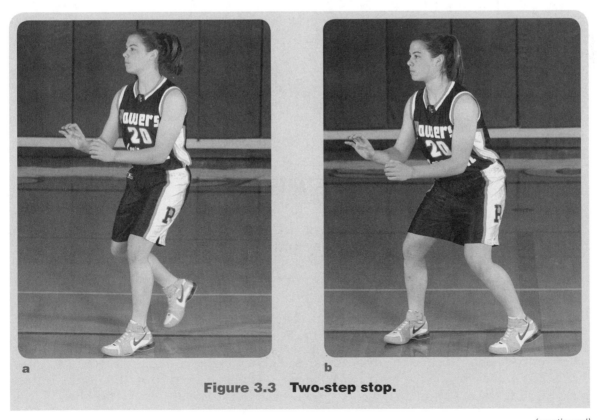

Figure 3.3   **Two-step stop.**

(continued)

Jump Stop

In the jump stop, both feet land simultaneously (see figure 3.4, *a* and *b*). This allows the player to use either foot as the pivot foot. This stop is very effective when players catch the ball with their back to the basket, because either foot can be used to pivot to the basket.

a   b

Figure 3.4   Jump stop.

PIVOTS

One of the most important aspects of footwork is the pivot turn, both with and without the ball. Additionally, the rules of the game dictate that when a player is in possession of the ball, the player must keep one foot (the pivot foot) on the floor until after the player releases the ball to dribble. The only time players may lift their pivot foot is when they are attempting a shot or pass, as long as they release the ball before the pivot foot returns to the floor. When executing a proper pivot, the player's weight is on the ball of the pivot foot, which is planted on the ground and acts as a base used to rotate the body up to 180 degrees, forward or backward.

A front pivot moves the body forward around the pivot (see figure 3.5*a*). For a front pivot, the player will lead with the chest and pivot on the ball of the foot. The back pivot—also called a *drop step*—moves the body backward around the pivot (see figure 3.5*b*). For a back pivot, the player will lead with the back and drop the nonpivot foot back. Again, players should stay low in their athletic stance and keep their head level.

Figure 3.5 *(a)* **Front pivot and** *(b)* **back pivot.**

CHANGE OF PACE AND DIRECTION

The advantage of being on offense is that players know when they are going to move and where they are going. Offensive players need to change their pace (i.e., their speed) and direction properly in order to deceive the defender.

Change of pace is used by players to alter their speed for the purpose of losing a defender. If a player plays at the same speed all the time, the defender will not have to work hard to stay with this player. But, for example, if a player slows down and then bursts forward, the player will most likely be able to get open because the defender will not expect the sudden change of pace. To slow their speed, players should shorten their stride and decrease their speed, keeping their upper body forward as they slow down. To increase speed, players should lengthen their stride and push forcefully off of the back foot. This change of pace will be very effective in deceiving opponents when executing many types of cuts.

Change of direction is used in almost every basketball skill and is very important in getting open off the ball. When changing direction, the player begins with a three-quarter step with the non-pivot foot (see figure 3.6a) and then plants the pivot foot firmly on the ground. The player then turns sharply on the ball of the pivot foot—while keeping the knees flexed—and pushes off in the new direction (see figure 3.6b), taking a long stride with the other foot (see figure 3.6c). Players should be aware that change of direction is effective in getting open for a pass and that they should keep their lead hand up as a target.

> **At a Glance**
>
> The following parts of the text offer additional information on proper offensive footwork:
>

(continued)

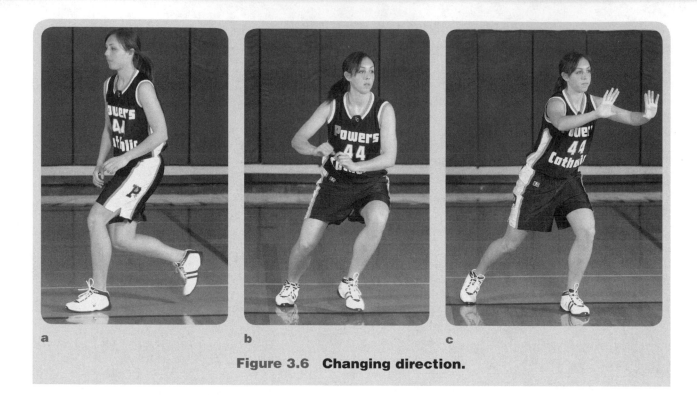

Figure 3.6 Changing direction.

Common Errors

You may run into several common errors when teaching your athletes proper offensive footwork.

Error	Error correction
The player's weight is forward in the offensive stance.	Emphasize that players need to bend the knees and get low instead of bending forward at the waist.
The player loses balance easily to either side.	Show players that they will have better balance in their stance if they keep the feet shoulder-width apart and the knees bent. Many tall players experience this problem because they don't bend the knees enough to get low.
When the player makes a cut and then uses a jump stop, one foot lands before the other.	Teach players that they need to stay low when making the jump stop. Make sure players realize that a jump stop is best in this situation because it enables them to use either foot when making a pivot for a post move.
The player lifts the pivot foot before beginning the dribble.	Remind players to maintain a balanced stance with the knees flexed and the weight on the ball of the pivot foot. This helps force the pivot foot to remain in contact with the floor until the ball is released.
The player does not change pace quickly.	Emphasize that players need to push off the back foot more aggressively when going from a slow speed to a faster speed. Players also need to keep the knees flexed because this will help them keep their balance when changing pace.
The player's cuts aren't sharp.	Emphasize that players need to keep the knees flexed and push off with the foot they are pivoting on, while taking a long first step in the new direction.

Triple-Threat Position

Every time a basketball player receives the ball on the perimeter, the player should assume what is called the *triple-threat position* by squaring up to the basket and achieving a balanced stance. From this position, players have three effective options—pass, shoot, or dribble—depending on their assessment of the game situation and which move they believe will gain them the best advantage.

SQUARING UP TO THE BASKET

Every time a basketball player receives the ball on the perimeter, the player should execute a pivot turn and "square up" to the basket, so that the basket is directly in front of the player. This enables the player to see the whole court and make the decision to shoot, pass, or dribble based on the situation and the location of teammates and opponents. The player's eyes should be focused on the rim and on the defender.

BODY POSITIONING

Once a player squares up to the basket, the player should assume the basic athletic stance (as discussed in "Offensive Footwork" on page 22). In this stance, the player's feet are shoulder-width apart, the knees flexed, and the back straight, with the head held over the waist and feet (see figure 3.7). The player should hold the ball between the waist and the chest with the shooting hand positioned on top of the ball and the nonshooting hand positioned under the ball. With this hand position, a player is able to pass, shoot, or dribble.

FAKING

When a player has squared up to the basket and assumed the proper body positioning, the player must now make a decision about his or her next move, depending on the game situation. If the player is closely guarded and cannot take a shot or make a pass, the player can use a fake by performing a jab step to force the defense to make

Figure 3.7   Body positioning for the triple threat.

(continued)

Figure 3.8   Jab step.

a move. The jab step will allow the player to get open off the dribble and can be an effective tool for your players. As the defensive player reacts to the fake, the offensive player can move in the opposite direction with the dribble. The fake often creates needed space for the offensive player.

The jab step is a short (approximately six to eight inches) and quick step made with the nonpivot foot straight toward the defender (see figure 3.8). The player's weight does not go forward, however, but remains on the pivot foot. If the defender reacts to the jab step by moving to the player's left or right, the offensive player should take a large step past the defender while putting the ball on the ground for a move to the basket (see figure

Figure 3.9   Moving past the defender after a fake.

3.9*a*). If the defender takes a retreat step, the offensive player can use this space to pull up for a jump shot or to pass to an open teammate in a better shooting position (see figure 3.9*b*). If the offensive player makes a jab step to the right and the defender reacts to the fake and moves to the player's right side as well, the offensive player can perform a quick crossover step with the right foot while moving the basketball across the body in preparation for dribbling to the left (see figure 3.9*c*).

In all cases, the player's hands should also move in the direction that the player is going. The player must be careful not to move too wide while maneuvering past the defender; instead, the player should move "shoulder to shoulder" around the defender so that the defender cannot recover easily. Players also need to remember that the pivot foot must remain on the ground until the ball leaves the hand so that traveling is not called.

At a Glance

The following parts of the text offer additional information on the triple-threat position:

Common Errors

You may run into several common errors when teaching your athletes the triple-threat position.

Error	Error correction
The player with the ball can only see the right side of the court.	Emphasize the importance of squaring up to the basket, which will enable players to see the whole court.
The defensive player on the ball gets his or her hands on the ball, and a jump ball is called.	Teach players to keep the ball close to their body when in the triple-threat position. This helps prevent the defender from stealing the ball or forcing a jump ball situation.
When using a jab step, the player with the ball is slow getting past the defender on the drive.	Emphasize that the jab step must be a short, quick step and that the player's weight should not go forward. This will help players be quicker when making the first step around their defender because they will maintain their balance. Players should then take a large first step to get by their opponent.
After the player with the ball takes a jab step and begins to drive toward the basket, the defender is able to recover.	The player is most likely going too wide on the drive, leaving the defender more than enough time to recover. Teach your players to pass by the defender at a close "shoulder to shoulder" range.

KEY POINTS

The most important components of dribbling are

- body positioning,
- protecting the ball,
- keeping the head up,
- using the hands, and
- proper footwork.

When players have possession of the basketball, they have two options for moving the ball: pass or dribble. Players can use the dribble to move the ball out of congested areas when a pass isn't available, to advance the ball up the court when receivers are not open (especially against pressure defenses), to penetrate the defense for a drive to the basket, or to draw defenders to them to create an opening for a teammate. The dribble can also be used to set up offensive plays, to improve positioning before passing to a teammate, and to create a shot.

Figure 3.10   Body position for the dribble.

BODY POSITIONING

When preparing to dribble, the player should be facing the basket in a well-balanced basic athletic stance, or the triple-threat position (see "Triple-Threat Position" on page 27), which allows the player to move quickly, change direction, change pace, and stop under control, while keeping the ball protected. The player's feet should be positioned at least shoulder-width apart, with the back straight and the player's weight evenly distributed on the balls of the feet (see figure 3.10). The knees should be flexed so that the player is prepared to move.

PROTECTING THE BALL

When dribbling, players should protect the ball by keeping their body in a position between the defender and the ball. For example, if a player is dribbling to the basket with the right hand and using the left side of the body to protect the ball, the defender is required to reach across the body to steal the ball, making it much more difficult to do. To protect the ball with the nondribbling hand and arm, the player should keep the forearm parallel to the floor, with the elbow flexed and the palm of the hand facing the ground (see figure 3.11).

KEEPING THE HEAD UP

Watching the ball when dribbling is a habit that many players must break, and this should be specifically addressed by coaches when covering the skill of dribbling. When dribbling, the player's head should be up, so that the player is aware of the location of open teammates and defenders (as shown in figures 3.10 and 3.11). Coaches should teach their players to always "see the rim" of the basket when they dribble; this will help players avoid the tendency to watch the ball.

Figure 3.11   Protecting the ball.

USING THE HANDS

To dribble properly, players must understand that the wrist and the fingers are responsible for making the ball bounce. Many players have the tendency to pump their arms rather than letting the wrist and fingers do the work when dribbling the ball. When dribbling, a player's dribbling hand should be in a relaxed position, with the wrist and thumb loose and the fingers comfortably spread (see figure 3.12). If the player's wrist and hand are tense, the player is more likely to slap the ball. A relaxed wrist will allow the hand to move up and down with the dribble, providing the correct amount of pressure needed for the dribble. The ball should be dribbled off of the finger pads with fingertip control, and the wrist and fingers should flex to impart force on the ball as it leaves the player's hand. The fingertips should be the last part of the hand to touch the ball as a player dribbles.

Figure 3.12   Hand positioning for the dribble.

Additionally, to be effective dribblers, players must also become skilled at dribbling with either hand. If players can only dribble with one hand, they will be much easier to guard and will essentially limit themselves to only one-half of the court. If a player cannot dribble with both hands, defenders will soon recognize this as a weakness and exploit it. For example, if the player can only go right when dribbling, the defense will recognize this and work to force the player left.

(continued)

PROPER FOOTWORK

To be an effective dribbler, the most important aspect of footwork that a player needs to work on is the first step, assuring that the ball leaves the hand before the player lifts the pivot foot. When the player catches the ball with both feet on the floor, the player may pivot using either foot (before dribbling). A pivot is when a player who is holding the ball steps once, or more than once, in any direction with one foot while the other foot (called the *pivot foot*) is kept at its point of contact with the floor. Once the player has picked one foot up, the other becomes the pivot foot. The pivot foot may not leave the floor until the ball leaves the dribbler's hand or else traveling will be called. To do this correctly, the first step and dribble should happen simultaneously. For example, assume that the dribbler needs to drive to the right and that the left foot is the pivot foot. In this case, the player will take a large step with the right foot to drive past the defender, making sure the ball leaves the hand before the pivot foot comes off the ground. Or, when the dribbler needs to drive to the left (and the left foot is the pivot foot), the dribbler must take a crossover step with the right foot, keeping the pivot foot on the floor until the ball is released from the hand.

Your players need to understand that the number of steps they will take when dribbling will not necessarily match the number of bounces of the ball. For example, when advancing the ball up the court or in a closely guarded situation, the ball may bounce more than once between a player's steps.

Common Errors

You may run into several common errors when teaching your athletes how to dribble.

Error	Error correction
The player looks at the ball when dribbling.	Teach players to keep the head up and to always "see the rim," which will put them in a position to see the entire court.
The player dribbles too high or too far away from the body.	Remind players that they should keep the ball close to the body and should dribble at waist level. Show players how to keep the body between the ball and the defender and how to keep the nondribbling hand up.
The player loses control of the ball when dribbling.	Players sometimes lose control of the ball because they slap at the ball instead of using their fingertips for control. Show players that they won't have much control if they dribble with the palm of the hand instead of the fingertips.
The player does not get enough force on the dribble.	Remind players that they should not pump the arm. Emphasize that wrist and finger flexion will create force on the dribble while giving the dribbler more control.
The player gets called for carrying the ball when changing direction.	Emphasize that the dribbling hand should be on the top of the ball and that players should not let the hand come to a rest at the top of the dribble. When switching hands or directions on a dribble, players should keep the hand to the side of the ball and not under the ball.

Speed Dribble

The speed dribble is a dribble performed while moving at top speed. It is typically used when a player is not closely guarded and needs to advance the ball up the court quickly, such as in a breakaway situation or after a turnover. The speed dribble may end in a layup when the player beats the opponents down the court, or it may end with a pass to a teammate who is in a position farther up the court than the dribbler.

BODY POSITIONING

Although players should strive to maintain the basic athletic stance (as discussed in "Dribbling Basics" on page 30) before and after executing the speed dribble, the body position during the speed dribble is much different. Since the speed dribble is executed on the run, players must be in an upright position as they move down the floor. This enables players to push the ball out in front of them as they run (see "Proper Footwork" for more information).

HAND POSITIONING

When using the speed dribble, the player's dribbling hand should be relaxed, with the wrist and thumb loose and the fingers comfortably spread (as shown in figure 3.12 in "Dribbling Basics" on page 31). The hand should be positioned behind the ball at approximately a 45-degree angle to the floor (see figure 3.13). This hand positioning will make it possible for players to extend their arm completely as they push the ball out in front of them.

KEEPING THE HEAD UP

As you learned in "Dribbling Basics," watching the ball while dribbling is a common habit that must be broken, and the speed dribble is no exception. Dribblers should always "see the rim" so that they can see open teammates out in front for a pass and can see the location of defenders. Additionally, the speed dribble often leads to a layup, and keeping the head up is very important in timing this properly (see "Layup" on page 74 for more information).

Figure 3.13 Hand positioning for the speed dribble.

(continued)

PROPER FOOTWORK

When using the speed dribble, players should not try to time the dribble with every step they take Players should strive to move the ball up the court quickly, rather than being focused on how many times the ball hits the floor. When using the speed dribble, a player must learn to push the ball several feet out in front and run after it. The ball's bounce should not be any higher than hip level, however, because a higher bounce increases the chances of the player losing control of the ball while sprinting down the court.

Common Errors

You may run into several common errors when teaching your athletes how to speed dribble.

Error	Error correction
The player's first dribble is at his or her side.	Teach players to focus on always keeping the ball out in front. Teach them to throw the ball a few feet out in front of them and then run after it.
The player takes too many dribbles.	Players should not tie the dribble to their steps. Try temporarily limiting the number of dribbles the player can take from end line to end line.
The player is called for carrying the ball while speed dribbling down the court.	Emphasize that players need to keep the hand slightly behind the ball because they must push the ball out in front when speed dribbling. Teach players not to dribble so high that they can't control the speed dribble.
The player loses control of the ball while speed dribbling down the court.	Emphasize that players need to push the ball out in front but not in the middle of the body or out too far in front of the body because they will lose control of the ball.

Control Dribble

KEY POINTS

The most important components of the control dribble are

- body positioning,
- protecting the ball,
- keeping the head up, and
- proper footwork.

The control dribble, sometimes referred to as the *low dribble*, is a protected and controlled dribble where the ball is kept low and close to the floor. The control dribble is used whenever a player is closely guarded—for example, when the defense is in a pressure situation and a defender is putting a great deal of pressure on the player with the ball. Players may also use the control dribble when they need to move the ball out of a congested area after a rebound.

BODY POSITIONING

When using a control dribble, players may have a tendency to bend over at the waist to keep the ball low. However, in doing so, the ball will be too far from the body, and it will be difficult for the player to keep the head up. Players must instead strive to maintain a well-balanced athletic stance, with the feet shoulder-width apart and the nondribbling foot forward in an effort to keep the body between the ball and the defender. For the control dribble, the player should keep the back straight and positioned over the waist (as in the normal dribbling stance shown in figure 3.10 on page 30) but should bend the knees to get lower to the ground (see figure 3.14).

Figure 3.14 Body positioning for the control dribble.

PROTECTING THE BALL

Since the control dribble is typically used when the dribbler is being pressured by the defense or when dribbling in congested areas on the court, the ball should be dribbled at or below the knees. Players will find that it is much more difficult for the defender to steal the ball when it is dribbled low. When players are closely guarded or moving the ball out of a congested area, they will be able to protect the ball more effectively if they keep the elbow of the dribbling arm at their side and close to the body. And, as you learned in "Dribbling Basics," the nondribbling hand and arm are also an effective tool for protecting the ball from the defender; the player should keep the nondribbling forearm parallel to the floor, with the elbow flexed and the palm of the hand facing the ground (see figure 3.11 on page 31).

(continued)

KEEPING THE HEAD UP

As you learned in "Dribbling Basics" on page 30, watching the ball while dribbling is a common habit that must be broken. When players are closely guarded, it is especially important for them to keep the ball away from the defender, and keeping the head up will help them do this. Dribblers should remember to always "see the rim" so that they can see the entire court and be aware of the location of defenders and any open teammates out in front.

Players should also be aware that they are only allowed five seconds to dribble the ball when being closely guarded; therefore, keeping the head up to assess opportunities is vital to good team play. Players do not want to stop their dribble until they know what they are going to do with the ball.

PROPER FOOTWORK

Footwork is very important in maintaining a good low, controlled dribble. A player's movement when using a controlled dribble requires that the player take small steps while keeping the feet apart. The dribbler's nondribbling foot (left foot for a right-handed dribble) should be positioned slightly in front of the dribbling foot on each bounce of the ball, with the weight distributed evenly on both feet. To move forward, then, the player will take a small step with the nondribbling (or lead) foot and then slide the dribbling (or back) foot forward on the bounce. To move backward, the player will take a small step with the back foot and slide the lead foot back.

Common Errors

You may run into several common errors when teaching your athletes how to perform a control dribble.

Error	Error correction
The player's dribble is weak and slow.	Teach players not to pump the arms. They need to flex the wrist in order to get enough force on the ball.
The ball is stolen often.	Teach players to keep the ball low and protect it with the nondribbling hand.
The player turns his or her back to the basket when feeling pressure from the defense.	Emphasize that players need to be square to the basket and should strive to keep the ball low, protecting it with the nondribbling hand, when a defensive player is applying pressure.

Reverse Dribble

The reverse dribble, sometimes referred to as a *spin dribble*, is a type of dribble that allows the player to change direction by combining a reverse pivot with a two-dribble move when being closely guarded by a defender. This type of dribble is used most often as an offensive move when a defender overplays the offensive player's dribbling side; in this situation, the reverse dribble can enable the offensive player to create his or her own shot in the opposite direction. The disadvantage of the reverse dribble, however, is that the player temporarily loses sight of teammates and the defenders' positioning on the court while the reverse move is being made. This loss of sight can provide opportunities for the defense to set up a double team and force a turnover or set up another defender for a blind-side steal.

BODY POSITIONING

The reverse dribble is typically executed in game situations where a player is closely guarded by a defender, so the player should maintain the same body positioning that was previously discussed in "Control Dribble" on page 35. Players should assume a well-balanced athletic stance, with the feet shoulder-width apart and the nondribbling foot forward in an effort to keep the body between the ball and the defender. The player should also keep the back straight and positioned over the waist (as in the normal athletic stance) but should bend the knees to get lower to the ground (as shown in figure 3.14 on page 35).

KEEPING THE HEAD UP

As with the other types of dribbles, players should try not to watch the ball while performing the reverse dribble. When using the reverse dribble, especially, players must avoid the tendency to look at the ball while they move backward and change hands. This tendency, coupled with the momentary loss of sight of the court while executing the reverse move, makes it especially important that players keep their head up when using this dribble. Additionally, some players may find that they have a tendency to bend over at the waist in an effort to keep the ball low. However, players must be aware that in doing so, the ball will be too far from the body, and it will be difficult for them to keep their head up.

(continued)

PROPER FOOTWORK

As the player moves toward the defender, the player should plant the lead foot and prepare to execute a back pivot on that foot. The player should turn counterclockwise on the lead foot so that his or her back is to the defender (see figure 3.15*a*) and then swing the body around, taking a large step with the back foot to complete the pivot (see figure 3.15*b*). Once the back foot has been brought around, the player must quickly turn that foot and point it in the new direction to help get the rest of the body moving in that direction (see figure 3.15*c*).

Figure 3.15 **Reverse pivot for the reverse dribble.**

HAND POSITIONING

As the player plants the lead foot (as described in "Proper Footwork"), the player must continue to dribble the ball with the same hand while moving into the pivot, keeping the ball close to the body. During the pivot, the player should shift the dribbling hand from the top of the ball to the outside of the ball and should pull the ball back to complete the turn. As the player brings the back foot around to move forward in the new direction, the player should perform a second dribble using the same hand—still keeping the ball close to the body—and then change hands for the next dribble.

At a Glance

The following parts of the text offer additional information on the reverse dribble:

Common Errors

You may run into several common errors when teaching your athletes the reverse dribble.

Error	Error correction
The player puts the head down to watch the ball while changing direction.	The reverse dribble forces the dribbler to momentarily turn the head away from the rim. Emphasize that players must not watch the ball because they need to see the rim the split second they complete the turn.
The dribbler is called for carrying the ball while switching hands on the dribble.	Emphasize the importance of switching the dribbling hand from the top of the ball to the outside of the ball and pulling the ball back to complete the turn. Players should not put the hand under the ball because this will result in a carry.
The player is double teamed when attempting a reverse dribble.	Emphasize the need to keep the head up. Teach players that the reverse dribble should not be used when a second defender is close enough to the dribbler to form a double team.

KEY POINTS

The most important components of the crossover dribble are

o body positioning,
o protecting the ball,
o keeping the head up, and
o proper footwork.

The crossover dribble is a type of dribble where the player moves the ball from one hand to the other while changing direction. The crossover dribble is a good technique for a dribbler to use when trying to lose a defender. For example, assume that the dribbler is using a control dribble and wants to beat the defender on a move to the basket. Or, assume that the defender is overplaying the dribbler's dribbling side in the open court on a fast break. In these situations, the dribbler can use the crossover dribble to change direction and move past the defender. On the flip side, however, if not executed properly, the crossover move can provide an opportunity for the defender to steal the ball, because as the ball is crossed over in front of the dribbler's body, the ball is unprotected.

BODY POSITIONING

When using a crossover dribble, players may have a tendency to bend over at the waist as they change direction. However, in doing so, the ball will be too far from the body, and it will be difficult for players to keep their head up. Instead, players must strive to maintain a well-balanced athletic stance, with the feet shoulder-width apart and the nondribbling foot forward in an effort to keep the body between the ball and the defender.

Figure 3.16 Protecting the ball on the switch.

PROTECTING THE BALL

Players should keep the ball low and close to the body when switching hands on the crossover because the ball can become vulnerable to a steal by a quick defender when it crosses in front of the body. When switching the ball from one hand to the other, the player should move the ball so that it crosses the body at a backward angle; the nondribbling hand should be positioned with the palm held parallel to the floor, ready to receive the ball (see figure 3.16). After the switch is made, the player should bring the other hand (previously the dribbling hand) up to protect the ball.

KEEPING THE HEAD UP

As mentioned previously, players must avoid watching the ball while dribbling. When executing the crossover dribble, the dribbler needs to see the defender, the basket, and teammates at all times. Additionally, dribblers may have a tendency to look down at the ball when changing dribbling hands and direction. When players are closely guarded, it is especially important for them to keep the ball away from the defender, and keeping the head up will help them do this. Dribblers should remember to always "see the rim" so that they can see any open teammates out in front and see the location of defenders.

At a Glance

The following parts of the text offer additional information on the crossover dribble:

Offensive Footwork	p. 22
Triple-Threat Position	p. 27
Dribbling Basics	p. 30
Speed Dribble	p. 33
Control Dribble	p. 35
Reverse Dribble	p. 37
Change of Pace Dribble	p. 43

Figure 3.17 Footwork for the crossover dribble.

PROPER FOOTWORK

When using the crossover dribble, the player must pivot and push off on the outside foot to facilitate the change in direction (see figure 3.17). The combination of these two moves will make the change of direction more sharp and effective. At the same time as the change of direction, the player will bounce the ball.

INSIDE-OUT DRIBBLE

If a defender reacts quickly to the player's change of direction, an inside-out dribble—simply a fake change of direction dribble—can be used effectively to deceive the defender so that the dribbler can get open for a shot or a drive to the basket. For the inside-out dribble, the dribbler sets up the deception by using a head fake to the opposite side so the defender thinks the dribbler is going to change direction. The dribbler starts the dribble across the body, but instead of releasing the ball to the other hand, the dribbler rotates the hand over the ball, and as the defender is anticipating the change of direction, the dribbler pulls the ball back and dribbles past the defender. When using the inside-out dribble, the player should dribble the ball at knee level, close to the body, and should protect the ball with the body and the nondribbling hand (just as the player normally would when executing the crossover dribble).

(continued)

Common Errors

You may run into several common errors when teaching your athletes how to use the crossover dribble.

Error	Error correction
The ball is stolen on the crossover.	The player is probably dribbling too high on the crossover. Teach players to push the ball low and close to the body. Players should also keep their body position low and stay low in their stance.
The player is called for carrying the ball.	Emphasize that players must have their hand to the side of the ball and not under the ball when making the crossover.
The player loses control of the ball on the crossover.	Many times players lose control of the dribble on the crossover because they slap at the ball or they don't have the receiving hand ready and mishandle the ball on the crossover. Show players that they need to dribble with the fingertips and must have the receiving hand ready.
The player watches the ball when crossing it over.	Emphasize that dribblers should not watch the ball. Teach them to always see the rim so that they know when to make a pass or when they have an opening to shoot or to make a drive to the basket.

Change of Pace Dribble

KEY POINTS

The most important components of the change of pace dribble are

- body positioning,
- protecting the ball,
- keeping the head up,
- deceiving the defender, and
- moving past the defender.

In the change of pace dribble, the player slows his or her speed while dribbling in order to deceive the defender into thinking the dribbler is going to pick up the dribble and either shoot the ball or pass it to a teammate. The goal of the change of pace dribble is to get the defender to slow down as the dribbler slows down; the dribbler then quickly moves back into a full-speed dribble to drive past the defender.

The basic concept behind a change of pace dribble is one that we discussed early in this chapter (see "Offensive Footwork" on page 22), which is that players should continually adjust their pace, or speed, to deceive the defender. It is much more difficult to defend a dribbler who changes speed. Dribblers have a definite advantage over the defender because they know when they are going to change speed.

BODY POSITIONING

When using the change of pace dribble, the dribbler's body position is very important in order to deceive the defender and set up the drive past the defender. When dribbling at top speed and preparing to move into a slower dribble, the player must assume a well-balanced basic athletic stance; the feet should be shoulder-width apart with the nondribbling foot forward in an effort to keep the body between the ball and the defender. The player should straighten the back as if looking to shoot or looking for a teammate to pass to, and as the defender begins to move into a position to closely guard the dribbler, the dribbler should push the dribble out and run after it, moving back into a full-speed dribble.

PROTECTING THE BALL

As discussed previously for other dribbling skills, the player must use the body to protect the ball and should strive to keep the body between the defender and the ball. The player must also try to protect the ball with the body while moving back into a full-speed dribble and passing by the defender.

KEEPING THE HEAD UP

As with other types of dribbling, players must avoid watching the ball while performing the change of pace dribble. When executing the change of pace dribble, players need to know when the defender slows up, so keeping the head up is very important. When dribblers are closely guarded, it is especially important for them to keep the ball away from the defender, and keeping the head up will help them do this. Dribblers should remember to always "see the rim" so that they can see open teammates out in front and see the location of defenders.

(continued)

DECEIVING THE DEFENDER

As mentioned, the dribbler is at an advantage during the change of pace dribble because the dribbler controls when the change of speed occurs. To properly execute the change of pace dribble, the player will first set up the deception by inviting the defender to slow up. In this case, the player will typically be moving down the court at full speed using a speed dribble. The dribbler will first slow the pace and then straighten the back as if looking either to pass the ball to a teammate or shoot the ball, which will invite the defender to guard the dribbler more closely.

MOVING PAST THE DEFENDER

As the defender reacts to the adjusted pace and slows down to guard the dribbler more closely, the dribbler should quickly push the dribble out hard and run after it, exploding by the defender at top speed and protecting the ball with the nondribbling hand. The effective deception coupled with a forceful push of the ball should put the dribbler at least one step ahead of the defender.

Common Errors

You may run into several common errors when teaching your athletes how to use the change of pace dribble.

Error	Error correction
The dribbler cannot beat the defender when changing from the control dribble to the speed dribble.	Emphasize that players must first deceive the defender by slowing up. They must then push the ball out on the first dribble.
The player loses control of the ball while changing from a speed dribble to a control dribble.	Show players that they can maintain control of the ball when changing speeds by dribbling the ball at knee level and widening the base for better balance.

Passing Basics

KEY POINTS

The most important components of passing are

o assessing the situation,

o body movement,

o accuracy and timing,

o faking the pass, and

o receiving the pass.

Passing is the fastest and most effective way to get the ball from player to player and move it around the court. Passing is used to move the ball up the court quickly on a fast break, to set up offensive plays, to get the ball to open teammates for scoring opportunities, or to get the ball out of congested areas after a rebound. Passing is one of the most neglected technical skills in basketball, and although scoring may be much more glamorous than making a great pass, your players must learn that passing sets up shots—the team will not be able to get a shot off without first using good passing techniques. Players must also understand that being a good passer makes for a better player, which in turn makes the team more successful.

ASSESSING THE SITUATION

Because a pass is always faster than a dribble, players should always assess the game situation and the location of teammates and defenders to see if there are opportunities to pass the ball before they choose to dribble it. On a related note, again, players should keep the head up and "see the rim" as they assess the situation and make the decision to pass or dribble.

BODY MOVEMENT

Passes must be quick so that the defender doesn't have time to react. Unnecessary motion, such as winding up to make a pass by starting the pass behind the body, slows the pass, and players need to work to eliminate this. Teach players to keep the elbows in and to release the ball with a snap of the wrist, which is created by forcing the wrists and fingers through the ball. Players should also impart spin to the ball using the index and middle fingers and the thumbs. This helps the ball travel in a straighter line and makes it easier to catch than a ball without any spin.

Additionally, the player should first be in a balanced stance with the feet shoulder-width apart and the knees flexed. The player should step into the pass in the direction of the receiver by extending the legs, back, and arms to give more power to the pass.

ACCURACY AND TIMING

All passes should be thrown accurately, and it is the passer's responsibility to get the ball to an open teammate away from the defender. The basketball will go where the fingers direct it to go, so accurate passing requires the correct follow-through—that is, pointing the fingers at the target.

Players need to know their teammates' location and the speed at which they are moving so they can accurately time passes to them as they cut to the basket or to an open area. The goal of passing to a teammate is to set that player up for a shot or to further advance the play. If the player has to stop to catch the ball on a fast break,

(continued)

for example, it slows down the break. Conversely, if the player receives the ball without breaking stride—because the pass was made accurately to where the player was moving—the fast break will be much more successful. The key to timing the pass is for a passer to be able to anticipate the teammate's speed and make a well-timed pass slightly ahead of the teammate.

FAKING THE PASS

Players should learn how to fake effectively before a pass in an effort to keep defenders on their toes. If a defender is overplaying the pass, a fake will help set up the teammate and decrease the chances that the pass will be stolen. Also, players should not look at the target or in other ways telegraph the pass. Players should focus on the basket and "see the rim," allowing them to see the entire court and see the location of teammates and defenders.

RECEIVING THE PASS

Of course, the best pass is one that is caught by the passer's teammate, and your players need to always be ready to catch a pass. The communication between the passer and the receiver is unspoken, and when the receiver is open and ready to receive a pass, the receiver should position the hands out from the chest, with the fingers spread and pointed up and the thumbs facing each other (see figure 3.18*a*). When the ball is caught, the receiver should bend the elbows slightly and bring the ball in toward the chest to cushion the impact of the ball (see figure 3.18*b*). Receivers should also strive to keep their eyes on the ball until the catch is made. Many balls are fumbled because of receivers taking their eyes off the ball while it is in flight.

a   b

Figure 3.18   **Receiving a pass.**

Receivers should also be ready to move to meet the pass using a two-step stop or a jump stop, allowing the player to be in a well-balanced basic athletic stance when receiving the ball. Also, moving to the ball decreases the chance that the defense will steal the ball by taking advantage of the space between the passer and receiver and stepping in front of the receiver.

At a Glance

The following parts of the text offer additional information on passing:

Offensive Footwork	p. 22
Triple-Threat Position	p. 27
Chest Pass	p. 48
Bounce Pass	p. 50
Baseball Pass	p. 52
Overhead Pass	p. 54
Sidearm Pass	p. 56
Behind-the-Back Pass	p. 59
Catching	p. 61

Common Errors

You may run into several common errors when teaching your athletes how to pass.

Error	Error correction
The player telegraphs the location of the pass.	Teach players that they must focus on the rim and not look at the intended target when preparing to make a pass. A good passer will be able to make the pass without giving away the location to the defense.
The player's pass lacks zip.	Emphasize that players must keep the elbows in and force the wrists and fingers through the ball. The passer should also step into the pass in the direction of the receiver by extending the legs, back, and arms to give more power to the pass.
The player's pass is off target.	Remind players that accurate passing requires the correct follow-through, which involves pointing the fingers at the target.
The pass is behind the intended receiver on the fast break.	Emphasize that the key to timing the pass is to be able to anticipate the receiver's speed and make a pass slightly ahead of the receiver.
The passer sees that the receiver is no longer open but is unable to stop the pass.	Emphasize that players need to keep both hands on the ball until the moment of the release. The nonpassing hand will help to protect, control, or stop the pass at the last second.

Chest Pass

KEY POINTS

The most important components of a chest pass are

o proper stance,

o hand and arm positioning, and

o stepping into the pass.

The chest pass is a two-handed pass that moves from the passer's chest to the receiver's chest. It is the most common type of pass used during a game because it can be thrown from so many different positions on the floor. The best time to use a chest pass, however, is when there isn't a defender between the passer and the receiver—for example, in the open court on a fast break or for ball reversal on the perimeter.

PROPER STANCE

As with all passes, an effective chest pass requires that the player first be in a well-balanced athletic stance, with the feet shoulder-width apart and the knees bent (as discussed in "Passing Basics" on page 45). The head should be positioned over the support base, slightly behind the knees and over the waist, with the back straight. This stance will allow the passer to impart more power and speed to the ball.

Figure 3.19   Initial hand and arm positioning for a chest pass.

Figure 3.20   Hand and arm positioning when making the chest pass.

HAND AND ARM POSITIONING

When preparing to make a chest pass, the player should hold the ball with two hands near the center of the chest, with the thumbs up and the elbows in (see figure 3.19). The ball is held close to the body to gain optimum power behind the pass when it is made.

When making the pass, the player stretches the arms out to their full length, rotating the elbows and wrists outward so that the hands finish in a thumbs-down, palms-out position (see figure 3.20). The player should release the ball with a snap of the wrist, imparting spin to the ball with the index and middle fingers and the thumbs as it leaves the hands, so that the ball will travel in a straight line to the receiver (as discussed in "Passing Basics" on page 45).

STEPPING INTO THE PASS

Players should also step into the pass using the nonpivot foot, with the toes pointed in the direction of the receiver, to create more power. The passer should not overextend the step because this tends to move the passer off balance and reduces the power behind the pass.

At a Glance

The following parts of the text offer additional information on the chest pass:

Offensive Footwork	p. 22
Triple-Threat Position	p. 27
Passing Basics	p. 45
Bounce Pass	p. 50
Baseball Pass	p. 52
Overhead Pass	p. 54
Sidearm Pass	p. 56

Common Errors

You may run into several common errors when teaching your athletes how to use the chest pass.

Error	Error correction
The player's chest pass lacks power.	Emphasize that players must keep the elbows in and force the wrists and fingers through the ball. Players should also step into the pass in the direction of the receiver by extending the legs, back, and arms to give more power to the pass.
The player's chest pass is off target.	Remind players that accurate passing requires the correct follow-through, which involves pointing the fingers at the target.
The player's chest pass is high.	Emphasize that players should pass from chest level and not from waist level because this can cause the ball to go high.

KEY POINTS

The most important components of a bounce pass are

- proper stance,
- hand and arm positioning,
- stepping into the pass, and
- accuracy on the bounce.

A bounce pass is very similar to the chest pass, except the ball is bounced when it is passed to the receiver. The bounce pass is recommended for backdoor cuts and for leading players to the basket. As previously mentioned, it is difficult to use the chest pass when a defender is between the passer and the receiver (see "Chest Pass" on page 48); however, the bounce pass can be used in this situation because the pass can be made under the arms of the defender. The bounce pass is most effective when used after a fake that causes the defender to raise the hands up. The bounce pass is not recommended for perimeter passes because it is a slower pass and can be picked off more easily by aggressive defenders playing the passing lane.

PROPER STANCE

As with all passes, an effective bounce pass requires that the player first be in a well-balanced athletic stance, with the feet shoulder-width apart and the knees bent (as discussed in "Passing Basics" on page 45). The head should be positioned over the support base, slightly behind the knees and over the waist, with the back straight. This stance will allow the passer to impart more power and speed to the ball.

Figure 3.21   Making a bounce pass.

HAND AND ARM POSITIONING

The initial hand and arm positioning for a bounce pass is the same as discussed previously for the chest pass (see "Chest Pass" on page 48), except the ball is initially held at the waist. When preparing to make a bounce pass, the player should hold the ball with two hands near the body at the waist, with the thumbs up and the elbows in.

When making the pass (see figure 3.21), the movement is the same as described for the chest pass—the passer stretches the arms out to their full length, rotating the elbows and wrists outward so that the hands finish in a thumbs-down, palms-out position (as shown in figure 3.20 on page 48). The player should release the ball with a snap of the wrist, imparting spin to the ball with the index and middle fingers and the thumbs as it leaves the hands, so that the ball will travel in a straight line to the receiver (as discussed in "Passing Basics" on page 45).

STEPPING INTO THE PASS

Players should also step into the pass—as they would for a chest pass—in the direction of the receiver to create more power. However, for the bounce pass, players should bend the knees to help them get low as they step into the pass. The lower the passer is when making the pass, the more the passer decreases the chance of the pass being picked off by a defender.

ACCURACY ON THE BOUNCE

When making the bounce pass, the player should aim the ball so that it bounces approximately two-thirds of the way between the passer and the receiver. This will result in the ball arriving at the receiver's waist. If the ball bounces too close to the passer, it is typically a slow, high pass that can be easily intercepted. If the ball bounces too close to the receiver, it is typically too low, making it difficult for the receiver to handle.

At a Glance

The following parts of the text offer additional information on the bounce pass:

Offensive Footwork	p. 22
Passing Basics	p. 45
Chest Pass	p. 48
Baseball Pass	p. 52
Overhead Pass	p. 54
Sidearm Pass	p. 56
Catching	p. 61

Common Errors

You may run into several common errors when teaching your athletes how to use the bounce pass.

Error	Error correction
The player's bounce pass has too much front spin on the ball after the bounce, making it difficult to catch.	Teach passers to keep the thumbs down in the release, letting the ball roll off the first and second fingers. This gives the ball backspin and makes it much easier to catch.
The player's bounce pass lands too close to the receiver, making it difficult to catch.	Teach passers to bounce the ball farther from the receiver. The general guideline is to aim the bounce about two-thirds the distance between the passer and the receiver so that the receiver can easily catch it at waist height.
The player's bounce pass lacks force or is too slow.	Emphasize that players should extend the elbows and snap the wrist by pushing the fingers through the ball. The arms should rotate inward so that the hands finish in a thumbs-down position with the fingers pointed toward the target.

The baseball pass, as the name implies, involves the same techniques as the overhand throw that is commonly used in baseball. The baseball pass is a long-distance pass and is usually thrown a distance of at least half the court. This pass is often used when passing to a teammate down the court for a quick two points, when making an outlet pass to start a fast break, or when inbounding the ball.

KEY POINTS

The most important components of a baseball pass are

- proper stance,
- hand and arm positioning,
- making the pivot, and
- follow-through.

PROPER STANCE

As with all passes, an effective baseball pass requires that the player first be in a well-balanced athletic stance, with the feet shoulder-width apart and the knees bent (as discussed in "Passing Basics" on page 45). The head should be positioned over the support base, slightly behind the knees and over the waist, with the back straight. For the baseball pass, this stance is especially important because players must shift their weight and pivot, which is done more effectively from a well-balanced stance.

Figure 3.22 Initial hand and arm positioning for the baseball pass.

HAND AND ARM POSITIONING

When preparing to execute the baseball pass, the player should bring the ball up to the ear with the passing hand positioned behind the ball (see figure 3.22). The arm of the passing hand should be held at a 45-degree angle with the upper arm parallel to the floor so that the player can throw a quick, hard, and straight pass. If the elbow drops below the shoulder, the pass will take on the nature of a sidearm pass, which is more difficult to direct because it forces the passer to throw across the body. The player should keep the nonpassing hand in front of the ball until the pass is released. This is especially important if the player decides at the last moment to stop the pass or if the player wants to use a fake.

The player should release the ball with a snap of the wrist, which is created by forcing the wrist and fingers through the ball. The player should also impart spin to the ball using the index and middle fingers and the thumb; this will help the ball travel in a straighter line and make it easier to catch than a ball without any spin.

MAKING THE PIVOT

When using the baseball pass, the player begins in a balanced stance (as in all passes) but must pivot on the passing-side foot. The player shifts his or her weight from the middle of the stance to the passing-side foot and then to the front foot as the player steps toward the target and passes the ball. The player steps toward the direction of the intended pass with the foot opposite the throwing arm. For example, a right-handed passer will shift the weight from the balanced stance to the right foot and then to the left foot when stepping into the pass.

As the player pivots on the back foot and shifts the weight, the player will bring the ball to the ear on the passing side. The passing hand should be behind the ball, and the nonpassing hand in front of the ball. The player should keep the elbows in close to the body.

At a Glance

The following parts of the text offer additional information on the baseball pass:

Offensive Footwork	p. 22
Passing Basics	p. 45
Chest Pass	p. 48
Overhead Pass	p. 54
Catching	p. 61

FOLLOW-THROUGH

On the follow-through, the player's legs, back, and arms should extend forward in the direction of the target, and after the ball is released, the palm of the passing hand should face the ground and the fingers should be pointed toward the target. The player should impart backward spin on the ball, as discussed in "Passing Basics," so that the ball will travel in a straight line to the receiver.

Common Errors

You may run into several common errors when teaching your athletes how to use the baseball pass.

Error	Error correction
The player's baseball pass lacks power.	Teach players to use their legs on the pass and to follow through to help increase the force of the pass.
The player's baseball pass is inaccurate.	Teach players to follow through and point with the fingers toward the target.
The player is called for traveling when making the baseball pass.	Emphasize that players must keep the pivot foot in contact with the floor until the ball is released. Players should shift their weight from the back foot to the front foot.

Overhead Pass

KEY POINTS

The most important components of an overhead pass are

o proper stance,
o hand and arm positioning, and
o stepping into the pass.

The overhead pass is a two-handed pass that is thrown from above the passer's head. This pass is most effective when a player is closely guarded and needs to pass over the defender. The overhead pass is often used by players as an outlet pass to start the break, a skip pass over the defense, or an option for feeding the post.

PROPER STANCE

As with all passes, an effective overhead pass requires that the player first be in a well-balanced athletic stance, with the feet shoulder-width apart and the knees bent (as discussed in "Passing Basics" on page 45). The head should be positioned over the support base, slightly behind the knees and over the waist, with the back straight. This stance will allow the passer to impart more power and speed to the ball.

HAND AND ARM POSITIONING

When preparing to make an overhead pass, the player must hold the ball above the head with the hands in a handshake position on both sides of the ball (see figure 3.23). The player should hold the ball in front of the forehead, with the elbows in and flexed at approximately a 90-degree angle. Players must make sure that the ball is not held behind the head because it can be stolen easily from this position. It will also take longer to get the pass off if it is started from behind the head.

When making the pass, players should extend the elbows and rotate the arms so that the hands move into a thumbs-down position in front of the forehead (see figure 3.24). The release is made using a snap of the wrist by forcing the wrists and fingers through the ball. Players should also impart spin to the ball using the index and middle fingers and the thumbs; this will help the ball travel in a straighter line and make it easier to catch than a ball without any spin.

STEPPING INTO THE PASS

Similar to when making a chest pass, players should step into the overhead pass with the non-pivot foot, with the toes pointed in the direction of the receiver, as shown in figure 3.24, to create more power. The passer should not overextend the step because this tends to move the passer off balance and reduces the power behind the pass.

Figure 3.23 Initial hand and arm positioning for an overhead pass.

Figure 3.24 Correct form and follow-through for an overhead pass.

Common Errors

You may run into several common errors when teaching your athletes how to use the overhead pass.

Error	Error correction
The player's overhead pass is slow and is easily intercepted.	Emphasize that players should not take the ball behind the head. Players should flex the wrist and fingers to snap the ball and should extend the legs, back, and arms.
The player's overhead pass is inaccurate.	Make sure that players point the fingers toward the target and that the ball comes off the first and second fingers to help guide the ball.
The ball is stolen before the pass is made.	Most likely the passer is starting the pass with the ball positioned behind the head, thus making it susceptible to a steal. Teach players to start the overhead pass with the ball in front of the forehead so that they can protect it from opponents.

KEY POINTS

The most important components of the sidearm pass are

o proper stance,
o hand and arm positioning,
o releasing the ball, and
o stepping around the defender.

The sidearm pass is a one- or two-handed pass that originates from the side of the body and can be executed from either side. The sidearm pass is used most often when a player is being closely guarded and needs to pass around the defender to a teammate. This can be an excellent pass to use for feeding the post.

PROPER STANCE

When preparing to make the sidearm pass, the player must first assume the basic athletic stance (as discussed in "Passing Basics" on page 45), with the feet positioned slightly wider than shoulder-width apart and the knees bent. This stance allows the player to maintain balance. The head should be positioned over the support base, slightly behind the knees and over the waist, with the back straight.

Figure 3.25 Initial hand and arm positioning for the sidearm pass.

HAND AND ARM POSITIONING

When preparing to make the sidearm pass, the player should move the ball to one side and position it between the shoulder and hip (see figure 3.25). The player should also take a step in the same direction (see the following section, "Stepping Around the Defender," for more information on footwork). The player should be careful not to bring the ball behind the body because it takes longer to execute the pass from this position. This position also makes it easier for a defender to steal the ball from behind. Rather, the player needs to pass from beside the body, between the shoulder and the hip. The player should keep both hands on the ball, with the nonpassing hand in front, until the release so that the player can stop the pass or make a fake if necessary.

RELEASING THE BALL

The release for the sidearm pass can be made with two hands on the ball or one hand. When passing with one hand, the ball should be released off the first and second finger (see figure 3.26a). The two-handed sidearm pass should be released off the first and second fingers of both hands (see figure 3.26b). The player should keep the elbows in, flexing the wrist and fingers and extending the legs, back, and arms. The player should follow through by forcing the wrist and fingers through the ball to put force into the pass. The player should also point the first and second fingers of each hand toward the target.

At a Glance

The following parts of the text offer additional information on the sidearm pass:

Offensive Footwork	p. 22
Passing Basics	p. 45
Catching	p. 61

a   b

Figure 3.26 Release for *(a)* a one-handed and *(b)* a two-handed sidearm pass.

(continued)

Figure 3.27 Stepping around a defender.

STEPPING AROUND THE DEFENDER

When being closely guarded, the passer may step around the defender when making a sidearm pass. The passer should first maintain a balanced stance, which is the most important component for quickness. As the player moves the ball to one side, the player will also take a step in that direction with the nonpivot foot. To start, the player's weight will be on the back foot, and as the pass is made, the weight shifts to the front foot (see figure 3.27). For example, if a player's left foot is the pivot foot, and he or she will be using a sidearm pass on the left side, the player will take a crossover step with the right foot to make the pass. The passing hand will always be to the outside, meaning that the lead foot (the foot that makes the crossover step) must always be the nonpivot foot.

Common Errors

You may run into several common errors when teaching your athletes the sidearm pass.

Error	Error correction
The player's sidearm pass lacks force.	The player may be bringing the ball behind the body, thus forcing the elbow out. Teach players that they can put more force behind the pass if they keep the elbow in while flexing the wrists and fingers—and extending the legs, back, and arms—on the release.
The player's sidearm pass lacks accuracy.	The player may be bringing the ball behind the body, thus forcing the elbow out and leading to an incomplete follow-through. Teach players to point the first and second fingers of the passing hand toward the target on the release (both hands when making a two-handed sidearm pass).

Behind-the-Back Pass

KEY POINTS

The most important components of the behind-the-back pass are

o proper stance,

o hand and arm positioning, and

o making the pivot.

The behind-the-back pass, as its name implies, is a pass made behind the body. It is typically used when a defender overplays the chest pass or during a two-on-one fast break when the defender comes between the two offensive players. This pass should only be used by players with more advanced passing skills because the player is required to wrap the arm behind the body, thus making the target much more difficult to hit.

PROPER STANCE

When preparing to execute the behind-the-back pass, the player must first assume a well-balanced athletic stance, with the feet shoulder-width apart and the knees bent (as discussed in "Passing Basics" on page 45). The head should be positioned over the support base, slightly behind the knees and over the waist, with the back straight. This stance will allow the passer to impart more power and speed to the ball.

HAND AND ARM POSITIONING

Initially, the player should hold the ball with both hands in front of the body until beginning the movement of the behind-the-back pass. When the player is ready to make the pass, the player should move the ball to a position behind the hip with both hands (see figure 3.28). The passing hand should be positioned behind the ball, and the nonpassing hand should be positioned in front of the

At a Glance

The following parts of the text offer additional information on the behind-the-back pass:

Offensive Footwork	p. 22
Passing Basics	p. 45
Catching	p. 61

Figure 3.28   Hand and arm positioning for the behind-the-back pass.

(continued)

Figure 3.29 Releasing the ball on a behind-the-back pass.

ball. The player should keep both hands on the ball until the release.

The player should release the ball with a snap of the wrist, imparting spin to the ball (as discussed in "Passing Basics" on page 45). The passing arm should be in contact with the player's back, and the hand should be positioned near the opposite hip, with the palm up (see figure 3.29).

MAKING THE PIVOT

As the player brings the ball behind the hip (as discussed in "Hand and Arm Positioning"), the player must pivot on the ball of the back foot, turning the body to the passing-arm side. As the player releases the ball, the player's weight shifts from the back foot to the front foot. The player should keep the shoulders in a direct line with the target until the ball is released.

Common Errors

You may run into several common errors when teaching your athletes the behind-the-back pass.

Error	Error correction
The player's behind-the-back pass is inaccurate.	Emphasize that the passer's shoulders should be in a direct line with the target and that the passing hand's fingers should be pointing at the target.
The player's behind-the-back pass lacks power.	Emphasize that the ball should be released with a snap of the wrist. The passer's weight should also shift from the back foot to the front foot as the ball is released to give power to the pass.
The ball hits the player's hip on the behind-the-back pass.	Show players that they must pivot on the ball of the back foot and turn the body to the passing-arm side. This will get the hip out of the way for the pass.

Catching

KEY POINTS

The most important components of catching are

o ready position,
o moving to the pass, and
o receiving the ball.

Because passing is the quickest way to move the ball and challenge the defense, it is the primary tool of the offensive team's attack. Getting the ball to an open player to set up a scoring opportunity is the basic objective of an offense, and passing and catching are the most effective way of achieving this. In essence, the best pass is one that enables the receiver to catch the ball in position to shoot (within the receiver's shooting range) or in position to set up another player to shoot. Therefore, players must always be ready to catch the ball, which is an often overlooked skill. Players must be able to anticipate when and where the pass will be thrown.

READY POSITION

When preparing to catch a ball, players need to first be in a ready position, which requires the player to be in a well-balanced stance with the feet shoulder-width apart and the hands up (see figure 3.30). Receivers often use an unspoken signal to communicate to the passer to pass the ball—the receiver raises the open hands to the passer, as if to say, "I'm open. Give me the ball." The hands need to be out from the chest, with the fingers pointed up and spread comfortably, and with the thumbs almost touching each other. Players must keep their eyes on the ball, watching the ball into the hands until the hands touch the ball. If players take their eyes off the ball, even for a split second, this can cause them to lose track of where the ball is and can increase the chances of a fumble or a steal.

MOVING TO THE PASS

As discussed in "Passing Basics" on page 45, players should always be ready to move to the pass and, when possible, use either a two-step

Figure 3.30 Ready position when receiving a pass.

stop or jump stop (see "Offensive Footwork" on page 22). Of the two, the jump stop is a quicker stop and is recommended when a player is playing with his or her back to the basket, because it allows either foot to be used as the pivot foot. Some players, however, like the two-step stop when playing on the perimeter because it helps them establish a rhythm for their shot by always pivoting on the inside foot.

When using the two-step stop, the player's first step is toward the ball—with the arms out in an effort to prevent a defender from moving in front and stealing the ball—as the player pivots on the inside foot, that is, the foot closest to the basket (see figure 3.31a).

(continued)

The second step would be a takeoff step used for the shot or to square up in a triple-threat position (see figure 3.31*b*). When using the jump stop, the player will move toward the ball, with the arms out to prevent a defender from moving in front and stealing the ball (see figure 3.32*a*), and then use the jump stop when catching the ball (see figure 3.32*b*). The player can then pivot on either foot to square up to the basket.

a   b

Figure 3.31   **Two-step stop when catching a pass.**

a   b

Figure 3.32   **Jump stop when catching a pass.**

RECEIVING THE BALL

Because a pass is not always thrown accurately to the chest area, different methods for catching the ball should be taught, depending on where the ball is aimed. When the pass is thrown near the receiver's chest area and above the waist, the receiver should position both hands up, meaning that the thumbs are together (see figure 3.33a). When the pass is thrown near the middle of the receiver's body and below the waist, the receiver positions both hands down, meaning that the thumbs are apart (see figure 3.33b). When a pass is thrown to one side of the receiver, the receiver blocks the pass with one hand and tucks with the other hand (see figure 3.33c).

a   b   c

Figure 3.33 Hand positioning for the catch.

When catching any pass, however, a player should place both hands on the ball immediately. The receiver should "give" with the ball while catching it by bending the elbows slightly and bringing the ball in toward the chest. This cushions the impact of the pass and gives the receiver better control of the ball. As the player receives the pass, he or she should always square up to the basket.

At a Glance

The following parts of the text offer additional information on proper catching and receiving:

Offensive Footwork	p. 22
Passing Basics	p. 45

(continued)

Common Errors

You may run into several common errors when teaching your athletes how to catch and receive the ball.

Error	Error correction
The player is not ready to receive the pass from his or her teammate.	Emphasize that receivers need to communicate with the passer by raising the hands out from the chest, with the fingers pointed up and spread comfortably.
The ball is intercepted.	Show players that they cannot stand still and wait for the ball to get to them. They must always be ready to move to the pass. This will prevent a defender from moving in front and stealing the ball.
The receiver fumbles the ball when catching the pass.	Emphasize that receivers should "give" with the ball as they catch it by bending the elbows slightly and bringing the ball in toward the chest. This cushions the impact of the pass and gives the receiver better control of the pass. Receivers must also watch the ball into the hands.
The player travels when catching the pass.	Emphasize that players should always move to the pass and should use either a two-step stop or a jump stop when receiving the ball.

Shooting is one of the most important individual technical skills a player must learn in order to become a successful basketball player. The basic objective in the game of basketball is to score by making shots. Proper technique and form are critical components to becoming a good shooter.

BALANCED STANCE

Figure 3.34   Initial stance for shooting.

When preparing to shoot the ball, players should first assume a well-balanced stance in order to sustain both power and rhythm. The base, or foot position, of this stance is the foundation of the player's balance. When assuming this stance, the player should face the basket, but the shooting shoulder should be turned slightly toward the basket (see figure 3.34). The player's knees should be slightly bent, and the feet should be shoulder-width apart with the shooting foot positioned slightly ahead of the nonshooting foot. Typically, this means that the toe of the back foot should be aligned with the heel of the shooting foot. The toes should be pointed straight ahead, which will align the knees, hips, and shoulders to the basket. Additionally, the player's head should be positioned slightly forward over the waist and feet to help the player maintain proper balance.

FOCUSING ON THE TARGET

For most shots, the player should focus on the rim as the target. Players should be taught to concentrate on the rim, or more specifically, the eyelet that holds the net. If the player is positioned at a 45-degree angle to the backboard, as a player typically would be for a layup, the target is the top corner of the square on the backboard. For all shots, however, players should keep their eyes on the target and should resist the urge to follow the flight of the ball until after it reaches the goal. Concentrating on the target is very important in developing a consistent, accurate shot.

HAND POSITIONING

When preparing to shoot, the player first holds the ball in the *shooting pocket*—in front of and above the shooting shoulder, between the ear and shoulder. The player should place the shooting hand directly behind the ball, with the first finger and thumb positioned at approximately a 70-degree angle. The wrist should be bent and locked,

(continued)

forming an L-shape, and the fingers should be spread comfortably with the ball touching the fingers and pads (see figure 3.35a). Many players mistakenly hold the ball with the heel or palm of the hand, but when the hand is held correctly, a natural cup is formed that allows the ball to contact the pads of the player's fingers and not the palm. The nonshooting hand will act as the balance hand and is used to steady or balance the ball, not to shoot it. The player should position the balance hand at the side of the ball, with the fingers spread and touching the ball slightly to maintain balance in the shot (see figure 3.35b).

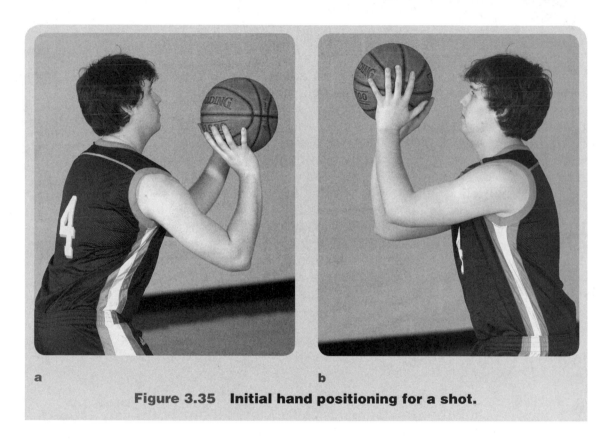

a   b

Figure 3.35   Initial hand positioning for a shot.

RELEASE

To release the shot properly, the player's stance, hands, and arms must first be in the correct positions (as discussed previously), and they must all move in a continuous upward direction. The player should move the arm, wrist, and fingers up and toward the basket at a 45- to 60-degree angle, with a complete extension of the shooting arm. The player should release the ball "up and over" by thrusting the fingers up and forward through the ball and releasing the ball off of the index finger of the shooting hand. To keep the ball aligned with the basket, the shooter must keep the shooting elbow in, within the frame of the body. If the elbow is out when shooting the ball, it is much more difficult for the player to get correct rotation on the ball. The player should keep the balance hand on the ball until immediately before the release, at which point the player will move the hand slightly away from the ball. Your players may better understand this motion by visualizing that they are shooting out the top of a glass telephone booth. The player will generate the final force and control of the shot by flexing the wrist and fingers forward and down.

FOLLOW-THROUGH

After the release, the index finger of the shooting hand should point straight at the target, the thumb should point down, and the palm should be facing down, with the wrist flexed. The nonshooting hand will finish in a vertical position with the fingertips even with the wrist of the shooting hand (see figure 3.36). Players should visualize putting their hand over the rim and into the basket.

Figure 3.36 Follow-through on a shot.

Common Errors

You may run into several common errors when teaching your athletes how to shoot.

Error	Error correction
The player's mechanics look okay, but the shot is way off the mark.	Emphasize the importance of focusing on the rim. Players should not watch the flight of the ball.
The player's shot hits the right side of the rim (right-handed shooter).	The player's balance hand may be too involved with the shot. Make sure they keep the elbow in and under the ball and that they use a proper follow-through.
The player's shot hits the left side of the rim (right-handed shooter).	The player may be pushing the ball and not using the legs. Make sure players keep the elbow in and under the ball and use proper follow-through.
The player's shot hits the front of the rim and is flat.	Emphasize that players should work on getting the release up and over the rim. They should use the legs and work on their shooting rhythm. Make sure players keep the wrist under the ball and use proper follow-through.
The player's shot is consistently short.	Show players that they need to use the legs and have a smooth rhythm to their release. Players should work on follow-through and should make sure their eyes are on the target.
The player's shot rims out instead of falling in.	The player's balance hand may be too involved with the shot. Remind players that the nonshooting hand should release before the ball leaves the shooting hand. Players must also make sure that they get the thumb of the shooting hand down in the follow-through.
The player's shot hits hard on the rim.	Emphasize that players need to work on touch. Players need to make sure the ball is not in the palm of the hand. They also need to relax the thumb of the shooting hand and release the ball off the index finger with backspin.

KEY POINTS

The most important components of a set shot are

- o balanced stance,
- o focusing on the target,
- o hand and arm positioning,
- o release, and
- o follow-through.

The set shot—the type of shot most commonly used when a player is not closely guarded—is the most basic shot in the game of basketball. The advantage of the set shot is that the shooter does not have to worry about timing the jump as he or she does when performing the jump shot; for this reason, many players consider the set shot an easier shot to use. The set shot is also the preferred shot at the free throw line, and many three-point shooters use the one-hand set shot because it is too difficult to shoot a jump shot from that far away from the basket.

BALANCED STANCE

When preparing to take a set shot, players should assume a well-balanced stance with the feet shoulder-width apart and the toe of the back foot aligned with the heel of the shooting foot (see figure 3.37). When the player is shooting a free throw, however, the shooting foot should be aligned with the middle of the basket at the free throw line, and the toe of the nonshooting foot should be aligned with the heel of the shooting foot (see figure 3.38). For all shots, though, the player should point the toes forward and bend the knees to provide crucial power to the shot.

Figure 3.37 Proper stance for a set shot.

Figure 3.38 Proper stance for a free throw.

FOCUSING ON THE TARGET

For the set shot, players should focus on the rim as the target (as discussed in "Shooting Basics" on page 65). Players should be taught to concentrate on the eyelet that holds the net, and they should resist the urge to look up at the ball because this can affect the aim of the shot. Players should also remember to avoid following the flight of the ball and should not look at it until after it reaches the basket.

HAND AND ARM POSITIONING

When a player is taking a set shot, the player's shooting hand should be comfortably spread, with the index finger lined up with the valve on the ball. The player should position the nonshooting hand at the side of the ball; this hand is used for balance in the shot. The player should keep the shooting elbow in and in front of the wrist and shooting foot.

RELEASE

To begin the release, the player generates an initial force by performing a down and up motion with the legs; as the body moves up, the player moves the arm up and over, thrusting the fingers up and forward through the ball. When the arms and hands

At a Glance

The following parts of the text offer additional information on the set shot:

SHOOTING FREE THROWS

The set shot is the most common shot that players use at the free throw line. Many games are won or lost at the free throw line, so it is very important to teach your players the proper mechanics of the free throw to ensure their success at the line.

Establishing a Routine

Establishing a specific routine during free throws will help your players check the proper mechanics before the shot and will help players focus on the proper mechanics. Many players like to use a set number of dribbles before the shot. Visualization of the made basket—that is, shooting the basket mentally before the actual shot—is another common part of a routine.

Learning to Relax

Deep breathing while preparing for the shot can be effective in helping players relax. The player should take a deep breath and relax the shoulders and other muscles. As the player takes a deep breath, the player should work to let go of any self-doubt or negative thoughts he or she might have regarding the shot.

Reciting Positive Affirmations

Saying key words or phrases to themselves will also help players in the relaxation process. "I will make this shot" or "All net" are examples of words or phrases that can be used. To increase their success at the free throw line, players should practice not only the mechanics of the shot, but also the routine, relaxation, and affirmations—every day.

(continued)

have reached approximately a 60-degree angle, the player first flexes the wrist of the shooting hand back, and then brings the hand forward to release the ball. The nonshooting, or balance, hand should stay on the ball until just before the point of release.

Players need to learn that the legs establish rhythm for the release by helping to synchronize the movements of the shot. For example, the knees are flexed when the shot begins, and the rhythm of the shot comes from the extension of the player's legs, back, shoulders, and shooting elbow and the flexion of the wrist. As the legs reach full extension, the back and shoulders extend in a smooth upward direction.

FOLLOW-THROUGH

In the follow-through, the player should point the index finger straight at the target, with the palm and fingers of the shooting hand facing down (see figure 3.39). The palm of the nonshooting, or balance, hand should face inward, with the thumb pointing toward the shooter's head. The player should hold this position for approximately a one-second count on a field goal attempt or until the ball reaches the basket on a free throw.

Figure 3.39 Follow-through on the set shot.

Common Errors

You may run into several common errors when teaching your athletes how to shoot the set shot.

Error	Error correction
The player's nonshooting hand is pushing against the ball at the release.	Emphasize that the nonshooting hand should only be used to guide the ball during the shot. Players should keep the palm facing the ball and the thumb facing the forehead to help keep the hand out of the shot.
The player's shot is flat and often hits the front of the rim.	Emphasize that the elbow needs to flex upward, not forward, in the shot. Also, teach shooters that the hand should go up and over (the rim) in the release instead of at the basket.
The player's shot is often short.	Show players that they need to work on using the legs and having a smooth rhythm to the release. Make sure that players use a proper follow-through and that their eyes are on the target.

Jump Shot

KEY POINTS

The most important components of a jump shot are

- balanced stance,
- focusing on the target,
- hand and arm positioning,
- making the jump,
- release, and
- follow-through.

The jump shot, a shooting technique used by players as they advance in their skill level, is similar to the set shot except that the ball is aligned higher and the player shoots after jumping. The jump shot is an ideal shot to use when players are close to the basket, because it is a much more difficult shot for a defender to block. The jump shot can be a very effective shot, but because the player is in the air when he or she shoots the ball, this type of shot requires the player to have great upper body strength.

BALANCED STANCE

When preparing to take a jump shot, the player must be in a well-balanced stance with the feet shoulder-width apart, the back straight, the head up, and the shoulders square to the basket (see figure 3.40). (At times, a player may begin the jump shot with the shoulders not square to the basket, such as when beginning the jump shot as the player cuts to a pass. In these situations, the player will square up in the jump.) In this stance, the knees are bent much lower than they would be for the set shot, and the buttocks should be positioned just above the knees. This lower positioning gives the player more time to put more power behind the shot and to get the body into the air.

FOCUSING ON THE TARGET

As mentioned in "Shooting Basics" on page 65, for most shots, the player should focus on the rim as the target; for shots where the player is positioned at a 45-degree angle to the backboard, the target should be the top

Figure 3.40   Initial stance for the jump shot.

corner of the square on the backboard. For all shots, however, players should keep their eyes on the target and should resist the urge to follow the flight of the ball until after it reaches the goal. The biggest difference when executing a jump shot is that the shooter is focused on the basket from underneath the ball instead of over the ball as in the set shot.

(continued)

Figure 3.41 Hand positioning for the jump shot.

HAND AND ARM POSITIONING

To begin the jump shot, the player should place the shooting hand and nonshooting hand in the same positions as for the set shot; the shooting hand should be comfortably spread, with the index finger lined up with the valve on the ball, and the nonshooting hand should be at the side of the ball. As the player makes the jump (as discussed in the following section), the player will raise the ball from the shooting pocket to a position at the top of the forehead, with the forearm of the shooting arm at a right angle to the floor and the upper arm parallel to the floor (see figure 3.41). The player uses the nonshooting hand to provide balance to the shot (as discussed in "Shooting Basics").

In situations where the player will take a jump shot off of a pass, the player should step with the inside foot—that is, the foot closest to the basket—using a two-step stop (as discussed in "Offensive Footwork" on page 22) to receive the pass. The player should flex the knees when starting the jump shot. The use of the two-step stop when receiving the ball will help the shooter gain balance and rhythm for the beginning of the shot.

MAKING THE JUMP

The basic mechanics covered for the set shot are essentially the same as those used for the jump shot. Most important, the shooter should be in a well-balanced, low stance to help prepare for the jump, because the shooter will need to explode off both feet for the shot.

When jumping, the player should execute a controlled jump straight up into the air, moving the ball from the shooting pocket to a position at the top of the forehead (as mentioned in "Hand and Arm Positioning" and shown in figure 3.41). The height of the jump depends largely on the range of the shot; however, players should know that they don't need to jump too high, but rather they should jump a height that is comfortable to them. Maintaining balance and control is more important than the height of the jump. For example, when a player is closely guarded and is playing close to the basket, the player will want to generate at least enough force in the jump to jump higher than the defender.

RELEASE

Players should release the ball at the peak of the jump, and the arm, wrist, and fingers should provide most of the force for the shot. When shooting from farther away from the basket, players will release the ball on the way up to avoid putting too much strain on the arm and shoulder. The player should snap the wrist, and backspin will be produced on the ball as the fingers thrust the ball up and over. When releasing the ball on the jump shot, some players have reported that they feel as though they are hanging in the air as they release the ball. When coming down from the jump, the player should land with both feet in a well-balanced stance in the same spot as when the jump was started.

At a Glance

The following parts of the text offer additional information on shooting jump shots:

Offensive Footwork	p. 22
Catching	p. 61
Shooting Basics	p. 65

FOLLOW-THROUGH

After the release, the index finger should point straight at the target, the thumb should point down, and the palm should be facing down, with the wrist flexed. To help your players achieve proper positioning, you can teach them to visualize putting their hand over the rim and into the basket.

Common Errors

You may run into several common errors when teaching your athletes how to shoot a jump shot.

Error	Error correction
The player's shot doesn't make it to the rim.	The player may be shooting out of his or her range for a jump shot. Have the player move closer to the basket to see if the shots go in. If so, the player should practice jump shots regularly to help build strength.
The player falls into the defender when taking a jump shot.	The player is moving on the jump, rather than jumping straight up and landing in the same spot. During practice, you may want to put tape on the floor to help players better visualize where they take their jumps and where their landings should be.

Layup

Simply put, the layup is executed by "laying" the ball on a spot on the backboard so that the ball will fall into the basket. This shot is a soft shot taken near the basket on the right, left, or middle of the basket. The layup is most commonly—and most effectively—used when a player receives a pass and cuts to the basket or when a player dribbles past a defender and is able to lay the ball off the backboard off the dribble. The layup is considered the easiest shot in the game of basketball because it is taken so close to the basket; however, it is quite often missed because of a lack of concentration or a lack of fundamental skill.

Figure 3.42 Approaching the basket on a layup.

APPROACHING THE BASKET

When a player approaches the basket for a layup (assuming that the player is coming in from the right), the player grasps the ball in both hands as the right foot hits the floor, keeping the body between the ball and the defender (see figure 3.42). The player comes down hard on the left foot and thrusts sharply upward as high as possible by lifting the right knee while holding the ball in both hands; the right hand should be behind the ball, with the wrist cocked and facing the basket, and the left hand should be in front of the ball, with the wrist facing away from the basket. This last step with the left foot is a shorter step that enables the shooter to convert his or her forward motion into a vertical jump (see "Making the Jump" for more information).

FOCUSING ON THE TARGET

As mentioned in "Shooting Basics" on page 65, the player should focus on the top corner of the square on the backboard because the player will be coming in at a 45-degree angle for the layup. The player should aim for the corner of the box on the side the player will be shooting from. For example, when coming in from the left side for a layup, the player will focus on the left corner. Players should keep their eyes on the target and resist the urge to follow the flight of the ball until after it reaches the goal. Because the player is moving toward the basket, focusing directly on the corner of the square can be difficult; therefore, while moving in for the shot, the player may watch the defender up ahead or just keep the general basket area in sight.

MAKING THE JUMP

To properly shoot a layup, the player must jump off of the inside foot, which would be the left foot when coming in from the right and vice versa (as discussed previously in "Approaching the Basket"). The player uses a takeoff step, coming down hard on the inside foot (see figure 3.43a) and thrusting upward by pushing off the foot and lifting the shooting knee (see figure 3.43b). This movement will change the player's momentum from a forward motion to a vertical jump. The player should not get too far under the basket when executing the layup because this decreases the angle; furthermore, if the takeoff step occurs too far from the basket, the player will still have forward momentum. For best results, the player should begin the takeoff step at the lower block to create the best angle.

a　　　　　　　　　　　　　　　b

Figure 3.43　Making the jump on a layup.

(continued)

At a Glance

The following parts of the text offer additional information on shooting layups:

Offensive Footwork	p. 22
Catching	p. 61
Shooting Basics	p. 65

TAKING THE SHOT

As the player approaches the basket, the ball should be positioned between the ear and the shoulder on the shooting side; the player should keep the elbow inside the frame of the body. When the jump is made, the player extends the shooting arm in an upward motion, releasing the ball at the height of the jump (as shown in figure 3.43*b*). At the release of the ball, the arm should be fully extended with the palm of the shooting hand facing the backboard. The player should keep the nonshooting hand on the ball until it is released.

FINISHING THE SHOT

When the player comes down from the jump, the player should land in a balanced position, with both feet in the same spot where they started under the basket. The player's hips should be down, the arms up at chest level with the hands pointed up, the knees bent, and the center of gravity low. In this position, the player is ready to rebound or to move on defense.

Common Errors

You may run into several common errors when teaching your athletes how to perform a layup.

Error	Error correction
The player takes a broad jump on the approach to the basket.	Teach players to shorten the step that is taken before the last takeoff step. This will help players create an upward momentum, rather than forward, as they take the ball up toward the basket.
The player swings the ball across the body as he or she goes up for the shot.	Teach players to lift the ball straight up on the shot. If players swing the ball across their body when shooting a layup, the defender can make the steal more easily.
The player shoots the ball hard off the glass.	Players are most likely out of control on the layup if they are throwing the ball at the basket. The layup should be a soft shot. Teach players to lift the ball as they move into their upward momentum on the shot. They should then be able to lay the ball softly off the glass.

Offensive Rebounds

In basketball, the team that controls the boards usually controls the outcome of the game. When an offensive player is able to get the rebound after a missed shot, this gives the team a second chance to score. In addition, offensive rebounds often lead to an inside, high-percentage scoring opportunity. Offensive rebounding can be difficult against a team that is good at blocking out and playing good defensive position. However, your players can gain an advantage on offense by knowing when and where a shot is going to be taken and by getting into the proper position on the floor. Offensive players should know their teammates and know when the shot is likely to be taken, and they can use this information to their advantage.

PROPER STANCE

When preparing to rebound, offensive players must strive to maintain a balanced stance to help counter the physical play that they may encounter in rebounding, such as shoving, pushing, and bumping. In this stance, players should be positioned with the feet shoulder-width apart, the back straight, and the knees bent; players should always be on the balls of the feet and ready to move. The hands should be held above the shoulders, ready to rebound the basketball. In addition, players should keep the head up, with the eyes focused on the ball.

ANTICIPATING SHOTS

When rebounding, offensive players must be continuously aware of their teammates' positioning on the floor, especially the player with the ball, and of any shots that the team will attempt. Offensive players must be ready to move at any time and go for the ball. Being able to effectively anticipate shots is important in getting a quick first step on a defender—and that split second jump can mean the difference between a second shot for the offense or the defense getting the rebound.

ACHIEVING AN INSIDE POSITION

An inside position—in other words, a position inside the opposing player's position, or closer to the basket—is very important in securing a rebound. It is very difficult to rebound if a player isn't in this position. Defensive players naturally have an inside position for a rebound because they play between their offensive player and the basket. To get the rebound, offensive players will need to use one of the following four methods to achieve an inside position.

(continued)

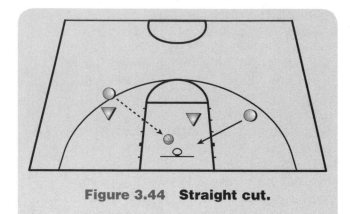

Figure 3.44   Straight cut.

Straight Cut

As mentioned, the defensive player typically plays between the offensive player and the basket, thus having the inside position. However, if the defensive player is playing out of position or is in help position, the offensive player can use a straight cut to the basket in order to gain an inside position for the offensive rebound. To do this, the offensive player uses a quick first step past the opponent before the box out is complete. For example, assume a shot is taken from the right wing and the defender from the weak side (i.e., left side, or help side) is positioned in the middle of the key for good help position. The offensive player on the left side can use this opportunity to make a straight cut to the basket and gain an inside position before the help defender can box the player out (see figure 3.44). The straight cut can also be used when the defender has the inside position. When the defender begins to block out the offensive player with a front turn, the player will make a straight cut by the defender to gain inside position.

Figure 3.45   Fake-and-go.

Fake-and-Go

If the defensive player is in an inside position and boxes out the offensive player with a reverse turn, a fake-and-go is an excellent countermove for the offensive player to use to get inside. To execute the fake-and-go, the offensive player will make a fake toward the defender's reverse step and then cut to the other side (see figure 3.45).

Figure 3.46   Step back.

Step Back

If the defensive player is in an inside position and leans back on the offensive player while boxing him or her out, the offensive player should use a step back move to get inside. When executed correctly, the step back will throw the defender off balance. When the defender loses balance, the offensive player cuts around the opponent and goes for the rebound (see figure 3.46).

Spin Move

If the defensive player is in an inside position and holds the offensive player's body while boxing him or her out, the offensive player can use a spin move to get inside. The offensive player places the forearm on the defender's back, makes a reverse pivot, cuts around the opponent, and goes for the rebound.

GETTING THE REBOUND

When going for the rebound, offensive players must time their jump so that they reach the ball at the top of the jump. This takes a lot of practice, because the exact timing of the jump will change from shot to shot and rebound to rebound. At the height of the jump, the player should have the hands positioned above the shoulders and approximately ball-width apart (see figure 3.47a). Offensive players should snatch the ball with two hands, get the elbows out, and bring the ball down aggressively to the chin (see figure 3.47b). When coming down from the jump, players should strive to land in a balanced stance with the feet approximately shoulder-width apart, ready to shoot, pass, or dribble.

a   b

Figure 3.47   Jumping to secure the rebound.

(continued)

MAKING DECISIONS AFTER THE REBOUND

After securing a rebound, a player has several options. The best option after getting an offensive rebound is to shoot the ball. Offensive players who are skilled enough can try to shoot the ball before returning to the floor—at the height of the player's jump, the player puts the ball back on the glass before coming down. In situations where offensive rebounders must come down with the rebound first, they should go right back up with the shot and not take a dribble. Putting the ball on the ground takes too much time and gives the defense a chance to recover. (An exception would be on a long rebound where the player is able to take one dribble in for a layup.) If the rebounder is not in a position to take a shot after the rebound, the player also has the option to either pass to an open teammate or use a power dribble to move out of the congested area.

Common Errors

You may run into several common errors when teaching your athletes how to rebound on offense.

Error	Error correction
After the player gets the rebound, an opponent strips it away.	Emphasize that players must keep the ball above the forehead (and not bring the ball down) in order to better protect the ball.
The player is too late when going for the rebound.	Teach players to be aware of their teammates' positioning and to anticipate the shot. They shouldn't watch the shot, but should instead move quickly into position for the rebound.
The player's shot is blocked when attempting a shot after getting the rebound.	The defense has also been taught to anticipate a shot attempt after a rebound, so they will be ready for this. Teach players to try tipping the ball or using a fake before the shot in an effort to deceive the defense.

Cuts

KEY POINTS

The most important components of cuts are

o proper stance,

o hand and arm positioning, and

o making the cut.

In basketball, a cut is a move performed by an offensive player without the ball in order to get open and free of the defender. Most cuts are preceded by a purposeful deceptive movement, or fake, that helps the offensive player get open on the cut by deceiving the defender. Players use cuts to get open against full-court pressure or to get open in the half-court offense against denial defense. Post players can also use cuts to get open in the lane. Cuts are an important element in effectively using screens and opening up opportunities for easy shots. Every player on the offensive team needs to know how to make cuts. It doesn't matter how good a player is with the ball if that player cannot get open to receive a pass.

PROPER STANCE

Every cut that a player will make in a game requires the player to first be in a well-balanced stance, with the feet shoulder-width apart (as discussed in "Offensive Footwork" on page 22). Cuts involve changes in direction and speed, and they require players to be quick and deceptive; therefore, players must stay low, with their weight on the balls of the feet.

HAND AND ARM POSITIONING

The primary goal of a cut is to get open for the ball, so players must strive to have their hands up and ready for a pass from a teammate immediately upon making the cut. The player should flash the hands at approximately chest level with the fingers pointing up and the arms slightly outstretched in front of the body (see figure 3.48). This will communicate to the passer that the cutter is open and ready for the ball.

MAKING THE CUT

To effectively deceive the defense and get open, players need to have a variety of cuts that they can use based on the game situation. Following are several basic cuts that are commonly used by players:

Figure 3.48   Hand and arm positioning to communicate that a cutter is open for a pass.

(continued)

Cuts (continued)

At a Glance

The following parts of the text offer additional information on using cuts:

Offensive Footwork	p. 22
Triple-Threat Position	p. 27
Catching	p. 61
Shooting Basics	p. 65
Layup	p. 74

L-Cut

An L-cut is a cut that takes on the shape of the letter *L*, starting at the block on the edge of the free throw lane and moving up the side of the lane (see figure 3.49*a*). This cut is used when a player is being closely guarded and needs to get open for a pass. To execute the L-cut, the player, when seeing that a teammate is ready to deliver the pass, steps into the defender, making contact, and changes speed quickly by pushing off of the inside foot to pop out to the wing.

V-Cut

A V-cut is a basic zigzag or change of direction cut that takes on the shape of the letter *V* (see figure 3.49*b*). The V-cut is used when a player is attempting to get the ball on the perimeter, but it can also be used at the post. Typically, this cut is used any time a player is unable to get a pass because the defender is in the passing lane. To execute the V-cut, the offensive player places his or her weight on the foot opposite the direction the player needs to go, thus sinking the hips into the cut, then points and steps with the opposite foot. For example, a player may plant and push on the right foot and then step to the left with the left foot. If the player's defender has a foot and hand in the passing lane to deny a pass to the player at the wing, the player should take the defender toward the basket and then sharply change direction, cutting back to the outside.

Backdoor Cut

The backdoor cut is a cut in which the offensive player goes behind the defender toward the basket (see figure 3.49*c*). This cut can be used anywhere on the floor if the player's defender is overplaying the passing lane between the player and the passer. Backdoor cuts are also effective when offensive players who are being denied a pass see that their defender has taken his or her eyes off of them to look at the ball. To perform a backdoor cut, the offensive player must first realize that the defender is overplaying the passing lane. To execute the backdoor cut, a player on the wing will take the defender high (a step above the free throw line extended), push off with the outside foot, and then take a quick step with the inside foot.

Flash Cut

A flash cut is simply a quick cut toward the ball by an offensive player and is often used when a defender is preventing one of the offensive player's teammates from receiving the ball (see figure 3.49*d*). The next closest player to the passer should make a flash cut to an open area between the passer and the overplayed teammate to help relieve some of the defensive pressure and give the passer another option. A flash cut used by a post player can be very effective in relieving pressure from defensive denial on the wing. For example, the low-post player on the weak side can flash high to receive the ball if a teammate at the low post on the ball side is being denied; the high-post player can make a flash cut to the low box if it is open; or a post player on the weak-side low block can flash to the ball-side low post if the high-post player is being denied. To execute the flash cut, the player pushes off hard with the outside foot, followed by several quick steps. The player should complete the cut by landing using either a two-step stop or a jump stop.

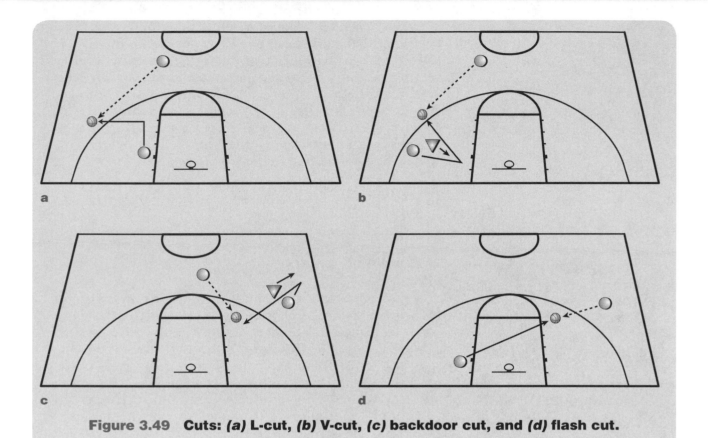

Figure 3.49 Cuts: *(a)* L-cut, *(b)* V-cut, *(c)* backdoor cut, and *(d)* flash cut.

Common Errors

You may run into several common errors when teaching your athletes how to execute proper cuts.

Error	Error correction
The player is not deceptive when making a cut and is unable to lose the defender.	Emphasize that players must be able to change direction and speed in their cuts in order to be deceptive.
The player's cuts are not sharp and are circular in direction.	Emphasize that players need to flex the knees on the pivot and push off in the new direction with the planted foot. The first step in the new direction must be toward the direction the player wants to go.
After a cut, the player is not ready to receive a pass.	Show players the importance of giving a target to the passer by putting the hands up to communicate to the passer, "Give me the ball."

Setting a screen (also referred to as *setting a pick*) is a move by the offensive player to position him- or herself to block the path of a teammate's defender in order to set up an advantage for the teammate. A player may set a screen off the ball for a teammate who is not able to get open because a defender is guarding the teammate very closely. A player may also set a screen for a teammate who has the ball. This will allow the teammate to get open off the dribble for a drive to the basket, a shot, or to make a pass to a teammate.

Figure 3.50 Proper stance when setting a screen.

PROPER STANCE

When setting a screen, the offensive player should plan on putting the center of the body on the teammate's defender at an angle that can prevent the defender from going through the screen (see figure 3.50). The player should use a two-footed jump stop to avoid an illegal moving block; the player must be stationary when setting the screen and is not allowed to move any part of the body into the defender. The screener must be prepared to take the blow from the teammate's defender moving into the screen. Therefore, the screener needs to be positioned in a well-balanced stance with the feet wider than shoulder-width apart and the knees bent. The player's hands are not part of the screen and should be crossed across the chest (for females) or crossed in front of the crotch area (for males).

SETTING THE SCREEN

Screens can be categorized according to the area of the body where contact is made. Screens can be set as a front screen, side screen, or back screen.

Front Screen

A front screen is often set as an off-the-ball screen when an offensive player needs to free a teammate to get open for the pass. The offensive player setting the screen approaches the defender, uses a two-foot jump stop, and assumes a well-balanced stance. The player must be stationary when setting the screen and is not allowed to move any part of the body into the defender. The player sets a screen on the front side of the defender as the screener's teammate cuts up to receive the ball.

Side Screen

A side screen is an on-the-ball screen set on the side of the defender; the offensive player will cut off of the screen in a way similar to when cutting off of a front screen. The difference is that the player making the cut is probably going to cut across the court and that the path of the defender being screened would be to the side. The screener approaches the defender, uses a two-foot jump stop, and assumes a well-balanced stance. The player must be stationary when setting the screen and is not allowed to move any part of the body into the defender. The screener screens for the teammate with the ball, who goes shoulder to shoulder past the screen for a penetration drive or a shot.

Back Screen

When screening an opponent from behind, the screener must allow the opponent one normal step backward without contact. The screener approaches the defender, uses a two-foot jump stop, and assumes a well-balanced stance. The player must be stationary when setting the screen and is not allowed to move any part of the body into the defender. The back screen is often an on-the-ball screen set on the defender's blind side, or back side. The dribbler runs the defender into the teammate setting a back screen. This can also be used to set a screen on a post player's defender. An example of this would be when the low post sets a back screen on the high post player's defender. Another example would be when a skip pass is being made, the low post player will set a back screen on the other post player's defender's blind side as the post player cuts off the screen. The important difference is that the screen is set on the back side of a defender.

SETTING UP THE DEFENDER

The player whom the screen is being set for has an important role in setting the defender up and running the defender into the screen. Players must remember that if the screener is still moving while setting the screen, this constitutes an illegal moving screen and the player setting the screen will be called for an illegal block. Therefore, the teammate needs to see the screen and wait until the screen is set before running the defender into the screen.

CUTTING OFF THE SCREEN

The player for whom the screen is being set must cut off the screen by going "shoulder to shoulder" with the screener so that the defender cannot slip through the screen (see figure 3.51). The player should be in a well-balanced stance and should approach the screen with control and then explode while moving by the screener. Players who are

Figure 3.51   Proper body positioning when cutting off the screen.

(continued)

At a Glance

The following parts of the text offer additional information on how to set screens:

Offensive Footwork	p. 22
Catching	p. 61
Shooting Basics	p. 65
Cuts	p. 81

cutting off a screen off the ball should have the hands up and be ready to receive the pass from their teammate as they go by the screener. Four types of cuts are commonly used when cutting off a screen, depending on how the player is being defended.

Front-Door Cut

When the defender is trailing the cutter around the screen, the player can use a front-door cut, also known as a *curl cut*, to curl around the screen to the basket, looking for a pass from the tcammate with the ball. Again, the cutter needs to move shoulder to shoulder with the screener, stay low, and push off with the outside foot when making the cut to the basket.

Pop Cut

When the defender attempts to fight through the screen, the player can use a pop cut to move out to receive the pass instead of curling to the basket. The pop cut is made by pushing off the inside foot and stepping out for the pass. This is essentially the same move as the L-cut discussed in "Cuts" on page 82. It is called a *pop cut* because the player pops out to receive the pass.

Backdoor Cut

When the defender overplays the pop cut, the offensive player can use a backdoor cut. Refer to "Backdoor Cut" on page 82 for more information.

Fade Cut

When the defender overplays the pop cut, the cutter can also use a fade cut to move away from the defender and the screener by cutting out away from the ball. This can be done by simply backpedaling off the screen.

Common Errors

You may run into several common errors when teaching your athletes how to set screens.

Error	Error correction
The screener is called for a blocking foul.	Emphasize that players need to use a jump stop when setting the screen and need to stay set until the teammate uses the screen.
The defender is able to stay with the cutter.	Show players that they need to have a wide base and should set the screen at an angle that can prevent the teammate's defender from going through it. Emphasize that players running off the screen need to go shoulder to shoulder on the cut.

To be successful, an offensive team needs to establish an inside game by getting the ball to the post players who are playing inside, near, or just outside the free throw lane (in the area sometimes referred to as *the paint*). This inside game can serve several purposes for the offense. First, by getting the ball to the post, the offensive team creates more frequent opportunities for high-percentage shots—the closer to the basket a shot is taken, the higher chance it has of going in. Getting the ball inside can also create three-point scoring opportunities because post players in the congested area are difficult to defend and are often fouled when they attempt a shot. Getting the ball to the post also forces the defense to collapse inside, which may give the offense an opportunity to pass back to the perimeter for an open three-point shot. Post players are generally the tallest and largest players on the team, but each player on the team should learn how to play the post.

KNOWING THE POST AREAS

There are three post positions—low, mid, and high post—with the low post obviously being the most dangerous to defend because it is the closest position to the basket. Some offensive sets use a single post player, others use two players, and still others use three players rotating in the post positions (a triple-post offense). The low-post area is just above the low block on either side of the free throw lane (see figure 3.52a). The mid post is between the free throw line and the low block (see figure 3.52b). The high post is at the free throw line area (see figure 3.52c). Depending on the offensive set used by the team, a single post player can move from high post to mid post to low post as the ball moves on the perimeter. Some coaches like to use two post players, and these players may play either at both of the low blocks or in a high and low position. Following is a closer look at each of the post positions.

Low Post

When a post player sets up in the low-post area, the player should be positioned outside the free throw lane (paint) with the back foot slightly above the low block and with his or her back to the free throw lane. This positioning allows the best angle for a shot. An offensive team should get the ball to the post player playing at the low-post position whenever possible. The low-post area is a very vulnerable position for the defense because it is considered a high-percentage shot area.

Mid Post

When a post player sets up in the mid-post area, the player is positioned halfway up the lane toward the free throw line. The same moves used in the low post can also be applied from the mid post. If the low-post player's defender is playing on the high side (closest to the free throw line), the post player wants to keep moving the defender up the free throw lane; this will give the post player more room for a pass. And, in doing so, the player will actually be playing the mid-post position. The

(continued)

mid-post position is often open against a zone defense. For example, the 2-1-2 zone defense has a defender at the high post and at the low post. A post player can take advantage by posting up between those two defenders.

High Post

When a post player sets up in the high-post area, the player should be positioned at the free throw line with his or her back to the basket. The high-post player should play on the ball side of the high post when the ball is below the free throw line. A post player who receives the ball in the high-post area has several options. Once the high-post player receives the ball, a pass to the low post is difficult to defend. This position is also a good means to get ball reversal when the defense makes the pass back to the point guard difficult. Yet another option is a jump shot from the high post or a dribble move to the basket.

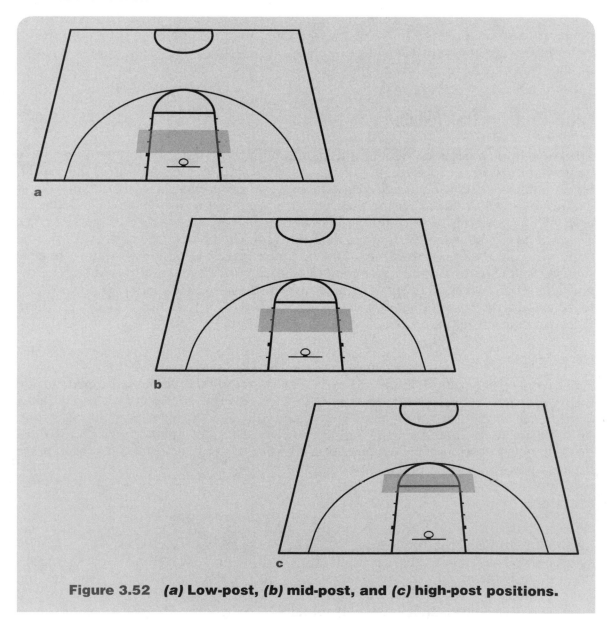

Figure 3.52 *(a)* Low-post, *(b)* mid-post, and *(c)* high-post positions.

BODY POSITIONING

Post players play with their back to the basket, and their chest should always be facing the passer (see figure 3.53). The stance at the post is basically an exaggerated version of the basic defensive stance (as discussed in "Defensive Positioning" on page 94). The post player should be in a well-balanced stance, with the feet slightly farther than shoulder-width apart; the player should bend the knees (as if the player is sitting down) in order to maintain a low center of gravity. The post areas, especially the low-post position, are physical areas of play, and keeping the feet apart and a low center of gravity will help players stay balanced so that they will not get pushed easily by the defender. The player should keep the shoulders square to the passer, showing the passer the player's number; the player's elbows should be out, with the forearms at a 45-degree angle and the upper arms parallel to the floor. The post player should position the hands up and slightly forward, with the fingers spread and pointing toward the ceiling. The passer can then pass to either hand of the low-post player, depending on which side the defender is playing.

Figure 3.53 **Proper body positioning at the post.**

GETTING OPEN IN THE POST

Post players need to maintain and hold their position so there is a passing lane between themselves and the teammate with the ball This can be done by using V-cuts and flash cuts or by stepping into the defender and making a reverse pivot (see "Offensive Footwork" on page 22 for more information). In each post area, the offensive player has to use proper footwork to get open and then maintain contact to move the defender to one side or the other. If the defender is on the high side, the offensive player will need to keep the feet active and move the defender higher; the player can then call for the ball low, with the target hand being the hand opposite the defensive player. The same is true if the defender is playing the offensive player on the low side; the offensive player must keep the feet active and move down the lane to create an open pass on the inside.

When attempting to get open, offensive players should move in the direction of the defender. They should not allow a defender to get a foot in front of their foot. Offensive players should try to get the defender on their backside or hip so they can seal the defender and make an offensive post move in the opposite direction. They do this by making contact with the defender and working to keep the defender behind them. The offensive player should keep the feet active and use the hips and buttocks to seal the defender by "sitting" on the defender's legs and maintaining contact.

(continued)

CATCHING THE BALL

After the post player has sealed the defender, the player should call for the ball with the hand farthest from the defender (see figure 3.54). The player should not turn sideways, but should continue to show his or her numbers to the passer. When the pass is made, the post player must step to the pass and use a jump stop when catching the ball so that either foot can become the pivot foot. The player should catch the ball with two hands on either side of the ball, with the fingers up. After the catch, the player should pull the ball close to the body and position it under the chin, keeping the elbows out (see figure 3.55).

Figure 3.54   Calling for the ball at the post.

Figure 3.55   Receiving a pass at the post.

MOVING AT THE POST

Once a post player receives the ball from the wing, the baseline, or the high post, the player will need to make a strong move inside to the basket. The post player can use several moves to get inside.

Drop Step Move

When the defender is positioned on the high side of the post player, the post player should use a drop step move. This move is preferred over the baseline power move when the post player is close to the basket, clearly has the defender beaten, and doesn't need to put the ball down. The drop step move is simply a big step with the foot closest to the basket followed by a layup. To execute the drop step, the post player uses a jump stop while catching the ball and then assumes a well-balanced, low stance with the elbows out and the ball at the chin. The player then uses a ball fake to the middle, takes a drop step back toward the baseline, and lays the ball off the glass.

Baseline Power Move

The baseline power move is another option when the defender is positioned on the high side of the post player. This move is similar to the drop step move, but the player uses a hard dribble and jumps off both feet, taking a jump shot instead of a layup. The baseline power move is often used when the player is slightly farther from the basket. It may also be used because a player prefers using a power layup, which is a jump shot, instead of a regular layup. The down side to this move, however, is that the ball is put on the floor (which does not occur in the drop step move). To execute the baseline power move, the post player uses a jump stop while catching the ball and then assumes a well-balanced, low stance with the elbows out and the ball at the chin. The player then uses a ball fake to the middle and pivots with a rear turn on the foot closest to the baseline, sealing off the defender with the hips and buttocks. The post player power dribbles the ball (uses one strong dribble) while making a two-foot power jump to the basket at the same time and shooting a power layup off the glass. The power jump is a two-step move where the player drops the lead foot back and slides the other foot to regain balance. The power lay-up, sometimes called a power move, is executed by jumping off both feet and taking a jump shot.

Drop Step Middle Hook

When the defender is positioned on the baseline side of the post player, the post player can use a drop step middle hook move. To execute the drop step middle hook, the post player uses a jump stop while catching the ball and then assumes a well-balanced, low stance with the elbows out and the ball under the chin. The player uses a ball fake to the baseline and takes a drop step to the middle of the paint. The player should point the toe to the middle of the paint to open up the hip and should protect the ball with the head and shoulder. On this move, the player should not lead with the ball, but should lead with the elbow instead. The player then executes a hook shot with the outside hand. The player should pivot in while taking the step, turning the body toward the basket, and then lift the knee on the shooting side and jump off the pivot foot. The shot is performed by lifting the ball to the basket with a hook motion as the player extends the shooting arm. The player must flex the wrist and fingers toward the target and release the ball off the index fingers, keeping the balance hand on the ball until the release.

(continued)

Front Turn Move

When the defender is playing off of the post player, the post player can use a front turn move. To execute the front turn move, the post player uses a jump stop while catching the ball and then assumes a well-balanced, low stance with the elbows out and the ball at the chin. Because the defender is playing off the post player, the post player does not need to seal the defender in order to get an advantage. The post player simply uses a front pivot to the baseline and shoots a jump shot off the glass.

Common Errors

You may run into several common errors when teaching your athletes how to play the post.

Error	Error correction
The post player picks up the pivot foot when receiving the ball and is called for traveling.	The player is most likely not using a jump stop when catching the ball at the post. Teach players to use a jump stop, which will allow them to then use either foot as the pivot foot when making the post move.
The defender forces the post player out of the post area.	Show players that when playing the post they must maintain a balanced stance and must "sit down" to keep their center of gravity low.
The post player receives the ball, and a defensive player from the perimeter gives help on the post player, causing a jump ball to be called.	Emphasize the importance of keeping the ball below the chin with the elbows out. Post players must be quick with their move or pass back out to a teammate in the area where help came from.
The post player tries to get open, and the defender knocks the ball away on the pass.	The player is probably positioning the body sideways to the passer, which makes the player more susceptible to getting the ball knocked away. Teach players to stay square to the passer, with a wide stance and the arms out. This gives the passer a much wider target and makes the post player more difficult to defend.
The post player puts the ball on the floor as soon as he or she catches it without making a move to the basket.	Emphasize that players should make their post move without the dribble if possible, because the defender has a better opportunity to steal the ball whenever it is put on the floor. Players should only dribble if they're using a power dribble or if they can make a one-dribble layup (after squaring up to the basket).
The post player attempts to drop step to the baseline, and the defender is there.	Show players the importance of reading the defender. They should peek over their shoulder or feel which side the defender is playing them on, and they should fake one way before making a move in the other direction.

chapter 4

Defensive Technical Skills

This chapter covers the defensive technical skills that you and your players must know to be successful. In this chapter, you will find the following skills:

Defensive Positioning

KEY POINTS

The most important components of proper defensive positioning are

- proper stance,
- hand positioning, and
- moving defensively.

An effective defender must be able to react instantly to the moves of the offensive player and must also have the ability to be proactive in applying pressure to the offense. To be ready to move in any direction or to stop and start with balance and quickness, defensive players must use good footwork and proper body positioning. A good defender is always keeping the feet active, ready to move.

PROPER STANCE

As mentioned, a defender must be able to move quickly in any direction while maintaining balance. To do this, a defensive player must be in a well-balanced defensive stance that allows the player to move quickly, change direction, jump, and stop under control.

In this defensive stance, the player's feet should be positioned slightly wider than shoulder-width apart and should be staggered, with one foot in front of the other (see figure 4.1). The front foot, sometimes called the *lead foot*, should be positioned outside the opponent, and the back foot should be positioned in line with the middle of the opponent's body. This allows the defensive player to be in control of dictating the direction the offensive player will move. Additionally, when positioned in the defensive stance, the player should bend the knees and keep the weight evenly distributed on the balls of the feet. The player's back should be kept straight, and the head should be positioned over the support base, slightly behind the knees and over the waist. Additionally, defenders should strive to always keep their eyes focused on the opponent's midsection so that they don't react incorrectly to a head or ball fake by the opponent.

Figure 4.1 **Basic athletic stance for defense.**

HAND POSITIONING

Hand positioning is important for a defender. The hands can be used to pressure an opponent in a closely guarded situation, or they can be used to deter and deflect passes. It becomes much more difficult for an offensive player to see an open teammate when the defender's hands are up and active. Your players can use three basic hand positions to their advantage when playing defense:

1. To pressure the shooter, the defender should keep one hand up (the hand on the side of the lead foot) to defend against a shot. The other hand should be held to the side to guard against a pass (see figure 4.2a).

2. To pressure the dribbler, the defender should keep the lead hand at waist level with the palm up. The defender can then flick at the ball with the hand that is closest to the ball. The trail or back hand should always be near the back shoulder of the defender, moving back and forth like a windshield wiper to cover the passing lane by the head (see figure 4.2b).

3. To pressure the passer, the defender should keep both hands up above the shoulders, making it difficult for the offensive player to make an effective pass (see figure 4.2c). Ideally, this will force the offensive player to use a lob or bounce pass, which can be intercepted more easily. The defender will also be in a good position to block shots because the hands are already up. Defenders should be careful not to spread the hands too far apart because this may cause them to lose balance.

MOVING DEFENSIVELY

When moving to take away an offensive player's move, defensive players should use a step-slide motion, commonly referred to as the *push step*. Defenders should take very short, quick steps; the first step is crucial because if the defender is late with the first step, the offensive player will gain an advantage. From the balanced stance, the defensive player should take a short first step with the nearest—or lead—foot while shifting weight in the

Figure 4.2 **Defensive hand positioning:** *(a)* pressuring a shooter, *(b)* pressuring a dribbler, and *(c)* pressuring a passer.

(continued)

95

At a Glance

The following parts of the text offer additional information on proper defensive positioning:

direction the offensive player is going (in an effort to stop the opponent). The defender uses the trail foot to push the weight to the lead foot and then performs a pulling slide step to regain basic position. For example, when moving to the right, the defender shifts the weight to the right and takes a step in that direction with the right foot, keeping the feet wide and moving in straight lines at all times. Defenders should use the floor to their advantage, pushing off the floor with the opposite foot as they step.

Common Errors

You may run into several common errors when teaching your athletes proper defensive positioning.

Error	Error correction
The player is off balance and forward in the defensive stance.	Emphasize that players should not bend at the waist. Players should bend the knees and stay low.
The opponent attacks the defender's lead foot.	Teach defenders to keep the lead foot outside the opponent and the back foot in line with the middle of the opponent's body. This will help defenders protect the lead foot.
The opponent is able to use ball and head fakes effectively.	Teach defenders to keep their eyes on the midsection of the opponent instead of the ball or the opponent's head.

KEY POINTS

The most important components of blocking shots are

o anticipating the shot,
o proper body positioning,
o aligning with the opponent, and
o flicking the ball.

A blocked shot can be a huge momentum builder in a game—and sometimes can even alter the outcome of a game. A successful shot blocker can force the opposing team to change their offensive style and take more shots from the perimeter. The most difficult teams to score against are those that have a defender who can disrupt and alter high-percentage shots in the key. Not every player on your team will be a shot blocker; however, if you are able to teach this skill to players who have height, long arms, the ability to jump, and good instincts, this will benefit the team immensely.

ANTICIPATING THE SHOT

In preparing to block a shot, timing and anticipation play a critical role. The defender should not jump too early because this will allow the offensive player to use a step-through move as the defender is in the air. A defender is better off waiting for the offensive player to leave the ground (rather than reading the fake as an actual shot) and then going up for the block. On the other hand, defenders also want to avoid leaving their feet too late because they will not be able to make the block if the ball is already in the net.

PROPER BODY POSITIONING

When preparing to block a shot or when defending an opponent with the ball, the defender should be positioned in a balanced stance with the weight on the balls of the feet and the knees slightly bent (see figure 4.3). As discussed previously in "Defensive Positioning," one of the player's hands should be up at eye level or higher as if they are ready for a rebound, and the other hand should be held out to the side. The player has only a fraction of a second to react and extend both hands to block or deflect a shot once it has left the shooter's hand (as discussed in the next section "Blocking the Shot"). If it takes the defender another half second to raise the hand because it is in a low position, the chances of making the block are diminished greatly.

Figure 4.3 Proper stance against an opponent with the ball.

(continued)

Figure 4.4 Proper body positioning when an opponent takes a shot.

ALIGNING WITH THE OPPONENT

When preparing to block a shot, the defender must also align the body so that it is square to the offensive player taking the shot, as shown in figure 4.3. If the body is turned sideways when attempting a block, the defender will find it difficult to elevate on the jump (see "Flicking the Ball" for more information on the jump) and will be susceptible to a shot fake and step-through move by the opponent. Turning the body sideways also makes it easier for the shooter to draw body contact from the defender because the defender's feet are not in a position to react and move in any direction; as a result, space is created between the shooter and shot blocker, commonly resulting in a foul by the defender.

FLICKING THE BALL

As soon as the ball leaves the shooter's hands, the defender must be ready to explode off the floor with a two-step jump, raising the arm to full extension and flicking at the ball with the fingertips of the hand—just enough so that the ball may be deflected and possession retained by the shot blocker (see figure 4.4). The majority of young players feel most comfortable using their dominant hand to block shots, while more advanced players will have the skill level and the flexibility to use either hand for the block.

Also note that many young players think it's flashy to swat the ball completely out of bounds when blocking, but this isn't necessary to be an effective and strong shot blocker. Teach your players that the ideal result of a blocked shot is for yourself or a teammate to be able to catch the ball after the block, giving your team possession.

At a Glance

The following parts of the text offer additional information on blocking shots:

Common Errors

You may run into several common errors when teaching your athletes how to block shots.

Error	Error correction
The defender jumps too soon for the shot block, and the offensive player executes a step-through move for a shot.	Emphasize that defenders should not jump too soon when attempting to block a shot. They should wait until the offensive player leaves the floor.
The defender fouls the shooter when attempting to block the shot.	Emphasize that defenders should not turn sideways to the shooter. When attempting to block a shot, defenders should go straight up with a two-step jump, raising the arm to full extension and flicking at the ball with the fingertips of the hand.
The defender is too late in attempting to block the shot.	Emphasize the importance of anticipating the release for timing the jump. Teach players to keep the hands up at eye level or higher.

Defensive Rebounds

KEY POINTS

The most important components of the defensive rebound are

o maintaining a defensive position,

o anticipating the shot,

o achieving an inside position,

o getting the rebound, and

o making decisions after the rebound.

As previously mentioned, in basketball, the team that controls the boards usually controls the outcome of the game. By rebounding the ball effectively on the defensive end of the court, a team can limit the offense to fewer scoring opportunities. Defensive rebounding also creates opportunities for fast breaks. Players need to understand that defensive rebounding plays a critical role in the success of the team. The defensive players' aggressiveness on missed shots by the offense will help prevent the offense from getting easy second chances.

MAINTAINING A DEFENSIVE POSITION

Maintaining a good defensive position enables players to have a better chance at securing the defensive rebound. To assume the basic defensive position, the defensive player should be in a balanced stance with the feet shoulder-width apart, the knees flexed, and the back straight (as discussed in "Defensive Positioning" on page 94). The player should keep the arms up, with the hands at shoulder height or above, so that the player is ready for a rebound that comes off the boards quickly.

ANTICIPATING THE SHOT

When playing defense, all players need to know where the ball is at all times, especially when and where a shot is taken. Once a shot is taken, the defender closest to the ball should shout, "Shot" to alert teammates that the shot has been taken. All defenders should assume that the shot is a miss and should not watch the ball while it is in flight to the basket. Instead, defenders should immediately prepare to rebound the ball and should locate the offensive player they are responsible for blocking out.

ACHIEVING AN INSIDE POSITION

Gaining an inside position—one that is between the basket and the opponent—is essential to a player's success in defensive rebounding. If an offensive player gains the inside position, that player has a better chance of making shots, and the defender will likely foul by going over the back of the offensive player when the shot is attempted. Since defenders usually try to stay between the offensive player they are guarding and the basket, defenders often have an inside position at the time a shot is taken. To maintain inside position and get the rebound, defensive players first need to "box out" their opponent. Boxing out is simply blocking the offensive player's path to the ball to prevent the player from getting the rebound. To box out, a defensive player puts his or her back to the opponent's chest and then goes to the ball. The most effective means of boxing out and maintaining inside position is to use either a front or reverse pivot.

Front Pivot

Defensive players should box out using a front pivot when they want to keep the best offensive rebounder off the boards or when they are defending a player far from the basket. For example, assume the offensive player is moving to the basket on the right side of the defender. In this situation, to execute the front pivot, the defender pivots on the right leg and steps in front of the offensive player with the left leg, blocking the player's path to the basket. When using a front pivot, the defender momentarily loses sight of the ball, but since the main objective is to keep the offensive player off the board, this is okay because the defender never loses sight of the offensive player. If the offensive player attempts to go around the defender, the defender should then take short choppy steps in either direction so that the offensive player cannot step around the defender.

Reverse Pivot

Defensive players should box out using a reverse pivot when they are defending a player close to the basket. For example, assume the offensive player is moving to the basket on the right side of the defender. In this situation, to execute the reverse pivot, the defender steps toward the offensive player with the foot closest to the offensive player; then, while keeping the pivot foot in contact with the floor, the defender turns on the other foot with his or her back leading the way. If the offensive player attempts to go around the defender, the defender should then take short choppy steps in either direction so that the offensive player cannot step around the defender.

GETTING THE REBOUND

When going after the rebound, defensive players must time their jump so that they reach the ball at the top of the jump. This takes a lot of practice because the exact timing of the jump will change from shot to shot and rebound to rebound. At the height of the jump, the player's arms should be extended, with the hands approximately ball-width apart (see figure 4.5a). Defensive players should snatch the ball with two hands, get the elbows out, and bring the ball down aggressively to the chin (see figure 4.5b). When coming down from the jump, defensive players should strive to land in a balanced stance with the feet approximately shoulder-width apart, ready to pass or dribble.

a

b

Figure 4.5 **Securing the rebound.**

(continued)

MAKING DECISIONS AFTER THE REBOUND

After securing a rebound, a player has several options. The best option after getting a defensive rebound is usually the outlet pass. This pass is a two-handed overhead pass (see "Overhead Pass" on page 54) to a teammate. Ideally, the teammate is positioned on the same side of the court as the rebound, in the area from the free throw line extended to the sideline. The sides of the court are not nearly as congested as the lane, so an outlet pass to the outside has a much greater chance of being successful and not being stolen. After capturing the rebound and landing in a balanced stance, the player with the ball should use a front pivot to the outside so that the player is facing the rebound side of the court. For example, if the rebound is secured on the right side of the basket, the front pivot is performed so that the rebounder is facing the right side of the court in order to make the outlet pass. After the front pivot, the player then makes the outlet pass to the teammate positioned at the free throw line extended to the sideline. If a defender is working to take away that pass by occupying the teammate at this position, the player with the ball can take a couple of hard dribbles toward the sideline. This may enable the receiver to get open when the defender reacts to the power dribble.

Common Errors

You may run into several common errors when teaching your athletes how to rebound on defense.

Error	Error correction
The player is called for holding an opponent when attempting to box out.	Emphasize that players must keep the hands above the shoulders when boxing out the opponent. This allows them to get to the ball more quickly and avoid the temptation to hold the opposing player.
The player gets pushed under the basket when attempting to rebound.	Emphasize the need for players to keep a wide stance so they are more balanced and able to withstand the physical play that occurs at the basket.
After the player gets the rebound, an opponent knocks the ball out of his or her hands.	Teach players that they need to rebound with both hands. Players should snatch the ball with two hands and bring it to the chin, with the elbows out.
The opponent cuts around the player who is attempting to box out.	Emphasize that players need to make contact when boxing out. Players should feel the opponent and keep the opponent on their backside by taking chop steps in the direction the opponent is cutting.
The shooter gets the rebound.	Teach players that they shouldn't watch the ball. They should front pivot and box out the shooter.

Defending Cuts

On offense, more and more teams are using systems known as *motion offenses*, which revolve around the passing game, with players cutting on each pass to create scoring opportunities or gain better positioning to receive the pass. Therefore, defenders need to be aware of the different types of cuts and must be prepared to defend each of them.

PROPER DEFENSIVE POSITIONING

When defending cuts, the first thing your players need to know is proper defensive position both on and off the ball (as we will discuss in "On-the-Ball Defense" on page 154 and "Off-the-Ball Defense" on page 157). Players must know the difference between ball-side defense and help-side defense, and they must play both positions correctly. In the most general sense, the side of the court where the ball is located is considered the "ball side," and the side of the court opposite the ball is considered the "help side." An imaginary line down the middle of the key divides the court into ball side and help side.

MOVING WITH THE PASS

To effectively defend cuts, defenders must be aware of where the ball is in relationship to the player they are defending. Defensive players must not only move when the player they are guarding moves, but must also move as the pass is made, while the ball is in the air. This is true for the defender playing the ball as well as the defenders off the ball. When defenders are playing off the ball, moving with the pass allows them to maintain the ball–you–man triangle position (see figure 4.6, *a* and *b*, for two examples of this positioning). This is effective in defending cutters from the help side, because the defenders are better able to see their player as well as the ball. When a defender is playing on the ball, jumping to the ball will take away the give-and-go cut by the passer. If an on-the-ball defender waits until the receiver gets the ball, the cutter—whether it's the passer or a player from the weak side—will beat the defender to the spot.

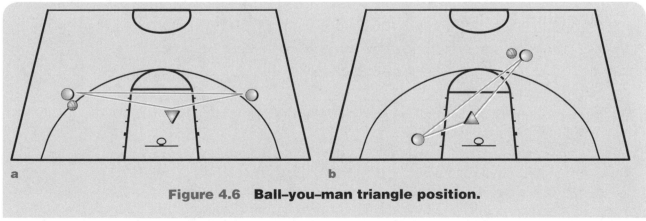

Figure 4.6   Ball–you–man triangle position.

(continued)

REACTING TO CUTS

A defender always needs to be in a good defensive position to take away the advantage from the offense and to take away the angle of a cut. The types of cuts that a defender should be prepared to defend are as follows:

L-Cut

The L-cut is made by a player cutting to the high-post area and then cutting straight out to the wing area. The defender must keep the hand and lead foot in the passing lane to take away the quick pass to the cutter.

V-Cut

A V-cut is when a player makes a move to the basket and then cuts back to the wing. The defender needs to move with the player as he or she cuts back up, keeping the lead hand and foot in the passing lane and attempting to make the receiver catch the ball outside of the shooting area.

Backdoor Cut

A backdoor cut is when the defender forces the cutter to go behind the defender (because the defender is overplaying the passing lane between the player and the passer). The defender must open to the pass against the backdoor cut. The defender is in a denial position and must maintain the closed stance while moving with the cutter and then open to the ball as the pass is made.

Flash Cut

A flash cut is when a player makes a quick cut from weak side to ball side. When the offense uses a flash cut, weak-side defenders need to be in the correct position, assuming an open stance and maintaining the ball–you–man triangle between the ball and the player they are defending. As soon as the weak-side offensive player begins the flash cut, the defender must bump the cutter and move from an open stance to a closed stance to deny the cutter the ball.

Common Errors

You may run into several common errors when teaching your athletes how to defend cuts.

Error	Error correction
The player gets beat on the give-and-go.	Emphasize that players need to move on the pass toward the ball (i.e., jump to the ball).
The player misses a flash cutter.	Teach players to maintain the ball–you–man triangle position. Defenders always need to see the player they are guarding and the ball.
The player gets beat on a backdoor cut.	Emphasize that players should play off the offensive player just a little while in the closed stance and then must open to the ball as the offensive player makes a backdoor cut.

Defending Screens

Setting a screen (also referred to as *setting a pick*) is a move by an offensive player to position him- or herself to block the path of a teammate's defender in order to set up an advantage for the teammate. Defensive players want to avoid screens whenever possible. The best way for defensive players to do this is to always be in motion when offensive players approach them to set a screen, because it is much more difficult to screen a moving target.

PROPER DEFENSIVE POSITIONING

Screens that are set off the ball are often successful if the defender is playing too close to his or her offensive player or if the defender is not moving to avoid the screen. To effectively play off-the-ball defense, players must first understand the concept of strong side (or ball side) and weak side (away from the ball). In addition, they must always maintain a ball–you–man triangle (as shown in figure 4.6 on page 103), which will be discussed in detail in chapter 6. Players should strive to maintain an open stance when they are on the weak, or help, side because this will help them see the offensive player attempting to set a screen. When a defender is in good help position, it is much more difficult for the offense to set the screen because the defender is able to see the screen and react accordingly. The defensive player should position in a defensive stance with the feet shoulder-width apart, the knees bent, and the player's weight evenly distributed on the balls of the feet. The player should keep the back straight and the head positioned over the support base, slightly behind the knees and over the waist.

When screens are set on the ball, defenders need to be in a good defensive position (as discussed in "Defensive Positioning" on page 94). The defensive player should position in a defensive stance with the feet shoulder-width apart, the knees bent, and the player's weight evenly distributed on the balls of the feet. The player should keep the back straight and the head positioned over the support base, slightly behind the knees and over the waist. This basic on-the-ball defensive position will allow the player to either fight over the top of the screen, slide through, or switch (as discussed later in this section).

COMMUNICATING WITH TEAMMATES

When playing defense against the screen, teammates must communicate with each other and must alert a teammate when a screen is about to be set. They must also be ready to help if a teammate is screened until the teammate is able to recover. The defender on the offensive player who is setting the screen must communicate to the defender being screened by calling out the direction of the screen (e.g., "screen left" or "screen right"). The defender on the screener should also communicate how the screen will be defended (e.g., "through," "over the top," or "switch"). These methods are discussed later in this section. Tactical skills for defending the screen will also be discussed further in chapter 6.

(continued)

PROPER FOOTWORK

A defender must be able to move quickly in any direction to effectively defend a screen. To do this, a defensive player must be in a well-balanced defensive stance (as discussed previously), allowing the defender to move quickly to fight over the top of the screen, slide through the screen, or switch on the screen.

Fighting Over the Top

Fighting over the top of a screen is a defensive technique used when the defender must stay with a good shooter. When the screen is being set, the player who is defending the screener must yell, "Get over" and step in the direction the offensive player is going in order to fake the switch. This will make the cutter go wider and give the player being screened a little more time to fight over the top of the screen. In this move, the defender being screened must work to first get the foot over the screen by taking a big step on the top side of the screener, followed by the rest of the body.

Sliding Through

Sliding through the screen is a defensive technique used when defenders can afford to give the opponent a little room, either because the opponent is out of his or her shooting range or the opponent is not a particularly good shooter. In this move, the defender being screened drops back, below the screen, and slides through between the screener and the defender's teammate to regain defensive position on the cutter. The defender must have quick feet on the slide through in order to stay with the cutter. Once again, the player defending the screener must communicate by yelling out, "Screen right" or "Screen left." This player should also yell, "Through" to help pull the defender being screened through and should step back to make room for the teammate to slide through.

Switching

Switching on a screen is a defensive technique used when the defensive players involved with the screen are of equal size and ability. Switching is not effective, for example, when a guard and big forward are involved with the screen, because they could end up guarding an offensive player who is much quicker or much bigger than them. In this move, the player defending the screener must communicate "Screen right" or "Screen left" and then yell, "Switch." When the player being screened hears "Switch," the player must aggressively pick up the screener on the ball side and must anticipate the roll to the basket or a cut outside for a quick pass and shot.

At a Glance

The following parts of the text offer additional information on defending the screen:

Common Errors

You may run into several common errors when teaching your athletes how to defend a screen.

Error	Error correction
The defensive player runs into a screen when playing on the help side.	Emphasize that defensive players need to avoid screens whenever possible. The best way for players to do this is by always being in motion when offensive players approach them to set a screen.
The player being screened is not aware that a screen is being set.	Emphasize that players need to call out a screen (and its direction) so that players being screened from the backside will be aware of the screen.
The defender has a difficult time getting over the top of the screen.	Emphasize the importance of getting the lead foot over the screen and then the rest of the body.
The defender attempts to slide through the screen but bumps into the teammate who is defending the screener.	Teach players that the defender guarding the screener needs to call out the screen and yell, "Slide." This defender must then move back to give the teammate room to slide through.

Defending the Post

KEY POINTS

The most important components of defending the post are

o maintaining a defensive position,

o denying entry, and

o defending a post player with the ball.

The most important area a team must defend is the post—that is, the area inside, near, or just outside the free throw lane. When playing defense, a team must strive to keep the offense out of this area for three main reasons. First, the offensive team has a better chance of making any shots they attempt inside this area. Second, if the offense gets the ball inside this area, the defense may need to collapse inside to take away a shot; this often gives the offense an opportunity to pass outside to an open three-point shooter. And third, offensive players are difficult to defend in this congested inside area, and defenders often foul when the offense is attempting a shot, leading to a potential three-point play. Because the post area is a vulnerable area for defenders, defensive players must have the attitude that the ball should never enter into the post, particularly the low-post area, and defenders should strive to keep offensive players out at all costs.

MAINTAINING A DEFENSIVE POSITION

Maintaining a good defensive position enables players to have more success in defending the post. To assume the basic defensive position, the defensive player should be in a balanced stance with the feet shoulder-width apart, the knees flexed, the back straight, and the hands above the shoulders (as discussed in "Defensive Positioning" on page 94).

DENYING ENTRY

When defending the post, the defender should strive to maintain a position in front of the offensive post player to deny the entry pass into the post area. When the ball is on the high side of the free throw line extended, the defender must deny the low-post player from the top side, the side closest to the free throw line (see figure 4.7a). When the ball is below the free throw line extended, the defender should deny the post from the low side, the baseline side (see figure 4.7b). Defensive players will use two types of stances when denying entry passes into the post area: a closed stance and a front stance.

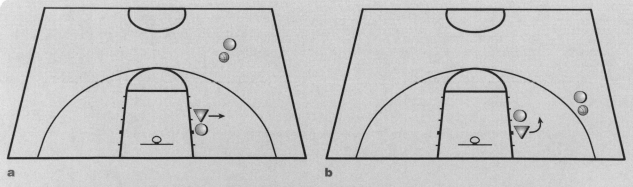

Figure 4.7 **Denying entry when the ball is *(a)* above and *(b)* below the free throw line extended.**

Closed Stance

One of the techniques used to deny entry passes into the low-post area is the closed—or half-front—stance. In the closed stance, the player positions the lead foot and lead hand in the passing lane, with the thumb down and the palm facing the ball (see figure 4.8). If the ball moves from above to below the imaginary line of the free throw line extended (toward the baseline), the defender should step in front of the post player and maintain the same position on the baseline side of the post.

Front Stance

Another technique used in denying the low-post player is the front stance. A front stance is when the defender is completely in front of the offensive post player—between the ball and the low-post player (see figure 4.9). When in a front stance, the defender must see the ball and not get pushed out of the post area. This stance allows a defender to move quickly to a pass and often makes it more difficult for the offense to get the ball to the low post. This is an effective stance when the defender has a height advantage and is difficult to throw over. However, this stance makes it more difficult to rebound because the defender is giving the offensive player inside position.

At a Glance

The following parts of the text offer additional information on defending the post:

Playing the Post	p. 87
Defensive Positioning	p. 94
Defensive Rebounds	p. 100
Flash Cut	p. 143
Defending the Flash Cut	p. 196

Figure 4.8 Closed stance.

Figure 4.9 Front stance.

(continued)

DEFENDING A POST PLAYER WITH THE BALL

If a defensive player allows the post player to receive the ball, the defender must stay in defensive position. When the post player receives the ball, the post defender should take a step back and establish a ball–you–basket position. This distance will give the defender time to react to the offensive move of the post player.

Common Errors

You may run into several common errors when teaching your athletes how to defend the post.

Error	Error correction
The defender has a difficult time getting around the post player when the ball goes to the baseline.	The defender is likely playing too close to the post player. Teach defenders to step through with the inside foot in front of the post player, using a two-step move.
The defender is unable to deny the pass to the post player.	The defender may be on the wrong side. Defenders should be on the top side when the ball is above the imaginary line that is the extension of the free throw line, and they should be on the low side (baseline) when the ball is below that line.
The defender gets called for holding the post player.	Emphasize that defenders should play slightly away from the post player. Encourage defenders to play defense with the feet and not the hands.

PART III

Teaching Tactical Skills

Tactical skills get at the heart of basketball. Without the proper understanding and execution of tactical skills, your players will often commit basic errors in game situations. You can empower your athletes by teaching them how to read situations, apply the appropriate knowledge, and make the correct decisions.

This part focuses on the basic and intermediate tactical skills in basketball, showing you how to teach your athletes to make good decisions. These skills include offensive tactical skills such as moving without the ball, playing against man and zone defenses, executing backdoor and flash cuts, and using the inside-out pass. Defensive tactical skills such as defending the pass, switching on a screen, and double teaming the post are also included.

For each skill, we first present an overview that paints a picture or puts you and your athletes into a specific scenario in the game in which you would be likely to use the particular tactical skill. The "Watch Out!" element highlights the distractions that may affect your athletes' ability to make appropriate decisions and provides insight on what to look for. The "Reading the Situation" element offers important cues that your athletes need to be able to read so that they can make the appropriate decisions for the situation. The next section, called "Acquiring

THINKING TACTICALLY

Throughout the presentation of tactical skills, you will see references to athletes needing to know the game situation. As described in Rainer Martens' *Successful Coaching, Third Edition*, the game situation includes the score and the time remaining in the quarter or game. In other words, your players need to know specific information when your team faces a specific situation. For example, when leading late in a game, you may ask yourself, How important is it that we maintain possession of the ball? Do we want to work for inside shots only? Does the opponent spread the offense to pull us out of a zone when we're on defense?

You and your team must have the key information you need to make the best decision. Following are a few questions that you and your team must keep in mind when facing tactical situations during a game:

- What is your strategy?
- How does your game plan affect your strategy?
- How does the game situation (the score, the strengths and weaknesses of the players involved at that particular time, and so on) affect your game plan?

the Appropriate Knowledge," provides the information that your athletes need to understand in order to make the proper decision and successfully execute the skill. Finally, as in the technical skill chapters, the "At a Glance" section refers you to the other important tools in the book that will help you teach the skill.

chapter 5

Offensive Tactical Skills

This chapter covers the offensive tactical skills that you and your players must know to be successful. In this chapter, you will find the following skills:

Playing Against Man Defense

When playing against a man defense, an offensive team's objective is to use a combination of techniques that, in the end, will get a player a good shot and put the other players in good rebounding position or a good defensive position to stop the opponent's fast break if they get the ball. Against a man-to-man defense, players should use cuts and screens as the primary way to get open for shots (see "Cuts" on page 81 and "Screens" on page 84 for more information). Cuts and screens will cause mismatches in size and ability that the offense can take advantage of for easy baskets. Effective cuts will put extreme pressure on the defenders, making it difficult for them to defend consistently.

 WATCH OUT!

The following circumstances may distract your athletes:

- Letting the size or speed of the defender rule out some of the offensive player's options.

- Focusing on the time left in the game or the score rather than on the defender and the defender's movements.

- Dribbling excessively. If the player with the ball dribbles excessively, this may cause other offensive players to stand and watch the dribbler.

- Getting too far away from the ball on the court.

READING THE SITUATION

How can your players gain the best advantage when playing against man defense? Teach your players to do the following:

- Change speed and direction quickly when being guarded. This will keep the defender watching the offensive player instead of the ball and will allow the offensive player to make better cuts to the ball to get open.

- Work to avoid the baseline when in possession of the ball, unless planning to drive or shoot. The baseline is a restrictive area because it essentially acts as another defender and cuts down on the area where an offensive player can move.

- Set good screens, especially against pressure defenses, to free up teammates. Against a man defense, screens may be the only way to get a teammate open for a shot.

- Make good cuts, especially backdoor cuts, when being overplayed by the defense. This will help release the pressure that the defenders are trying to apply.

ACQUIRING THE APPROPRIATE KNOWLEDGE

To ensure your team's success in playing against man defense, you and your players must know about the following:

Rules

You and your players need to know several main rules related to playing against man defense:

- An offensive player who has the ball may not dribble or hold the ball for longer than 5 seconds when being closely guarded or a violation will occur, resulting in a turnover.

Offensive teammates need to be aware of this rule and help out by cutting to the ball if the dribbler has trouble getting rid of the ball.

○ Players setting screens must not be moving when contact is made with the defender or an illegal block will be called.

○ The offensive team must advance the ball into the frontcourt within a 10-second time limit. This can be a challenge against teams that apply a pressing man-to-man defense in the backcourt.

○ When trying to get open on a cut or a screen, players must be careful not to hook the defender with the hands. This could result in a foul being called.

REMINDER!

You and your players must understand the team strategy and game plan and must assess playing against man defense based on those plans and the situation at hand. Make sure that you and your players consider the questions on page 112.

Strengths and Weaknesses of Opponents

You and your players must account for the opponent's strengths and weaknesses to know how to play against man defense properly. Consider the following about your opponents:

○ What is the size of the opponent? The size of the opposing players will determine how an offense should attack the defenders. Offensive players should use more screens and more cuts to the basket when playing against bigger opponents.

○ How quick is the opponent? If the defenders are quick, offensive players may need to use more screens because it is difficult to get open using cuts against a quick defender.

○ How good is the opponent's shot-blocking ability? If the defense has an effective shot blocker in the lane, offensive players will need to stay out of the lane. A blocked shot is just like a turnover and can start the fast break for the defensive team.

○ Does the opponent provide strong help-side defense on drives? If the opponent has good help-side defense, offensive players' cuts may not get them open all the way to the basket, and skip passes will be a more available and more effective choice.

Self-Knowledge

Besides being aware of your opponent's abilities, you and your players need to know about your own team's strengths and weaknesses. Teach your players to be aware of the following when playing against man defense:

○ Does your team have a player who can drive to the basket effectively? If so, this should help determine where players are positioned in the offense. A good driver will draw an extra defender to help stop the drive, and this will subsequently leave another offensive player open for a jump shot. The driver can then "penetrate and pass" the ball to the open player who is ready for the jumper.

○ Does your team have a good post-up player who can score effectively on the inside? If so, players should work to get this player the ball in the lane area in order to create high-percentage scoring opportunities.

○ Does your team have a player who can easily get shots off over the defender? This may be a player who has a size or quickness advantage over the defender. Teammates should try to get passes to this player in a position to catch and shoot over the defender.

○ Does your team have a player who is quick and can easily take the defender off the dribble? If so, players should get the ball to this player so that the team can get the ball into the frontcourt to start the offense. When this player has the ball, the other offensive players must keep proper spacing and not get too close to the dribbler. This will help prevent the defenders from double teaming the dribbler.

(continued)

Decision-Making Guidelines

When deciding how to gain the best advantage when playing against man defense, you and your players should consider the previous information as well as the following guidelines:

- Offensive players must know where the ball is located in relation to how the defenders are playing them because this will determine if they need to use a screen or if they can get open using a cut. If the ball is on the opposite side of the floor, a cut to the ball may be the best way to get open. If the offensive player is on the same side of the court as the ball (for example, the player is at the top of the key with the ball at the wing), a screen on the ball would be a good option to free up the dribbler.

- The defense may try to force a dribbler to go baseline or to go to the middle of the court when guarding an offensive player on the wing. This will determine where the offense should set screens to get a dribbler open. If the defender guarding the ball is forcing the dribbler to go to the middle, a baseline screen could be set to free up the dribbler to go baseline instead of where the defender wants the dribbler to go. If the defender wants the dribbler to go to the baseline, an offensive player can set a screen for the dribbler to go to the middle.

- Offensive players should work to create mismatches by using screens or dribble penetration, forcing a defender to guard an offensive player that the defender is not used to guarding. This usually takes place when a post defender must guard a perimeter player or vice versa.

- If the player with the ball is being defended by a slower player, the offensive player should try to take the defender off the dribble by taking the dribble up to the defender, using a quick crossover dribble, and then going to the basket. Typically, the slower defender will try to reach, rather than moving the feet in the defensive stance, and a foul will be called.

- When a screen is being set, offensive players must be aware of switching on defense, and they should watch for mismatches that may result. Players should try to get the ball to the teammate who has a mismatch. When players hear a defender yell "Switch," they should try to get the ball to the screener, who will roll to the basket.

- Offensive players should be aware of the positioning of both their teammates and the defenders on the court, and they should move when necessary to create better passing angles. For example, if a dribbler is working to get the ball into the post area, and the defender is guarding on the top side of the post player, the dribbler will need to dribble the ball toward the baseline to create a better passing angle to the post. A good rule is to pass the ball away from the defender and not directly to the offensive player.

- Offensive players must know where their defender is at all times and especially when making a cut to get open. For example, if the ball is above the free throw line and a player's defender is too low, the player can make a flash cut to the ball at the free throw line area to get the ball. Players should always take the defender in the opposite direction of where they want to end up on the cut. If a player wants to make a low cut, the player should take the defender higher toward the centerline before making the cut. This will get the defender leaning in the opposite direction from where the player plans to go. If a player wants to make a high cut, the player should take the defender lower toward the baseline before making the cut.

At a Glance

The following parts of the text offer additional information on playing against man defense:

In zone defense, defenders guard an area instead of a particular player, and any offensive player who moves into the defender's area of the zone is the responsibility of that defender. When playing against a zone defense, offensive players will need to attack gaps in the defense by using dribbles, passes, or offensive movement. Playing against a zone defense is very different from playing against a man defense—players will set fewer screens and will use cuts more often. Having more than one offensive player in a zone area will force the defender in that area to make a choice of which player to guard.

 ## WATCH OUT!

The following circumstances may distract your athletes:

- Facing zone defenses that extend different lengths of the court—full-court, three-quarter-court, half-court, or quarter-court zones. In each type of zone defense, the defenders pick up the offensive players at different points on the court.

- Facing an opponent with bigger players. This can make it difficult for offensive players to see over the zone to make passes.

ACQUIRING THE APPROPRIATE KNOWLEDGE

To help ensure your team's success in playing against zone defense, you and your players must know about the following:

Rules

You and your players need to know several main rules related to playing against zone defense:

- An offensive player cannot be in the lane for longer than 3 seconds. This rule is more crucial against the zone because offensive players tend to stand around more when playing against a zone defense.

- An offensive player who has the ball may not dribble or hold the ball for longer than 5 seconds when being closely guarded. Offensive teammates need to be aware of this and make a flash cut to get open if the dribbler cannot get rid of the ball.

READING THE SITUATION

How can your players gain the best advantage when playing against zone defense? Teach your players to do the following:

- Make sure offensive movement and positioning are dictated by the gaps in the zone defense, or the areas in the zone where a defender is not located. For example, in a 2-3 zone defense, the gap would be between the top two defenders, and an offensive player should be positioned in this gap.

- Use ball reversal when attacking a zone defense. This will force the zone to shift from one side to the other, typically providing the offense with an opportunity for a shot.

- Stretch the zone defense by passing the ball from side to side. This creates bigger gaps in the zone, and the larger spacing makes it much more difficult for the defenders to cover the offensive players.

- Understand that good post play is essential to scoring against a zone defense. Post players must make their cuts in gaps in the zone and catch the ball in the post. If they are covered in the post, the post players can reverse the ball to the opposite side of the court for good perimeter shots.

(continued)

REMINDER!

You and your players must understand the team strategy and game plan and must assess playing against zone defense based on those plans and the situation at hand. Make sure that you and your players consider the questions on page 112.

○ The offensive team must advance the ball into the frontcourt within a 10-second time limit. A full-court zone defense may make this difficult for the offense to do.

○ Help defenders who work to stop the drive must be aware of rules about charges. Offensive players driving through gaps in the zone must not charge into help defenders who have established a stationary position.

Strengths and Weaknesses of Opponents

You and your players must account for the opponent's strengths and weaknesses to know how to play against zone defense properly. Consider the following about your opponents:

○ How big is the opponent? If the defense has a size advantage, offensive players must be diligent about being quick in their attack and making crisp and accurate passes in an effort to avoid steals. Offensive players should also use more fakes to get the hands of the defenders moving in the opposite direction of their passes.

○ How quickly does the zone shift? If the zone shifts quickly from one pass to another, offensive players may want to use pass fakes to force the zone to shift without the pass. This will allow them to effectively set up their passes by getting the zone to react to the pass fake.

○ Is the opponent's strength in the middle of the zone or on the perimeter? Offensive players should attack the weaknesses of the zone depending on what the defenders cover best. If the zone is weak in the middle or a mismatch can occur in the lane (e.g., the defender in the middle of the zone is small), the offense must be ready to take advantage of this by passing the ball into the post.

Self-Knowledge

Besides being aware of your opponent's abilities, you and your players need to know about your own team's strengths and weaknesses. Teach your players to be aware of the following when playing against zone defense:

○ Who is your best baseline shooter? This player should work to get open for passes along the baseline because the baseline is a very good shooting area against a zone defense. A player on the baseline is often outside of the defenders' vision, and the defenders will react more slowly to the ball if they cannot see the player at all times.

○ Are your players effective at getting into the gaps in the zone on shots? One of the best methods for getting offensive rebounds is by getting into the gaps as the shot goes up. When playing zone defense, the opponent may have a difficult time blocking out because the defenders are not responsible for a specific player.

○ Does your team have a strong inside presence with good post players? If so, this will be one advantage to getting the ball inside against a zone defense.

○ Does your team have a good perimeter shooting game? If the offense has wing players who can shoot the ball well, this will make the zone defense cover farther out than the defenders would like. Bigger gaps open up in the zone when the defenders are drawn out to cover the wing shooters.

Decision-Making Guidelines

When deciding how to gain the best advantage when playing against zone defense, you and your players should consider the previous information as well as the following guidelines:

- If the zone shifts hard to the ball side, so that four defenders are on the same side of the court as the ball, the skip pass will be open. If this happens, offensive players should look to the opposite wing, because the defender on the help side of the floor will be covering the low-post area for a possible rebound.

- Offensive players should be aware of which defender covers the wing when the ball gets reversed from one wing to the opposite wing. If the back defensive player who normally covers the post comes out to cover the wing player who receives the ball on the reverse pass, this will leave only two defenders to cover the post areas, and the offense should get the ball inside to the post player, who should be open on the block.

- If the zone defense uses traps, quick ball movement is important. In many zone defenses, the defenders will trap the ball in different areas of the floor. When this occurs, the offensive player must make the pass before the trap is complete. If the ball is passed quickly—quicker than the zone defenders can move—offensive players will be open for shots.

- Offensive players should attack gaps in the zone with the dribble to draw two defenders to the ball. This will leave one of the dribbler's teammates open for a shot in an area vacated by one of the defenders.

- If the defenders in the back line of the zone step up, a cutter on the baseline—usually a player who goes from ball side to ball side as the ball is passed from one wing to the other wing—should stay behind the zone so that the player is out of the defenders' vision. When this offensive player is out of the defenders' vision, this makes it easier for the player to get open for passes by making cuts from behind the zone to an open area.

- The high-post area is a key to attacking the zone defense. If the offense can get the ball to the high-post area, this will put pressure on the defenders because the high-post player has many options for passes or a shot. If the ball enters the high-post area, the center defender may come out of the lane to cover the high-post area. If this happens, the offense should pass the ball to the baseline area and then into the lane area that the post defender vacated.

- In a zone defense, the guards will sometimes come out above the three-point line to pressure the ball. This leaves the high-post area wide open for a pass. As mentioned, the high post is a very good place for the offense to get the ball because it is in the middle of the court and provides good passing angles.

- When the ball goes into the post player, the best place for other players to spot up for a pass from the post is the wing area on either side of the floor. The defenders in a zone defense tend to help when the ball goes to the post, and this leaves the wing areas open for passes.

At a Glance

The following parts of the text offer additional information on playing against zone defense:

Moving without the ball involves using intuitive and purposeful movements within the flow of a game in order to get open or get a teammate open. All movements without the ball—such as making cuts, setting screens, or coming off screens—are dependent on team organization within the offensive set that is being used. But, essentially, an offensive player becomes difficult to guard when the player learns to move efficiently without the ball.

 WATCH OUT!

The following circumstances may distract your athletes:

- Watching the dribbler or the ball instead of focusing on moving to open areas.
- Standing and watching a play instead of moving to keep the defensive player occupied.
- Allowing the physical play of the defenders to hinder the movement on cuts or other attempts to get open.

ACQUIRING THE APPROPRIATE KNOWLEDGE

To help ensure your team's success in moving without the ball, you and your players must know about the following:

Rules

You and your players need to know several main rules related to moving without the ball:

- Players setting screens must not be moving when contact is made with the defender or an illegal or moving screen will be called. Therefore, players should always use a jump stop when setting a screen.
- An offensive player may not go out of bounds and then step back on the court to receive the ball.

READING THE SITUATION

How can your players gain the best advantage when moving without the ball? Teach your players to do the following:

- Do not watch the ball unless moving to get open or cutting to the basket.
- Be conscious of changing speed and direction when moving without the ball. Sharp cuts and changes in direction will make the offensive player much more difficult to guard than a player who always moves at the same speed or on the same path.
- Recognize the best angle to take when cutting to the basket. This angle is determined by the defender's position. For example, if the defender follows the offensive player around the screen, then the player should use a curl cut. If the defender goes on the ball side of the screen, the offensive player should use a flare cut.
- Make sure that cuts to the basket or around screens are made in a direct line to the basket or ball. Using a rounded path will allow the defender to more easily defend the cut and stay with the offensive player.

- An offensive player cannot be in the lane for longer than three seconds or a violation will be called.
- When using the screen, players should be careful not to hook the defender with the hands. This could result in a foul being called.

REMINDER!

You and your players must understand the team strategy and game plan and must assess moving without the ball based on those plans and the situation at hand. Make sure that you and your players consider the questions on page 112.

Strengths and Weaknesses of Opponents

You and your players must account for the opponent's strengths and weaknesses to know how to move without the ball properly. Consider the following about your opponents:

- How quick are the opponent's defenders? If the defender is quicker than the offensive player, the offensive player needs to set the defender up by first moving in the opposite direction of the intended cut. This will force the defender to lean in one direction, reacting to the fake, and then the cutter can cut in the opposite direction. If the defender is slower than the offensive player, the offensive player may be able to make a direct cut and beat the defender to the basket or the ball (without using a fake to set the defender up).
- Does the opponent play good help-side defense? The proper positioning for a help-side defender would involve maintaining a triangle between the defender, the ball, and the offensive player being guarded. If the help-side defender maintains this positioning well, the offensive player that the defender is guarding could use a skip pass. If the defender stays too close, the offensive player may use a quick cut and beat the defender to the ball or the basket.
- Is the opponent physical? If the defenders are physically aggressive when offensive players cut, the offensive players will need to use quickness or screens to get open and to get away from the physical play of the defenders.
- Do the opponent's players maintain a good defensive stance when the player they are guarding doesn't have the ball? If a defender tends to stand straight up when on the help side, the defender will be unable to move quickly from this position. When an offensive player sees the help-side defender stand straight up, the player can take advantage of this by using a quick change of direction move to get open.
- Do the defenders turn their head when the player they are guarding makes a cut? If a defender turns the head during an offensive player's cut, the defender will lose sight of the ball. Offensive players can take advantage of this by communicating with the teammate who has the ball and looking for the pass when the defender's head is turned.

Self-Knowledge

Besides being aware of your opponent's abilities, you and your players need to know about your own team's strengths and weaknesses. Teach your players to be aware of the following when moving without the ball:

- Who has the ball when a cut is made? This will determine the type of pass the cutter will expect to receive. If a post player has the ball, the cutter can typically expect a high pass because post players are usually the taller players on the team. If a guard has the ball, the cutter can typically expect a bounce pass. Because the guards are generally the smaller players on the team, they often need to use a bounce pass in order to get the ball by the defender.
- Is the player with the ball in a good position to drive to the basket? If so, the player making the cut should stay away from the driving lane. If the player with the ball is at the wing

(continued)

and the cutter is making a move to the basket, the cutter should stay clear of the lane if the teammate is a good driver and is likely to put the ball on the floor for the drive.

- Does the player with the ball drive to the basket well or is this player a spot-up shooter? This determines if the player with the ball will draw weak-side help. Players who drive to the basket tend to draw help, but shooters usually do not because defenders are too far away to provide any weak-side help on the shooter.
- Do your players communicate well? Communicating with teammates is necessary to create good continuity when moving without the ball.

Decision-Making Guidelines

When deciding how to gain the best advantage when moving without the ball, you and your players should consider the previous information as well as the following guidelines:

- Understanding spacing is very important when moving without the ball. There should always be at least 12 feet of space between players after cuts or screens take place. This will allow the players to move without much restriction from the defenders, and it makes the passes much easier to complete. When moving without the ball, players should put themselves in a position to use a screen as well as to screen for a teammate.
- When the team is leading late in a game, offensive players should make hard cuts to the basket because the defenders may be overplaying the passing lanes. By doing this, an offensive player may get open on a backdoor cut for an easy basket.
- Players should be aware of how the player with the ball got the ball. This information will help the offense know how to best beat the defender and determine if screens must be set to get players open for shots.

- Players for whom a screen has been set must keep a close watch on their defender and make their moves accordingly. For example, if the defender tries to go over the top of the screen, the offensive player must recognize this and use a front-door cut, also known as a *curl cut*, to the basket to get open (see "Screens" on page 84 for more information on this cut).
- Players should set up their cuts by first taking a step in the opposite direction of the cut. This will force the defender to lean in the opposite direction of the cut.
- When a screen is set for a player, the player should stay low when coming off the screen, with the shoulder at the screener's hip. Staying low allows the offensive player to maintain better balance and to be more physical in taking over space that the defender is trying to use.
- When receiving a pass, if the defender is playing soft defense, the offensive player should catch and square up in order to read the situation. This will allow the offensive player to see the court well and "window-shop," reading the cuts of teammates and choosing the proper pass to make.

At a Glance

The following parts of the text offer additional information on moving without the ball:

Inbounds plays are specific plays that the offensive team will try to run when taking the ball out of bounds anywhere on the court. Inbounds plays can have a definite impact on the outcome of games. When running an inbounds play, a team usually has one of two main objectives: scoring from the inbounds play or getting the ball inbounds to run a set offense. Inbounds plays should be set up so that they are effective against both man and zone defenses, because the offense will often not know which defense the opponent is playing until they take the ball out of bounds.

WATCH OUT!

The following circumstances may distract your athletes:

- Focusing on the score or the amount of time left in the game rather than on the proper execution of the inbounds play.
- Letting the defender who is guarding the inbounder disrupt the play.
- Facing a team with bigger defenders. This is especially challenging if the offense would like to get the ball inside the paint area on the out-of-bounds play.
- Facing a trapping defense on the out-of-bounds play. This can often result in a quick turnover.

ACQUIRING THE APPROPRIATE KNOWLEDGE

To help ensure your team's success in running inbounds plays, you and your players must know about the following:

READING THE SITUATION

How can your players gain the best advantage when running inbounds plays? Teach your players to do the following:

- Recognize the defense being played. Each type of defense has its own strengths and weaknesses. Typically, against a man-to-man defense, screens will be the best choice when trying to get an offensive player open. If the defense is playing zone, the offense should use cuts in the gaps, forcing defenders to cover these gaps and leave other areas open for shots.
- Be careful not to initiate the inbounds play before the referee hands the ball to the player who is inbounding the ball.
- Understand that the inbounder's first option should always be to get the ball to the best shooter; however, this first option may not be available all the time, so the inbounder can look at this player to decoy the defense and then pass to another available option.

Rules

You and your players need to know several main rules related to running inbounds plays:

- The player who is inbounding the ball has 5 seconds to get the ball out of the hands.
- The 3-second lane violation rule does not start until a player on the court receives the ball from the player who inbounds the ball and the ball becomes live.
- The player who inbounded the ball must establish a position on the court (inbounds) before touching the ball again.
- By rule, if there is 0.3 seconds or less left in the game or the half, a shot off the inbounds pass must be a tip in order for the basket to count (there is not enough time to catch and shoot).

(continued)

REMINDER!

You and your players must understand the team strategy and game plan and must assess running inbounds plays based on those plans and the situation at hand. Make sure that you and your players consider the questions on page 112.

Strengths and Weaknesses of Opponents

You and your players must account for the opponent's strengths and weaknesses to know how to run inbounds plays properly. Consider the following about your opponents:

- Are the defenders slow to the corners after the ball is inbounded? Some defenses are slow in covering the baseline when guarding the inbounds play, and offensive players can use this opportunity for a quick cut to the baseline for a shot.

- How big is the opponent? Bigger defenders will take up more room in the defensive formation, and the offensive team may want to get the ball inbounds before setting up the offense, rather than going for an immediate score off the inbounds pass. If the offensive team has a size advantage over the opponent, the offense should look to get the ball inside the lane or use a lob pass on the inbounds play.

- How well does the opponent communicate? If the defenders do not communicate well, offensive players can use screens to get open on the inbounds play, because there is a great chance that the defenders will get caught off guard and run into the screens.

Self-Knowledge

Besides being aware of your opponent's abilities, you and your players need to know about your own team's strengths and weaknesses. Teach your players to be aware of the following when running inbounds plays:

- Is the player inbounding the ball the best passer on the team? When running an inbounds play, the most dangerous player on offense is the player who is inbounding the ball. This player should be the team's best passer and must also be a smart player who has the ability to see the options that open up.

- Do you have a tall post player? If so, this player can be your first option because the defense may have a more difficult time defending a pass to this player on the inbounds play.

Decision-Making Guidelines

When deciding how to gain the best advantage when running inbounds plays, you and your players should consider the previous information as well as the following guidelines:

- Offensive players should be aware that most teams will play a zone defense against inbounds plays. This is because zone defenses can be more effective against screens, and it is much easier to cover areas in a zone than to cover individual players on an inbounds play.

- The game situation will determine if the team needs to try to score off the inbounds play or if the team just needs to get the ball inbounded safely against pressure defense. For example, if very little time is left on the clock, the offense may need to use a quick pass (maybe a lob pass) to get the shot off before the clock runs out.

- When trying to get the team's best shooter an open shot on the inbounds play, other offensive players can help the shooter get to his or her strongest position on the floor by using a screen or a cut.

- The player who is inbounding the ball should always first look for an opportunity to pass the ball to the post player, because the post player is the closest player to the basket for a shot. Typically, the post player will be defended initially, but after the ball is inbounded, the defenders may go to the ball and leave the post player open for a pass.

- If the defenders switch on screens, offensive players should look for the screener to be open after the cutter uses the screen. The defender will usually go with the player using the screen, leaving the screener open.

- When trying to get the ball to the post player, the inbounder can fake a pass to a different option, which may cause the defenders to react and open up the passing lane to the post.

- Offensive players should remember that the inbounder is an additional option after the inbounds pass is made. Often, defenders tend to forget about the inbounder, and this player may be open for a pass and shot attempt after stepping back inbounds.

At a Glance

The following parts of the text offer additional information on running inbounds plays:

The skip pass is an overhead pass thrown by a player at the wing to a teammate on the opposite side of the court. The skip pass is a weapon that can be used by the offensive team in situations where a help-side defender gets too far away from an offensive player on the help side. This can occur, for example, when a help-side defender goes to provide defensive help on the ball. The offense can also use the skip pass to spread the defenders back out when the defense has collapsed to provide help on a good driver. In certain set plays that involve the skip pass, a help-side offensive player, typically the post player, will screen the help-side defender as the pass is made so that the defender cannot get to the offensive player who will receive the pass.

 WATCH OUT!

The following circumstances may distract your athletes:

- Attempting a skip pass when a weak-side defender fakes to the ball side but does not help.
- Letting the strong-side defender's actions (physical or verbal) distract the passer.
- Trying to pass over a bigger defender who is guarding the ball.
- The post defender's position in guarding the post player. If the post player is completely fronting the post player, the post player can pin the defender and make a flash cut across the key to receive a pass from the perimeter player.
- Facing a defense that traps quickly.

READING THE SITUATION

How can your players gain the best advantage when executing the skip pass? Teach your players to do the following:

- Be aware of the help-side defender's position. If the defender is in the lane with the head completely turned to the ball, the skip pass will be open.
- Recognize that screens may be used to set up the skip pass; when this occurs, the pass should go directly over the top of the screen to a teammate for the shot.
- Understand that offensive players at the help-side wing should be ready for the skip pass and should be prepared to take the shot as soon as they receive the pass.

ACQUIRING THE APPROPRIATE KNOWLEDGE

To help ensure your team's success in executing the skip pass, you and your players must know about the following:

Rules

You and your players need to know several main rules related to executing the skip pass:

- When receiving a skip pass, offensive players should be careful not to be in too big of a hurry with the ball, or a dribbling violation may occur because they may travel before gaining control of the ball.

- An offensive player holding the ball must keep the pivot foot stationary or traveling will be called. Therefore, when catching the skip pass for the shot, players should have the pivot foot planted and should be ready for the shot.

- An offensive player cannot be in the lane for longer than three seconds. Post players must be aware of this when setting a screen on the help side.

- An offensive player who has the ball may not dribble or hold the ball for longer than five seconds when being closely guarded. This may come into play if the wing player with the ball has a difficult time deciding if the skip pass is open.

REMINDER!

You and your players must understand the team strategy and game plan and must assess the skip pass based on those plans and the situation at hand. Make sure that you and your players consider the questions on page 112.

Strengths and Weaknesses of Opponents

You and your players must account for the opponent's strengths and weaknesses to know how to execute the skip pass properly. Consider the following about your opponents:

- Do the opponent's help-side defenders maintain proper defensive positioning at all times? If so, the proper positioning will allow the defender to quickly get back to cover the pass or even steal it. If the opponent does not maintain proper defensive positioning, the offensive player can use a skip pass or can use a quick fake skip pass and then look to the screener for the open pass.

- Is the defender at the top position tall? This player will be guarding the ball, and a tall defender creates even more risk for the skip pass. A deflection or steal is easier when the defender has an advantage in size.

- Is the weak-side defender a strong defensive player? A strong weak-side defender may be able to defend the skip pass or defend the player who receives the skip pass effectively, making the shot or drive difficult.

Self-Knowledge

Besides being aware of your opponent's abilities, you and your players need to know about your own team's strengths and weaknesses. Teach your players to be aware of the following when executing the skip pass:

- How well does your team understand offensive spacing and movement? The skip pass will be available more often if offensive players maintain proper spacing of 12 to 15 feet apart from each other. If the spacing is less than this, the defenders will be in a position to cover all passes more easily because the offensive players are close together.

- Does your team have a strong outside shooter? If so, the team strategy may be to feed the ball to that shooter. Thus, a skip pass to that shooter on the weak side may be a good option for creating an opportunity to score. If the team does not have strong outside shooters, the skip pass can be used to shift the defense when a post player is being denied the ball; the post player can use a flash cut to get open on the skip pass.

- How quick is the player who will be receiving the pass? This will determine if a screen is required and if there is any room for error on the pass. If the receiver is quick, the skip pass can be executed without the screen, and the receiver will be able to move effectively to catch the pass even if it is not right on the mark. If the receiver is slower, a screen may be needed in order to complete the skip pass.

(continued)

At a Glance

The following parts of the text offer additional information on the skip pass:

Decision-Making Guidelines

When deciding how to gain the best advantage when executing the skip pass, you and your players should consider the previous information as well as the following guidelines:

- If the weak-side defender reacts quickly to passes, the offensive player can set up the skip pass by using a fake pass into the post area or the baseline area before the skip pass is made.

- If the defender is able to maneuver easily around the screen, the screener may be open for a shorter skip pass. The defender guarding the screener may jump out over the screener to get to the skip pass, which would leave the screener open in the post area.

- If a team has just scored using the skip pass, the team may want to fake the skip pass and go to the post on the next play. A skip pass that leads to a jumper will set up the next option—a pass to the screener stepping into the post after the screen is set.

Inside-Out Pass

The inside-out pass refers to a pass that goes from the perimeter area to the post area, followed by a pass back out to the perimeter area for a shot. An inside-out pass is used when a defender guarding the perimeter player drops into the post for a double team on the post player. After the perimeter player passes to the post player, the perimeter player's defender goes to double team the post player in order to prevent an easy shot. This typically happens when the post player is a good offensive player and the defense has to use a double team in order to stop the player from scoring. When the double team occurs, the post player then passes back to the perimeter player, who was left open because of the double team, for a shot.

WATCH OUT!

The following circumstances may distract your athletes:

○ Facing a tall perimeter defender. The size of the defender doubling down on the post will make the pass more difficult to get back out to the perimeter player for a shot.

○ Facing a quick perimeter defender. The quickness of the defender doubling down will force the post player to make a quicker decision about passing or shooting.

○ Executing the inside-out pass against defenders who sometimes fake the double team. This makes the post player unsure if the double team is really coming.

○ Facing a double team that comes from a player other than the defender guarding the passer, such as the point guard's defender.

READING THE SITUATION

How can your players gain the best advantage when executing the inside-out pass? Teach your players to do the following:

- Be aware of passes to the post and watch for a double team on the post player. The player who made the pass must be ready to catch the return pass from the post.

- Understand that the post player must set up the shooter on the perimeter by using strong offensive moves to draw the double team.

- After making a pass to the post from the perimeter, move to any open area on the same side of the court as the post player who has the ball (if the defender leaves to double team the post).

- Understand that post players should keep their defender on their back. This is the best position for receiving the pass and drawing the double team.

- Be aware that if the post player is being played by a fronting defender, the pass to the post cannot be completed and another option, such as reversing the ball to the other side of the court, will need to be used.

ACQUIRING THE APPROPRIATE KNOWLEDGE

To help ensure your team's success in executing the inside-out pass, you and your players must know about the following:

(continued)

REMINDER!

You and your players must understand the team strategy and game plan and must assess the inside-out pass based on those plans and the situation at hand. Make sure that you and your players consider the questions on page 112.

Rules

You and your players need to know several main rules related to executing the inside-out pass:

- An offensive player cannot be in the lane for longer than three seconds. Post players must be aware of this when executing the inside-out pass.

- An offensive player who has the ball may not dribble or hold the ball for longer than five seconds when being closely guarded. This may come into play if extreme defensive pressure is placed on the passer at the wing position or on the post player.

- When the ball comes back out from the post player, the perimeter player must be careful not to double dribble.

Strengths and Weaknesses of Opponents

You and your players must account for the opponent's strengths and weaknesses to know how to execute the inside-out pass properly. Consider the following about your opponents:

- Does the opponent double at the post well? If the double team on the post player is a good one, the pass back out to the perimeter will be difficult to execute, so the post player should turn quickly and shoot the ball before the double team arrives. If the defenders are slow to execute the double team, they may be waiting until the post player dribbles the ball because this often takes away the pass to the perimeter player.

- Do the opponent's defenders help and recover well? The offense must recognize if the defender can break away from the double team and go back to defending the perimeter player quickly or if the defender is slow to do this. If the defender recovers well, the shot will not be available for the perimeter player, but the perimeter player can pass back into the post player. If the defender is slow to recover, the shot will be open.

- How big is the defender at the post? If the defender is bigger than the offensive post player, a double team on the post player will most likely not occur; therefore, the inside-out pass will not be an option.

Self-Knowledge

Besides being aware of your opponent's abilities, you and your players need to know about your own team's strengths and weaknesses. Teach your players to be aware of the following when executing the inside-out pass:

- Is your team's main strategy to get the ball inside? If so, the opponent may figure this out and try to prevent it by doubling from the outside, sending a player from the wing position to double the post before a pass is made into the post. When this happens, the offense should not pass the ball to the post but instead reverse the ball to the other side of the court. Another option would be for the help-side post player to set a screen for the ball-side post player to cut across the lane. The cut across the lane will get the post player open for the initial pass from the perimeter player and draw the double team.

- Is your post player a good passer? If not, the inside-out pass may not be the best option to use because the post player must recognize the double team and identify the player that is open after the double team occurs. Other options for this post player would be to shoot the ball immediately or to set a screen across the lane to get another post player open.

Decision-Making Guidelines

When deciding how to gain the best advantage when executing the inside-out pass, you and your players should consider the previous information as well as the following guidelines:

- If a double team on the post occurs, the post player must recognize where the extra defender came from and spot the teammate who is open for the shot. Typically, the extra defender has moved into the post off the perimeter player who made the pass to the post. However, in other cases, the extra defender could be from the outside, and the post player must know where the open teammate is located for the pass back out to the perimeter.

- The player whose defender has left to help in the post must move to create an open passing lane so that the post player is able to make the pass back outside. This perimeter player must move in a direction opposite the defender who left to make the double team so the defender will lose sight of the perimeter player.

- The post player needs to watch the perimeter defenders while catching the ball. The earlier the post player sees the double team coming, the quicker the player can make the pass back to the outside.

- After passing to the post, the perimeter player can also cut to the weak side of the floor, forcing the defender to make a decision to double team the post or to stay with the perimeter player on the cut to the weak side.

- If the team's best shooter is positioned on the same side of the court as the post player, this will make the inside-out pass much easier. The inside-out pass works much better if the wing player can shoot the ball well because this draws the defender back from the double team quicker to cover the wing player. This takes away the defense's ability to double team the post.

At a Glance

The following parts of the text offer additional information on the inside-out pass:

Penetrate and Pass

The penetrate and pass—sometimes called the *draw and kick*—occurs when the offensive ball handler drives toward the basket, draws an extra defender over to help stop the drive, and then passes the ball to the offensive player left open by the helping defender. The penetrate and pass is typically used against a zone defense when a player attempts to dribble through a gap in the zone and draws two defensive players who make an attempt to stop the dribble. It may also be used against a man defense—for example, when the defender is closely guarding the offensive player and the offensive player dribbles around or past the defender. The penetrate and pass puts extreme pressure on the defense to stop the dribble penetration to the basket. A team may use the penetrate and pass to create opportunities for the team's best scorer to shoot the ball, to break down the opponent's defensive strategy, or to draw the help defense.

 WATCH OUT!

The following circumstances may distract your athletes:

- Encountering a helping defender who is big or fast.
- Executing the penetrate and pass against a defender who fakes toward the dribbler but then does not help.
- Losing focus on the penetration and pass because of a helping defender who attempts to draw a charge on the dribbler.

READING THE SITUATION

How can your players gain the best advantage when executing the penetrate and pass? Teach your players to do the following:

- Dribble hard at the defender's outside shoulder. This will enable the dribbler to get around the defender or draw a helping defender to help stop the dribbler's penetration to the basket.
- Understand that offensive players near the dribbler must be ready for the pass if their defender leaves to help the defender on the ball.
- Work to keep good spacing so that the help defender will have a difficult time getting back to cover the offensive player who receives the pass for the shot.

ACQUIRING THE APPROPRIATE KNOWLEDGE

To help ensure your team's success in executing the penetrate and pass, you and your players must know about the following:

Rules

You and your players need to know several main rules related to executing the penetrate and pass:

- When attempting to penetrate to the basket, players should be careful not to commit any dribbling violations.
- An offensive player holding the ball must keep the pivot foot stationary or traveling will be called. Players must be aware of this when penetrating because they may get into the lane and need to pivot out of pressure without traveling.

- When an offensive player is penetrating and taking the ball to the basket, the five-second closely guarded rule does not apply.
- An offensive player cannot run into a defender who is stationary or a charge will be called. Therefore, when penetrating to the basket, the offensive player must use a proper jump stop.

REMINDER!

You and your players must understand the team strategy and game plan and must assess the penetrate and pass based on those plans and the situation at hand. Make sure that you and your players consider the questions on page 112.

Strengths and Weaknesses of Opponents

You and your players must account for the opponent's strengths and weaknesses to know how to execute the penetrate and pass properly. Consider the following about your opponents:

- Is the opponent quick when defending ball penetration? If the defender on the ball is quick and can defend the dribble well, the penetrate and pass will be more difficult to run because a helping defender may not need to be used to stop the dribbler. If the defender tends to be slower, the dribbler can get around the defender and draw another defender to the ball, thus getting the teammate open for a pass and shot.
- Does the opponent help and recover well? This determines how much time the shooter will have to get the shot off. If the helping defender is quick to recover, this will put more pressure on the shot because the defender will move to cover the shooter more quickly. If this is the case, the shooter should use a shot fake and then dribble before the shot. If the helping defender is slow to recover, the player receiving the pass should shoot the ball immediately upon receiving it.
- Does the opponent have a size advantage? If so, this will hinder the penetration of the dribbler to the basket. Bigger defenders will also make the pass to the teammate after the penetration a much tougher pass.

Self-Knowledge

Besides being aware of your opponent's abilities, you and your players need to know about your own team's strengths and weaknesses. Teach your players to be aware of the following when executing the penetrate and pass:

- How quick is the dribbler? If the dribbler, typically the perimeter player at the wing, is quick, the dribbler will be able to quickly get around the defender and to the basket.
- Is the dribbler good at executing one-on-one moves? If the dribbler can execute one-on-one moves, such as the crossover, this will allow the dribbler to get past the initial defender and force another defender to come over to help stop the dribbler, leaving the dribbler's teammate open.
- Is the player who will receive the pass a strong shooter? If the offensive player who receives the pass is not a good shooter, then the dribbler, after making the pass, must get into a position to receive a pass back from this player.
- Are your post players good offensive players? If the team's post players are good offensive players, the defender on the post player cannot help on the penetration, so the dribbler may be able to drive all the way to the basket.

(continued)

At a Glance

The following parts of the text offer additional information on the penetrate and pass:

Decision-Making Guidelines

When deciding how to gain the best advantage when executing the penetrate and pass, you and your players should consider the previous information as well as the following guidelines:

- Offensive players need to know that help from another defender can come from the top side or the baseline side. Knowing where the help comes from will let the dribbler know who is open for the shot.

- Every time an offensive player gets the ball, the player should square up to the basket and assume a triple-threat position. This gives the offensive player more options when receiving the ball—the player can either dribble, pass, or shoot from this position—and it keeps the defense guessing about the offensive player's next move.

- The dribbler must try to get even with the defender—that is, shoulder to shoulder—which will make the help defender slide over to stop the dribbler, opening up the pass.

Give-and-Go

In the give-and-go, an offensive player passes to a teammate ("give") and then makes a quick cut to the basket ("go") for a return pass from the teammate and a shot at the basket. A give-and-go is often used when an offensive perimeter player passes to another perimeter player (e.g., point guard to wing or wing to baseline) and then makes a sharp cut in front of the defender for a return pass going to the basket. This is most effective when the defender stays guarding the offensive passer closely and does not jump to the pass. The give-and-go play forces the defenders to drop to the basket to stop the return pass, opening the court up on the perimeter. If not defended properly, the give-and-go will lead to an easy basket.

WATCH OUT!

The following circumstances may distract your athletes:

- Trying to make the pass to the give-and-go cutter over a defender who has a size advantage.
- Facing a defense that puts good pressure on the ball, making the pass to the cutter more difficult.
- Executing the give-and-go against a defense that overplays off the ball and interferes with the cutter.

ACQUIRING THE APPROPRIATE KNOWLEDGE

To help ensure your team's success in executing the give-and-go, you and your players must know about the following:

Rules

You and your players need to know several main rules related to executing the give-and-go:

- An offensive player cannot be in the lane for longer than three seconds. The cutter must be aware of this when waiting for the pass.
- An offensive player who has the ball may not dribble or hold the ball for longer than five seconds when being closely guarded. This may come into play if the passer has to wait too long for the cutter to get open.
- When executing the give-and-go, players should be careful not to hook the defender with the hands. This could result in a foul being called.

Strengths and Weaknesses of Opponents

You and your players must account for the opponent's strengths and weaknesses to know how to execute the give-and-go properly. Consider the following about your opponents:

- How well does the opponent defend the cut? If the defender stays with the offensive player on the cut to the basket, the player should either go through opposite the passer or pop back to get the pass. If the defender is a step or two slow when defending the cut, the offensive player should be able to get open when making a quick give-and-go cut to the basket.

(continued)

READING THE SITUATION

How can your players gain the best advantage when executing the give-and-go? Teach your players to do the following:

- Understand that effective give-and-go plays are crucial to a strategy that takes advantage of the passing game because players are always on the move and making cuts to the basket.
- Recognize when the lane is clear after an offensive player at the top of the key passes the ball. This will indicate that the give-and-go is available because the cutter can get to the basket.

REMINDER!

You and your players must understand the team strategy and game plan and must assess the give-and-go based on those plans and the situation at hand. Make sure that you and your players consider the questions on page 112.

○ Does the opponent play tight defense at all times? If the defender plays tight defense when the offensive player doesn't have the ball, a quick give-and-go option will be much more effective and easy to complete. If the opponent doesn't play tight defense, the offensive player who receives the initial pass (before the give-and-go cut) may have an open outside shot.

○ Does the defender jump to the ball on passes or fakes? If the defender jumps to the pass quickly, the offensive player will need to cut behind the defender. If the defender reacts to the offensive player's head and shoulder fakes (moving in the opposite direction of the pass), the offensive player will be able to cut in front of the defender on the give-and-go cut for a pass.

○ Does the opponent sag, or play without much ball pressure, on defense? If the defense sags to the ball on the weak side, the give-and-go will not be as effective because the cutter will be double teamed on the cut. However, offensive players should be aware that other options will be open, such as the open jump shot and the pick-and-roll.

Self-Knowledge

Besides being aware of your opponent's abilities, you and your players need to know about your own team's strengths and weaknesses. Teach your players to be aware of the following when executing the give-and-go:

○ Does your team have a player who cuts to the basket well? If so, this player is crucial in setting up an effective give-and-go play. Typically, the give-and-go is started from the perimeter, and the purpose of the play is to get a player an open layup after an effective cut to the basket. A team should have set plays that allow the team's best cutter to perform the give-and-go.

○ Does your team have a player who can pass well from the perimeter? The give-and-go requires a strong, accurate, and quick pass. A perimeter player who has strong passing ability can increase the chances of success with this play. Again, the team's set plays should allow this player to pass the ball in the give-and-go.

○ Does your post player pass the ball well? If so, this post player may step out to the perimeter, which will bring the post defender to the perimeter. This will open up the lane for the give-and-go and a pass.

Decision-Making Guidelines

When deciding how to gain the best advantage when executing the give-and-go, you and your players should consider the previous information as well as the following guidelines:

○ If the defender overplays the give-and-go cut to take away the pass, the offensive player can follow up the play with a backdoor cut. The offensive player should take the defender higher and then make a hard direct cut to the basket for the backdoor cut.

○ After making the initial pass, the offensive player should take a step away before making the give-and-go cut. The step away may get the defender leaning and out of balance, which will help the offensive player get open on the cut.

○ If the pass to the cutter is not open immediately after the give-and-go cut, the cutter may assume a post-up position in the lane to look for the pass after the cut.

○ If the defender takes away the cut initially, the offensive player can make a quick cut back out to receive the pass for a jumper.

At a Glance

The following parts of the text offer additional information on the give-and-go:

Fast Break

The fast break is an attempt by the offense to get down the court and score quickly—before the opponent is able to get back on defense. By attacking quickly, the offense tries to get a favorable number of offensive players versus a lesser number of defenders as the ball gets to the frontcourt. Successful fast breaks often lead to an easy shot (e.g., a layup) for an offensive player. The fast break is started as soon as the team gains possession of the ball by getting a defensive rebound or a steal. The player who gains possession can start the break by using a power dribble out from the opponent's basket, a quick outlet pass to the point guard in the backcourt, or a long pass to the frontcourt.

 WATCH OUT!

The following circumstances may distract your athletes:

- Letting the opponent's actions (physical or verbal) disrupt the focus on the fast break.

- Trying to start the fast break after a rebound when defenders stay on the rebounder.

- Facing quick defenders who can get back on defense in time to stop the break.

- Facing bigger opponents who can affect the initial pass that gets the fast break started.

ACQUIRING THE APPROPRIATE KNOWLEDGE

To help ensure your team's success in executing the fast break, you and your players must know about the following:

Rules

You and your players need to know two main rules related to executing the fast break:

- When they gain possession of the ball, players must be careful not to try to start the fast break too quickly, or a traveling or double dribble violation may occur.

READING THE SITUATION

How can your players gain the best advantage when executing the fast break? Teach your players to do the following:

- Always look for the first option, called the *primary break*, when running a fast break. This is typically a 2 versus 1 situation and results in a layup. If the defenders are quick to get back on defense and take away the primary break, players can use the next available option, called the *secondary break*. The secondary break is typically a 3 versus 2 or 4 versus 3 situation and results in a jump shot

- Understand that the perimeter players should run the floor wide and close to the sideline on a fast break. This will make sure that one defender back on defense cannot guard two offensive players running the break.

- Understand that the post player should sprint down the middle of the floor on a fast break. This will ensure that the post player does not get in the way of the wings who are running wide to get open. Running down the middle may also help the post player beat the defensive post player down the floor. As a result, the post player may be available for a pass from the guard and an easy layup.

- Run the fast break off every steal. A steal often leads to an immediate layup before all defenders can get into position to cover the break.

(continued)

REMINDER!

You and your players must understand the team strategy and game plan and must assess the inside-out pass based on those plans and the situation at hand. Make sure that you and your players consider the questions on page 112.

○ An offensive player holding the ball must keep the pivot foot stationary or traveling will be called. Players must be aware of this when attempting to start the break off the rebound.

Strengths and Weaknesses of Opponents

You and your players must account for the opponent's strengths and weaknesses to know how to execute the fast break properly. Consider the following about your opponents:

○ How quickly does the opponent get back on defense? If the defenders are quick getting back on defense, this will limit the fast break layup opportunities because the defenders will outnumber the offensive players. The offensive players should not force the shot but instead set up the offense or look for a shot from the secondary break situation. If the opponent is slow getting back on defense, the offense should immediately look for the long pass to score. When the opponent's point guard penetrates to the basket and misses, this may often lead to an easy fast break basket because the point guard is slow getting back.

○ What is the size and speed of the opponent? When playing against a smaller or slower team, the fast break may be used more often because passes may be made over the top of smaller players to begin the fast break. Smaller defenders will have a difficult time stopping high passes to the offensive players running the break, especially passes to the post player sprinting down the floor to get the ball for a layup. The same advantage is gained when playing against a slower team. It is difficult for a team to successfully defend a fast break, if they get beat down the court.

○ Is the opponent effective at denying the outlet pass? If the outlet pass to the guard is taken away, the rebounder may need to power dribble the ball out to get the fast break started. In addition, the long outlet pass down the floor may be open if the defender stays back and guards the short outlet pass. The offensive player should then go deeper up the sideline for a longer outlet pass over the defender.

○ Does the opponent rebound well? It is more difficult to begin a fast break after a made basket. If the opponents are a good rebounding team and have the ability to turn the offensive rebounds into baskets, this can limit your team's fast break opportunities.

Self-Knowledge

Besides being aware of your opponent's abilities, you and your players need to know about your own team's strengths and weaknesses. Teach your players to be aware of the following when executing the fast break:

○ How big are your players compared to the opponents? This will determine if the fast break should be run more often after defensive rebounds or after made shots. Smaller teams should work on starting the fast break with a quick inbounds pass after the made basket, because the team may not be able to get many rebounds against a bigger opponent.

○ What is the size and speed of the player who rebounded the ball? If this player is slow, the player will not be able to beat many defenders down the court; therefore, the player should look to start the break with a pass. If the player rebounding the ball is bigger than the opponent, an outlet pass over another player will be more effective in starting the pass.

How well does your point guard handle the ball? If the point guard is a good ball handler, players should always look for the point guard on the outlet pass. After receiving the outlet pass, the point guard should keep the ball and dribble as quickly as possible to the frontcourt, and the wing players can concentrate on running the floor wide and looking for the pass in the frontcourt.

Decision-Making Guidelines

When deciding how to gain the best advantage when executing the fast break, you and your players should consider the previous information as well as the following guidelines:

- After securing the rebound, if the opponent uses a double team on the player with the ball to slow down the break, the player should look for a quicker outlet pass to a guard at the outlet wing position. If the opponent pressures the outlet pass and does not get back on defense, a long pass down the floor may be available.

- A good rule of thumb is to make no more passes than the number of defenders that are back on defense. For example, if the break starts quickly and only one defender is back on defense, the offensive team should get a good shot after one pass is made on the fast break. If more passes are used, a turnover may result because more defenders will have time to get in a position to stop the break.

At a Glance

The following parts of the text offer additional information on the fast break:

Dribbling Basics	p. 30
Speed Dribble	p. 33
Passing Basics	p. 45
Baseball Pass	p. 52
Overhead Pass	p. 54
Catching	p. 61
Offensive Rebounds	p. 77
Defensive Rebounds	p. 100

Backdoor Cut

The backdoor cut is used when an offensive player is being overplayed by a defender who is trying to prevent the player from receiving a pass. The backdoor cut takes place when the offensive player makes an initial cut to receive a pass from a teammate, but the defender attempts to prevent this pass or steal the pass by moving into the passing lane. When the offensive player recognizes this, the player plants the top foot and makes the backdoor cut directly to the basket, looking for a pass and an easy score. The backdoor cut is typically used in situations where defenders are playing aggressively and try to steal the pass or when defenders play in the passing lanes and try to deny the pass. The backdoor cut is a great offensive move to keep the defenders from overplaying the offensive players and to keep them from moving into the passing lanes. After several successful backdoor cuts, the defenders will think twice about positioning in the passing lanes and will not want to pressure the pass as much.

 WATCH OUT!

The following circumstances may distract your athletes:

- Focusing on the movements of a weak-side defender who is in good position, rather than on the backdoor cut.
- Facing aggressive help defenders with a size advantage who inhibit the cutter from getting the pass.
- Facing defenders who aggressively guard on the ball, making the backdoor pass difficult.
- Paying more attention to the communication by the defenders and what is being called rather than what is actually happening at that moment.

READING THE SITUATION

How can your players gain the best advantage when executing the backdoor cut? Teach your players to do the following:

- Be aware of situations when the defender moves into the passing lane, and know that the backdoor cut to the basket can be used for a pass to the offensive player who is being overplayed by the defender. Also be aware of situations where the defender is in a closed stance denying a player the ball on the perimeter, because this type of stance can also lead to the backdoor cut.
- Be ready to make a backdoor cut to the basket if the defender turns his or her head to the ball.
- Make sure that the backdoor cut is made in a straight line to the basket and not a curved "banana" route. A straight cut, or direct cut, to the basket will free up the cutter from the defender more effectively.

ACQUIRING THE APPROPRIATE KNOWLEDGE

To help ensure your team's success in executing the backdoor cut, you and your players must know about the following:

Rules

You and your players need to know several main rules related to executing the backdoor cut:

- An offensive player who has the ball may not dribble or hold the ball for longer than five seconds when being closely guarded. The player with the ball must be aware of this when waiting for the teammate to make the backdoor cut.

- When receiving the pass after making the backdoor cut, players should be careful to avoid a traveling violation, especially if the player receives an out-of-control pass or isn't fully prepared for the pass.

- An offensive player cannot be in the lane for longer than three seconds. The cutter must be aware of this and must work to keep the feet out of the lane, especially when the pass is made from the high-post area.

- An offensive player cannot run into a defender who is stationary or a charge will be called. When making a backdoor cut, players must be aware of help-side defenders who may be in position to draw the charge.

REMINDER!

You and your players must understand the team strategy and game plan and must assess the backdoor cut based on those plans and the situation at hand. Make sure that you and your players consider the questions on page 112.

Strengths and Weaknesses of Opponents

You and your players must account for the opponent's strengths and weaknesses to know how to execute the backdoor cut properly. Consider the following about your opponents:

- Do the opponent's weak-side defenders sag to the ball on defense? If so, backdoor cuts will rarely be a good option because the defender will be positioned in the way of the cut.

- Does the opponent defend cuts quickly and effectively? If the defender is good at getting in the passing lanes and is quick to cover the backdoor cuts, the offensive player should fake the backdoor cut and then look to receive the pass after the fake. This fake will get the defender off the cutter and allow the cutter to have an open jump shot.

Self-Knowledge

Besides being aware of your opponent's abilities, you and your players need to know about your own team's strengths and weaknesses. Teach your players to be aware of the following when executing the backdoor cut:

- Does your team strategy focus on using a passing offense? If your team prefers or can execute a strong passing game where the players move and cut after passes, backdoor cuts can be highly effective.

- Do you have a good shooter on your team? If the team has a good shooter that teammates often try to get the ball to, the defense may work to deny passes to this player. Backdoor cuts may be an effective way to get this player open.

- Is your team strong on the perimeter? If the team has three or four players who play well on the perimeter, the defense may be spread out more on the court. As a result, backdoor cuts may be open as the defenders work to overplay passes farther away from the basket.

- Are your perimeter players quick? If so, these players can use the backdoor cut to get open without the use of a screen because they can beat their defender to the basket.

(continued)

At a Glance

The following parts of the text offer additional information on the backdoor cut:

Decision-Making Guidelines

When deciding how to gain the best advantage when executing the backdoor cut, you and your players should consider the previous information as well as the following guidelines:

- If the defender has a habit of turning his or her head and watching the passer when a player makes the backdoor cut, the passer must see this and make a quick pass to the cutter. If the defender stays in a closed stance as the player makes the backdoor cut, there is a split second in which the defender cannot see the ball, and the cutter will be open for the pass. If the defender opens up and sees the ball on the backdoor cut, the offensive player can fake the backdoor cut and step back out to receive the pass for the jumper.

- If the post player has the ball away from the basket (and the player is confident in his or her passing ability), this is a good time to execute the backdoor cut. In this situation, the post player is taking the post defender away from the basket—thus taking the size away from the lane—which opens up the court for the backdoor cut.

- If the offensive player does not get the ball on the backdoor cut, the player must not stop in the lane. The player should keep going and clear the lane so that other options are available, such as the player with the ball driving to the basket.

- If the defender quickly backs off the cutter, the cutter should come back for a pass and a jump shot.

Flash Cut

A flash cut is simply a straight cut toward the ball by an offensive player in order to get open for a pass. Flash cuts can be used to get open for a score or to give a passer another option when teammates are being denied the pass. A flash cut is often executed by a post player or wing player when the ball is at the opposite wing and the player sees an opportunity to "flash" to the ball and receive the pass for a score. Many teams use the skip pass to set up a flash cut from the strong side to the weak side. For example, assume that the ball is on the strong side and the post defenders are full fronting the low- and high-post players. The help-side defense is sagging, so a lob pass is not possible, but a skip pass is open. While the ball is in the air, the low-post player maintains inside position on the defender, keeping the defender on his or her backside. The player who receives the skip pass then feeds the low-post player on the flash cut from box to box. This pass can also be made to the high post on the same cut. If your team is successful at executing flash cuts and scoring off those cuts, this puts a lot of pressure on the defenders to take away this cut and helps to open up other options.

 WATCH OUT!

The following circumstances may distract your athletes:

- Facing a defense that moves from weak-side defense to strong-side defense on the skip pass.
- Facing a defense that double teams the passer.
- Facing a big and quick defender who is guarding the passer.

READING THE SITUATION

How can your players gain the best advantage when executing the flash cut? Teach your players to do the following:

- Recognize when the opponent uses a zone defense. Zone defenses have many gaps between defenders, allowing offensive players to use flash cuts to get the ball.
- Look at the position of the help-side defenders. If a defender is playing too close to an offensive player on the help side, the offensive player should take advantage of this and flash cut to the ball immediately.
- When positioned on the weak-side wing, always be ready to catch a skip pass and then look for the flash cut to the ball by the post player.

ACQUIRING THE APPROPRIATE KNOWLEDGE

To help ensure your team's success in executing the flash cut, you and your players must know about the following:

Rules

You and your players need to know several main rules related to executing the flash cut:

- An offensive player cannot be in the lane for longer than three seconds. A flash cutter must be aware of this and must be careful not to stop in the lane.
- When making the flash cut, players should be careful not to hold the defender. This could result in a holding foul being called.

(continued)

REMINDER!

You and your players must understand the team strategy and game plan and must assess the flash cut based on those plans and the situation at hand. Make sure that you and your players consider the questions on page 112.

- When receiving the pass after making the flash cut, players must be aware of their footwork and must be careful to avoid a traveling violation.
- An offensive player cannot run into a defender who is stationary or a charge will be called. When making a flash cut, players must be aware of defenders who may be in position to draw the charge.

Strengths and Weaknesses of Opponents

You and your players must account for the opponent's strengths and weaknesses to know how to execute the flash cut properly. Consider the following about your opponents:

- Are the opponent's inside players big and strong? If the opponent's post players have an advantage in size and strength, the flash cut will not be as effective because the defender can step in front of the cut and use an arm bar to prevent it from being executed. Additionally, offensive players must be aware that the defender may choose to let the flash cut go but then use the size advantage in an effort to prevent a good shot.
- Are the defenders on the weak side tall and quick? If so, the offense may have trouble executing a skip pass over to the weak-side offensive player. The defenders' size and speed will increase their ability to stop or intercept the skip pass. The passer should first use a ball fake to the post and then execute the skip pass. This will better set up the flash cut for the weak-side post player.
- Are the opponent's post defenders slow? If the post defender is slow, the offensive post player will most likely be able to beat the defender just by making a quick flash cut to the ball.

Self-Knowledge

Besides being aware of your opponent's abilities, you and your players need to know about your own team's strengths and weaknesses. Teach your players to be aware of the following when executing the flash cut:

- Is your post player an exceptional athlete? If so, using the flash cut would be effective in getting the ball to this player at the post. The better the post player is athletically, the better the player will be able to perform the flash cut. Strong and athletic post players can often seal the defender effectively or make the quick flash cut needed to get open.
- Is the player who receives the skip pass a good shooter? If so, this player will draw the defender to him or her quickly, which will allow some room for the flash cut and the pass to the cutter. If this player is not a good shooter, the defender may not guard the player very close and this can potentially cause some problems for the pass into the flash cutter.
- Does your post player have good offensive skills in the post area? If the post player is a strong shooter, the player should be put in a position where he or she can execute the flash cut and receive the pass for a shot.

DECISION-MAKING GUIDELINES

When deciding how to gain the best advantage when executing the flash cut, you and your players should consider the previous information as well as the following guidelines:

- If a team uses the skip pass for ball reversal, the flash cut is critical because it will help keep the defenders from double teaming the ball. The defenders will need to respect this cut and try to prevent it from leading to a score.

- Sometimes the defenders will concentrate too much on the post player making the flash cut and forget about the wing player. When this occurs, the wing player may make a high-post flash cut to the ball and be open for the shot. The passer needs to watch for this from the wing.

- If the offense does not position a post player at the block on the weak side, this will allow the skip pass to be made much easier because there will be no defender on the help side.

- If the offensive post player is fronted on the strong side, and the weak-side defense is sagging into the lane, the skip pass will be open and should be made immediately. After the skip pass, the offensive post player will be in a good position to seal the defender who was fronting the post. The post player can then execute the flash cut.

At a Glance

The following parts of the text offer additional information on the flash cut:

Offensive Footwork	p. 22
Passing Basics	p. 45
Catching	p. 61
Cuts	p. 81
Playing the Post	p. 87
Skip Pass	p. 126

Pick-and-Roll

In the pick-and-roll, an offensive player sets a screen for the teammate with the ball, and if the defenders switch on the screen, the screener reacts by rolling to the basket for a pass. Usually, the player who sets the screen in the pick-and-roll is a bigger player, and the offensive team tries to create a mismatch by getting a smaller defender to switch onto the screener. The screener then tries to take advantage of this mismatch by rolling to the basket for the pass. When running this play, the two offensive players involved also have several other options based on how the defenders react to the screen. The pick-and-roll is typically used in situations where the defenders are applying good pressure on the player who has the ball. This play may be executed any time a player sees that the teammate with the ball needs help to get away from the defender.

WATCH OUT!

The following circumstances may distract your athletes:

○ Facing bigger defenders who can overpower the player setting the screen.

○ Facing defenders who double team the dribbler.

○ Executing a pick-and-roll that results in a mismatch in favor of the defense on the switch.

ACQUIRING THE APPROPRIATE KNOWLEDGE

To help ensure your team's success in executing the pick-and-roll, you and your players must know about the following:

READING THE SITUATION

How can your players gain the best advantage when executing the pick-and-roll? Teach your players to do the following:

- Wait for the screener to set the screen before starting to dribble. If the player with the ball dribbles too early and the screen is not set, the screener may be called for a moving screen.

- Keep good spacing for the pass to the screener by taking two dribbles past the screen. This allows the dribbler to get a better angle for the pass to the screener on the roll to the basket.

- Be alert to situations where a screen is not called out by the defense. In these cases, the dribbler will probably want to go all the way to the basket. It is difficult for a defender to stay with the dribbler if he or she does not know the screen is coming.

- Be aware that some opponents may switch defensively even if the switching defenders are of different size. This means that a mismatch on the offensive players may occur after the defenders switch on the screen.

- Understand that players not immediately involved in the pick-and-roll must stay away from the screener to make this option open enough to complete.

Rules

You and your players need to know several main rules related to executing the pick-and-roll:

- When coming off the screen, the player with the ball must be careful not to double dribble.

- An offensive player cannot be in the lane for longer than three seconds. The screener must be aware of this if he or she rolls into the lane.

- An offensive player who has the ball may not dribble or hold the ball for longer than five seconds when being closely guarded. The dribbler must be aware of this when waiting to make the pass to the teammate on the roll.

REMINDER!

You and your players must understand the team strategy and game plan and must assess the pick-and-roll based on those plans and the situation at hand. Make sure that you and your players consider the questions on page 112.

Strengths and Weaknesses of Opponents

You and your players must account for the opponent's strengths and weaknesses to know how to execute the pick-and-roll properly. Consider the following about your opponents:

- Do the defenders switch on the screen? If the defenders switch when the dribbler goes off the screen, a mismatch may occur, and the dribbler should make the pass immediately to the screener rolling to the basket. The pick-and-roll has a greater chance for success when the defense switches and a mismatch occurs, because this typically leaves a smaller defender on the screener, who is usually a bigger player.

- Are all of the defenders approximately the same size? If so, a switching defense will not create much of a mismatch because the defenders switching are the same size.

- Does the opponent have quick defenders at the guard position? Quick guards may be able to defend the pick-and-roll without switching.

- Are the defenders good communicators? If the defense talks and communicates well, the pick-and-roll will be better defended. The offensive players must listen for the communication of the defenders (for terms such as *switch* and *stay*).

Self-Knowledge

Besides being aware of your opponent's abilities, you and your players need to know about your own team's strengths and weaknesses. Teach your players to be aware of the following when executing the pick-and-roll:

- Do your players drive to the basket well? If so, a good strategy might be to use a screening offense where the pick-and-roll often comes into play. In the pick-and-roll, the dribbler may keep the ball after coming off the screen and look to make a hard drive to the basket, rather than passing it to the screener who rolls to the basket.

- Do your players screen well and are they quick to read a defensive switch? If so, the pick-and-roll is a good choice. If a switch is recognized early, a quick pass can be made to the screener, who rolls after setting the screen. If the team has more than one good screener, the pick-and-roll is even more effective because the defenders do not always know who the screener will be.

- Is the dribbler or the screener a strong shooter? If the dribbler can shoot the ball well, this player may try to clear the screen with several dribbles and then pull up for a jump shot. If the player setting the screen is a good shooter, the player can roll back to receive the pass for a jumper rather than rolling to the basket.

(continued)

Decision-Making Guidelines

When deciding how to gain the best advantage when executing the pick-and-roll, you and your players should consider the previous information as well as the following guidelines:

- If the opponent is a good, sound, well-balanced defensive team, the offense may not gain an advantage when the defenders switch. In this case, the player with the ball should keep the dribble longer and look for the screener (who has rolled to the basket) on a mismatch if the switch takes place.

- The dribbler should work to go close to the screener so the defender cannot get over the screen to stay with the dribbler. This forces the defenders to switch. If a mismatch occurs, the screener should roll all the way to the basket and post up against the shorter defender.

- Some opponents may opt to fight over or under screens and may rarely switch, thus not providing many opportunities for the pick-and-roll to be executed. In these cases, if the defender typically goes over the top of the screen, the dribbler should continue the dribble to maintain proper spacing in the offense and move to the basket. If the defender typically goes behind the screen, the screen should be set in the shooting area because the dribbler can pull up behind the screen for a jump shot.

- If the defense sags into the paint from the weak side, the pass to the screener on the roll will need to be quicker. Also, the screener cannot roll all the way to the basket for the pass because the help-side defender will be there to defend the pass if the screener goes too far.

- If the defense traps the dribbler coming off the screen, the screener must step back to receive the pass rather than roll to the basket.

A cross screen is when the offensive post player on the strong side goes across the lane to set a screen for the weak-side post player. The cross screen is an effective way to get the ball inside to the post player for an easy score or in a good position to make an offensive post move. The cross screen is most effective when a team has two good post players. Many teams use a cross screen to create a mismatch in the post. For example, assume that the post players are both at the low block, with the bigger player on the weak side. As the ball is passed to the wing, the strong-side post player is being fronted by the defender and is unavailable for the entry pass. The strong-side post player goes across the lane and sets the screen for the weak-side post player, who cuts off the screen to the strong side, looking for the pass. In this situation, a defensive switch will create a difficult mismatch for the defense. Your team can use cross screens to attack the inside, to create a mismatch with the defensive post players, or to keep your post players moving.

 WATCH OUT!

The following circumstances may distract your athletes:

- Continuing to battle for position on the strong-side post instead of going to set the cross screen once the post player recognizes that he or she isn't open.

- Being too focused on ball reversal and not recognizing that the cross screen is available.

- Facing defenders who switch quickly on the post screens.

- Facing an opponent with bigger post defenders.

- Facing an opponent whose perimeter defenders sag off to help.

- Paying too much attention to the communication by the defenders.

READING THE SITUATION

How can your players gain the best advantage when executing the cross screen? Teach your players to do the following:

- Know the situation in the post area. Other players should take advantage of the post players by getting them the ball for a shot after the cross screens.

- Recognize any mismatches when the screen is set.

- Pay attention to the post player on the ball side. The perimeter player should be aware that the ball-side post player may be open for a pass before setting the cross screen.

- After setting a cross screen, roll back to the ball and look for the pass. If the cutter goes high off the screen, the screener should roll back to the low post. If the cutter goes low, the screener should roll back to the high post.

ACQUIRING THE APPROPRIATE KNOWLEDGE

To help ensure your team's success in executing the cross screen, you and your players must know about the following:

Rules

You and your players need to know several main rules related to executing the cross screen:

- An offensive player cannot be in the lane for longer than three seconds. This may come into play when the cross screen is set in the lane.

(continued)

REMINDER!

You and your players must understand the team strategy and game plan and must assess the cross screen based on those plans and the situation at hand. Make sure that you and your players consider the questions on page 112.

- An offensive player who has the ball may not dribble or hold the ball for longer than five seconds when being closely guarded. The perimeter player must be aware of this when waiting for the cross screen to be set.

- Players setting screens must not be moving when contact is made with the defender, or an illegal or moving screen will be called.

Strengths and Weaknesses of Opponents

You and your players must account for the opponent's strengths and weaknesses to know how to execute the cross screen properly. Consider the following about your opponents:

- How big are the opponent's post players? If the opponent's post players are big and can effectively use their size when defending the post, the offensive post players must be sure to set the cross screen using good balance and solid contact with the defender. This will help the post player set effective screens that the defender cannot get through, allowing the offensive player to get open for a good shot by using the screen.

- How well do the defenders communicate? Poor communication by the defenders will allow the offensive team to use the cross screen more effectively. Lack of communication will cause confusion by the defenders about who is guarding the cutter on the cross screen.

Self-Knowledge

Besides being aware of your opponent's abilities, you and your players need to know about your own team's strengths and weaknesses. Teach your players to be aware of the following when executing the cross screen:

- Do your post players have a size advantage over the opponent's post players? When the offensive post player has a height advantage, the offense should work to get the ball inside and create a mismatch in the post on the screen.

- Are your post players strong inside scorers? This may determine if the ball gets passed back out for a shot. If the post players cannot make a good offensive move for a shot, they must pass the ball back out to the perimeter for a shot.

- Does your team have good perimeter shooters? If so, the defenders will pressure the shooter and leave more room for the cross screen to be executed.

- Are your post players quick? If so, they will be able to make the cut off the cross screen quicker to lose the defender on the screen.

Decision-Making Guidelines

When deciding how to gain the best advantage when executing the cross screen, you and your players should consider the previous information as well as the following guidelines:

- The offense should strive to keep the team's best perimeter shooter on the same side as the team's best post player so that a two-person game can develop as they work together on the pass. If the defenders are trying to stop the ball from getting into the post area after the cross screen, sagging defenders will leave the perimeter player open for the shot.

- If the opponent fights over screens and bumps cutters to take away the cut on top of the screen, the offensive player must read this situation and should go low off the screen. The cutter should initially attempt to go over the top of the screen because there is more room for the cutter coming off the cross screen on the high side of the screen than the low or baseline side of the screen. The screener should always roll back to the ball on a switch, meaning that the screener should pivot back to find the ball because the screener could be open if the defenders switch.

- If the defender sags from the perimeter wing into the post, the perimeter player must reverse the ball or shoot. The pass into the post will be too difficult because the sagging defender will be in the path of this pass after the cross screen.

At a Glance

The following parts of the text offer additional information on the cross screen:

chapter 6

Defensive Tactical Skills

This chapter covers the defensive tactical skills that you and your players must know to be successful. In this chapter, you will find the following skills:

On-the-Ball Defense

Simply stated, on-the-ball defense is when the defender is guarding the offensive player with the ball, whether the player is dribbling, passing, or shooting the ball. This may be the most important type of defense because the offensive player with the ball is the most dangerous player on the floor and the only player who can score. To play good on-the-ball defense, the defender guarding the ball must be able to force offensive players to do what they don't want to do with the ball. For example, if the offensive player wants to go to the right, the defender must make the player go left. If the offensive player is a good shooter off the dribble, the defender must not allow the player to put the ball on the floor before the shot. The defensive team should make the offensive player with the ball work extremely hard to pass, dribble, or shoot.

 WATCH OUT!

The following circumstances may distract your athletes:

- Guarding a tall or quick offensive player with the ball. This player may be able to shoot the ball over the defender or quickly get around the defender.

- Facing an offensive team that effectively uses screens to free up the ball handler or cuts to get into position for passes and shots.

READING THE SITUATION

How can your players gain the best advantage when defending on the ball? Teach your players to do the following:

- Stay low in the defensive stance when guarding the ball. This will ensure that the defender cannot be pushed out of position easily.

- Work to keep the inside hand down to discourage the offensive player from easily changing direction, and keep the outside hand up so the dribbler cannot easily see the open player for a pass.

- Force the offensive player with the ball to turn so that his or her back is to the basket. This gives the defender an advantage because the offensive player cannot always see an open teammate when the back is to the basket.

- Learn the ball handler's weak hand and force him or her to use this hand on the dribble.

- Keep the eyes focused on the offensive player's waist to avoid being faked out of position by the player's head or shoulder movement.

- Understand the need for communication with the defender who is guarding the ball so that he or she knows when screens may be coming and on which side.

ACQUIRING THE APPROPRIATE KNOWLEDGE

To ensure your team's success in defending on the ball, you and your players must know about the following:

Rules

You and your players need to know several main rules related to defending on the ball:

○ When defending on the ball, players should be careful not to get out of position and reach for the ball, or a foul could be called.

○ An offensive player cannot run into a defender who is stationary or a charge will be called. The defender on the ball can try to draw a charge by getting in the way of the dribbler's drive to the basket.

○ An offensive player who has the ball may not dribble or hold the ball for longer than 5 seconds when being closely guarded. The on-the-ball defender can force a turnover by not allowing the offensive player to get rid of the ball within this time limit.

○ The offensive team must advance the ball into the frontcourt within a 10-second time limit. If the on-the-ball defender can prevent the dribbler from moving up the court, a backcourt violation may occur.

○ An offensive player cannot be in the lane for longer than 3 seconds. If the on-the-ball defender can effectively slow the offensive player's drive to the basket, a 3-second violation could occur.

REMINDER!

You and your players must understand the team strategy and game plan and must assess on-the-ball defense based on those plans and the situation at hand. Make sure that you and your players consider the questions on page 112.

Strengths and Weaknesses of Opponents

You and your players must account for the opponent's strengths and weaknesses to know how to defend on the ball properly. Consider the following about your opponents:

○ How quick is the offensive player with the ball? This is probably the most important factor that will determine the defender's ability to play effective on-the-ball defense. If the offensive player with the ball is quicker than the defender, the defender must give the player more room on the dribble and shouldn't play so close to the player. The defender should try to stay at least one arm's length away so that the offensive player cannot go around the defender and drive to the basket.

○ Is the player with the ball a strong shooter from the perimeter? If so, the defender should play closer to the player when he or she goes up for the shot. If not, then the defender can focus more on defending the dribble rather than the shot.

○ Can the player with the ball drive to the basket well? If so, the defender must force the offensive player to pick up the dribble before getting to the basket. The player will not be as much of a threat shooting the ball away from the basket. To get the offensive player to pick up the dribble, the defender must move the feet quickly and keep the eyes on the offensive player's waist to avoid being faked out of position.

Self-Knowledge

Besides being aware of your opponent's abilities, you and your players need to know about your own team's strengths and weaknesses. Teach your players to be aware of the following when defending on the ball:

○ How quick are your defenders? If the defender has a quickness advantage, the defender may be able to put much more pressure on the ball without getting beat by the offensive player to the basket. If the opponent is quicker and can easily beat the defender, the defender must get at least an arm's length away from the offensive player. This will enable the defender to keep the dribbler in front of him or her more easily.

(continued)

On-the-Ball Defense (continued)

- How big are your defenders? If the defender on the ball has a size advantage, the defender can use pressure to prevent a shot or force the offensive player to take a quicker shot to get it off over the bigger defender.

- Does your team have good help defense? If so, this will allow the defense to guard the ball more closely because if a defender gets beat off the dribble, his or her defensive teammates will be in help position to stop the dribbler.

- Does your team have strong post players? If so, defenders can put more pressure on the player with the ball because they will have a shot blocker ready to help if they get beat off the dribble.

Decision-Making Guidelines

When deciding how to gain the best advantage when defending on the ball, you and your players should consider the previous information as well as the following guidelines:

- As the offensive player crosses the half-court line using the dribble, the on-the-ball defender should guide the player toward the sideline, making the player use the weak hand on the dribble.

- When the offensive player picks up the dribble, the defender on the ball should bring both hands up and block the vision of the offensive player.

- If the dribbler gets to the middle of the lane, the post defender must step up and help stop the penetration to the basket.

- When the dribbler goes baseline on a drive to the basket, this is a perfect area for the defense to trap the dribbler because he or she will have limited choices.

- When guarding the dribbler full court, the defender on the ball should work to keep the dribbler out of the middle of the court where the dribbler will have the entire court available for making a pass.

Off-the-Ball Defense

Off-the-ball defense is the type of defense played when the defender is guarding a player who doesn't have the ball, whether on the strong or weak side of the court. Typically, off-the-ball defenders on the strong side (or ball side) will work to deny passes to their offensive player, and off-the-ball defenders on the weak side will help protect the basket on drives or try to stop the offensive player from cutting to get the ball. Many of your players may not understand the important role of off-the-ball defense; these players may relax when their player doesn't have the ball. However, off-the-ball defense is more difficult than on-the-ball defense because the defender has to be concerned not only with the ball, but also with the offensive player that he or she is defending. The defender will have to defend cuts and screens as well as be ready to help cover the offensive player with the ball. Off-the-ball defense is a challenging skill and one that is very important to your team's overall success.

 WATCH OUT!

The following circumstances may distract your athletes:

○ Guarding a bigger offensive player. The size of the offensive player may prevent the defender from knowing where the ball is at all times.

○ Guarding a quicker offensive player. A quick offensive player may be difficult for the defender to stay with.

○ Losing focus on playing strong off-the-ball defense because of screens or cuts executed by the offensive players.

READING THE SITUATION

How can your players gain the best advantage when defending off the ball? Teach your players to do the following:

- Maintain a ball–you–man triangle so that the defenders are in a position between the offensive player with the ball and the offensive player they are guarding so that they can see the ball and their offensive player at all times. The defenders must continually adjust their position as the ball and their player move.

- Jump to the ball as it is passed. This will help ensure that the off-the-ball defenders are in proper help position—the ball–you–man triangle—when the ball reaches its target.

- Watch for an opportunity to double team. As the dribbler brings the ball up court, the off-the-ball defender closest to the dribbler should look for an opportunity to move in and double team with the on-the-ball defender (if the dribbler turns his or her back to the off-the-ball defender).

ACQUIRING THE APPROPRIATE KNOWLEDGE

To ensure your team's success in defending off the ball, you and your players must know about the following:

Rules

You and your players need to know several main rules related to defending off the ball:

(continued)

REMINDER!

You and your players must understand the team strategy and game plan and must assess off-the-ball defense based on those plans and the situation at hand. Make sure that you and your players consider the questions on page 112.

○ An offensive player cannot run into a defender who is stationary or a charge will be called. The off-the-ball defender on the help side can try to draw a charge by getting in the proper position to stop the dribbler's drive to the basket.

○ When defending off the ball on the help side, players should try to avoid being slow to help on the dribbler and then reaching out for the ball or holding the dribbler. This could result in a foul being called.

○ An offensive player who has the ball may not dribble or hold the ball for longer than five seconds when being closely guarded. The off-the-ball defender on the help side can create a turnover by helping on the dribbler and forcing the dribbler to hold the ball for longer than this time limit.

○ A foul may be called when an offensive player screens the off-the-ball defender on the help side and the defender runs through the screen.

○ When defending off the ball, players should be careful not to reach out and hold the offensive player they are guarding when that player makes a cut to the ball, or a foul could be called.

Strengths and Weaknesses of Opponents

You and your players must account for the opponent's strengths and weaknesses to know how to defend off the ball properly. Consider the following about your opponents:

○ How big are the opponent's players? If the offensive players are bigger, the off-the-ball defenders on the help side must block out farther away from the basket to reduce the chances of the bigger offensive players getting the rebound because of their size.

○ Are the opponent's players quick with the ball? If an offensive player is quick off the dribble and beats the on-the-ball defender, off-the-ball defenders on the help side will need to move in quickly to stop the offensive player's drive.

○ Does the offensive player with the ball shoot well from the perimeter? If so, off-the-ball defenders should be prepared for a rebound and must work to block their offensive player from getting the rebound.

○ Does the opponent's offense depend on drives to the basket? If so, the off-the-ball defenders on the help side must be sure to stay in good help position. On each pass, the defenders must be in position to help stop the offensive player on the drive, because the drive to the basket would typically be the offensive team's first option. If the defenders can take this option away, the offense is forced to take jump shots or use other options to score.

Self-Knowledge

Besides being aware of your opponent's abilities, you and your players need to know about your own team's strengths and weaknesses. Teach your players to be aware of the following when defending off the ball:

○ How big are your players? If the off-the-ball defenders are taller than the opponents, this will make the skip pass more difficult for the offense to pull off because the defenders can more easily deflect or steal the pass. The skip pass is often used against small teams to get the ball to the other side of the court when defenders are in good help-side position.

- Does your team have a strong shot blocker at the post? If the defense has a shot blocker in the middle, this will allow the off-the-ball defenders on the help side to stay closer to the offensive player they are guarding because the shot blocker can help on the drive to the basket.

- Does your team apply good ball-side pressure? If so, this may lead to more help-side opportunities because the defenders on the ball side are making it difficult to pass the ball. In this situation, the offensive player with the ball will resort to driving around the defender to the basket, thus forcing the help-side defenders to react.

Decision-Making Guidelines

When deciding how to gain the best advantage when defending off the ball, you and your players should consider the previous information as well as the following guidelines:

- If the ball is below the free throw line extended, off-the-ball defenders on the help side should be straddling the rim line (an imaginary line from rim to rim) to be in good help position. If the ball is above the free throw line extended, off-the-ball defenders should be one step off the rim line toward the offensive player they are guarding. This positioning will allow a defender to maintain the ball–you–man positioning so the defender can be in good help position when an offensive player is driving from the strong side.

- If the dribbler drives the ball to the baseline, the off-the-ball defender on the help side must move over to the ball to stop the dribbler outside the lane on the ball side of the court. This will prevent the dribbler from getting close to the basket for an easy shot.

- If the opponent uses the penetrate and pass as part of the team's offense, help-side defenders must be prepared to first help on the dribbler and then recover to the offensive player they are guarding to cover the shot.

- When an off-the-ball defender is guarding an offensive player who cuts to the ball, the defender should block the cutter's path to the ball by getting the arm and shoulder in the path of the cutter and forcing the cutter to take a different path. This will help prevent the cutter from getting the ball in good shooting position.

At a Glance

The following parts of the text offer additional information on defending off the ball:

Playing Man Defense

In man defense, each defender is responsible for a specific offensive player. Each defender also has a secondary responsibility of helping to guard the offensive player with the ball when necessary. Effective man defense requires players to have a strong understanding of help principles such as ball-side and help-side defense. Man defense is the best defense to use against a strong rebounding team because defenders are in a better position to block out when they are responsible for guarding a specific player.

 WATCH OUT!

The following circumstances may distract your athletes:

○ Guarding an offensive player who is bigger or has good speed or offensive ability. This may make it difficult for a defender to stop the offensive player from scoring.

○ Letting the communication on offense interfere with the defenders' communication with each other.

ACQUIRING THE APPROPRIATE KNOWLEDGE

To help ensure your team's success in playing man defense, you and your players must know about the following:

Rules

You and your players need to know several main rules related to playing man defense:

○ The offensive team must advance the ball into the frontcourt within a 10-second time limit. If the defender can prevent a dribbler from moving up the court, a backcourt violation may occur.

READING THE SITUATION

How can your players gain the best advantage when playing man defense? Teach your players to do the following:

• Maintain the proper defensive stance whether or not the player they are guarding has the ball so that they can move quickly when reacting to the game situation.

• When guarding the player who has the ball, work to limit the player's offensive ability. Defenders can do this by forcing the offensive player in one direction and eliminating the player's preferred option or forcing the offensive player to use the weak hand on the dribble.

• Maintain a ball–you–man triangle when guarding a player who does not have the ball. This will help ensure that the defender is always in a position to see the ball and is always ready to provide help if an offensive player dribbles the ball to the basket.

• Communicate with teammates. Defenders should warn teammates about screens being set by offensive players, let teammates know when cutters are going to the ball, specify who should guard the ball in a break situation, identify when a double team can be made effectively, and so on.

- An offensive player who has the ball may not dribble or hold the ball for longer than 5 seconds when being closely guarded. The defender can force a turnover by not allowing the offensive player to get rid of the ball within this time limit.

- An offensive player cannot run into a defender who is stationary or a charge will be called. Defenders can try to draw a charge by getting in the proper position to stop a dribbler's drive to the basket.

- When defending on or off the ball, players should be careful not to get out of position and reach for the ball. This could result in a foul being called.

> **REMINDER!**
>
> You and your players must understand the team strategy and game plan and must assess playing man defense based on those plans and the situation at hand. Make sure that you and your players consider the questions on page 112.

Strengths and Weaknesses of Opponents

You and your players must account for the opponent's strengths and weaknesses to know how to play man defense properly. Consider the following about your opponents:

- How big is the offensive player? If an offensive player is bigger than the defender guarding that player, the defense should use double teams or switches on screens to try to prevent the offensive player from using this size advantage to score.

- Can the offensive player drive to the basket well? When guarding a player who drives to the basket well, a defender must give that player more space and force the player to go to the weak hand on the drive. This will prevent the player from getting all the way to the basket for an easy shot using the strong hand. The defender must force the offensive player to go in the direction he or she does not want to go.

- Can the offensive player pass the ball well? When guarding a player who passes well, a defender may allow the player to shoot the ball in order to take away the player's passing ability. If the player is also a good shooter, the defensive strategy may be to deny the passes to the player's teammates. The defender who is guarding the offensive player one pass away from this player should play more aggressively or deny the ball in a closed stance so that the pass is not open.

- Does the opponent's offense depend on perimeter shooting? When playing against a team that shoots a lot of perimeter and three-point shots, the perimeter defenders must screen out their offensive players on the shots because long rebounds are likely.

Self-Knowledge

Besides being aware of your opponent's abilities, you and your players need to know about your own team's strengths and weaknesses. Teach your players to be aware of the following when playing man defense:

- Is the defender quicker than the player he or she is guarding? If a defender has a quickness advantage, the defender can apply more pressure in the man defense because the offensive player will not be able to beat the defender to the basket. The defender's quickness will allow the defender to stay closer to the offensive player without letting the player get around him or her. A team with a quickness advantage over the opponent could also extend the man defense and play a full-court or three-quarter-court defense.

- Is the defender physically stronger than the player he or she is guarding? It is much more difficult for an offensive player to drive around a defender who is stronger. Therefore, a stronger defender can guard the offensive player closer, eliminating the open shot and making the offensive player put the ball on the floor.

(continued)

○ Does your team have a size advantage over the opponent? If the defense has a size advantage, they will be able to control the boards more easily and start the fast break more effectively. If the defensive team is smaller, the defenders may want to block out farther away from the basket.

○ How effective are your weak-side defenders? If the weak-side players are well schooled in the help-side principles of man defense, the defensive team will be able to stop the offensive team's drives to the basket because the defenders will be in good help position. If the defenders do not understand the principles of weak-side help, this will allow the offense to get easy shots off the dribble going to the basket.

At a Glance

The following parts of the text offer additional information on playing man defense:

Decision-Making Guidelines

When deciding how to gain the best advantage when playing man defense, you and your players should consider the previous information as well as the following guidelines:

○ When the ball is below the free throw line extended, defenders on the weak side should position on the rim line (an imaginary line from rim to rim), creating a ball–you–man triangle, so that the defender can see both the ball and the offensive player he or she is guarding. This will put the defender in good help position, allowing the defender to stop the dribble penetration of an offensive player.

○ If the defensive team has a center who is a strong shot blocker, the defender guarding the ball should force the dribbler into the middle, toward the shot blocker. The shot blocker can cause a bad shot, which may lead to a fast break the other way.

○ When the ball goes into the post, the defense may need to double team the offensive post player to help prevent an easy shot.

Playing Zone Defense

In zone defense, defensive players guard a certain area instead of a particular player (as in man defense), and any offensive player who enters into a defender's area of the zone is the responsibility of that defender. Many of the principles used for man defenses are also required in order to play a good zone defense. Some teams may find that playing a zone defense is a better choice because of the size and quickness of their players. Different types of zone defenses can be used based on the opponent's offensive strengths. One type is an even-front zone, such as the 2-3 zone (which is best against a good offensive rebounding team that is good inside the paint) or the 2-1-2 (which works best against a team with a good high-post offensive player). Odd-front zones are also common, such as the 1-3-1 (which works best against a team that has excellent wing shooters and a good high-post player), the 1-2-2 (which works best against a team that is not real strong inside the lane but is strong at the wings and baseline), and the 3-2 (which works best against a team that has a strong wing, high-post, and baseline game but is weak inside the lane).

 WATCH OUT!

The following circumstances may distract your athletes:

- Facing a team with good shooting or passing efficiency. This may prevent defenders from focusing on other aspects of zone defense, such as stopping a pass to the lane or covering the baseline drive in the zone.

- Facing a team with a size advantage. The size of the opponents could prevent defenders from concentrating on covering their areas.

- Focusing on pressuring one specific player because of that player's quickness, rather than covering all offensive players in the defender's area of responsibility.

READING THE SITUATION

How can your players gain the best advantage when playing zone defense? Teach your players to do the following:

- Limit the gaps left open in the zone. The defense must strive to have a defender in place to guard the ball no matter where this may be.

- Keep the hands up to limit the offensive players' vision when they have the ball.

- Move quickly while the ball is in the air as it is passed between offensive players. This will help ensure that defenders are in position to cover their specific area when the pass is completed.

- Do not move to cover offensive players if they move outside their shooting range. Doing so would leave bigger gaps in the zone defense because the zone is stretched if the defenders come out too far on the court. Typically, defenders should focus their attention on offensive players closer to the basket, except in cases where the offensive team has a great three-point shooter.

ACQUIRING THE APPROPRIATE KNOWLEDGE

To help ensure your team's success in playing zone defense, you and your players must know about the following:

Rules

You and your players need to know several main rules related to playing zone defense:

(continued)

REMINDER!

You and your players must understand the team strategy and game plan and must assess playing zone defense based on those plans and the situation at hand. Make sure that you and your players consider the questions on page 112.

- An offensive player cannot be in the lane for longer than 3 seconds. If the defenders make it difficult for the offensive post player to get into a gap in the zone, this player may be caught in the lane for longer than 3 seconds, resulting in a turnover.

- The offensive team must advance the ball into the front-court within a 10-second time limit. The defense may force a backcourt violation if they make it difficult for the offensive team to get the ball across the centerline.

- An offensive player who has the ball may not dribble or hold the ball for longer than 5 seconds when being closely guarded. The defenders can force a turnover by trapping the ball and not allowing the offensive player to get rid of the ball within this time limit.

- When playing zone defense, players should avoid getting out of position and reaching for the ball. This could result in a foul being called.

Strengths and Weaknesses of Opponents

You and your players must account for the opponent's strengths and weaknesses to know how to play zone defense properly. Consider the following about your opponents:

- Are the opponent's players quick? If so, the zone defenders need to move quickly and focus on keeping dribblers from getting into the gaps in the zone.

- Do the opponent's players shoot well? If so, the defense will need to adjust by extending the zone to the area where the shooters are located when taking the shot. For example, if the offensive team shoots well from the perimeter and is making the shots from the wing, the defense may want to use a 1-3-1 zone because it covers the wing areas best. If the offensive team likes to take shots close to the basket, the defense may want to use a 2-3 zone, which will position more defenders at the post.

- Does the opponent rebound well? If the offensive team rebounds well, the defense should use a zone where the bigger players are positioned close to the basket, such as a 2-3 zone.

- How does the opponent move? If the offensive team likes to move the ball and keep the offensive players stationary, the defense can put more pressure on the passes to take away some of those passes. This can be done with the zone defender guarding the area where pressure can be put on the passer and passing lane. If the offensive team likes to use cuts to the ball, zone defenders should work to take the path of the cutter away as opposed to taking away the pass.

- Does the player with the ball handle the ball well? If so, zone defenders should try to force the dribbler to give up the ball and pass to another player who might not handle it as well. Defenders can do this by double teaming the dribbler to try to force the pass. When the good ball handler does not have the ball, defenders should try to deny passes to this player.

Self-Knowledge

Besides being aware of your opponent's abilities, you and your players need to know about your own team's strengths and weaknesses. Teach your players to be aware of the following when playing zone defense:

- Are your players quick? If the defenders are quicker than the offensive players, the defenders can place more pressure on the passer or dribbler and can use more double teams.

- Is your team big in the middle? If the defense has a size advantage up the middle, defenders should work to force the offensive players to put the ball on the floor and go to the basket up the middle, where these bigger defenders are positioned. This will force the offense to take shots where the defense has a size advantage.

- Are your players physically aggressive? If a team's players are more aggressive than the opponent, this can be a big advantage when playing a zone defense, making the zone more difficult to penetrate against. Because of the aggressiveness of the zone defenders—not allowing cutters in the lane and not allowing a dribbler to get to the lane—the offense will typically keep the ball away from the lane area.

Decision-Making Guidelines

When deciding how to gain the best advantage when playing zone defense, you and your players should consider the previous information as well as the following guidelines:

- Many offenses use the skip pass to get an open shot against a zone defense. The offense tries to take advantage of a zone defender on the help side who is in a position to help stop the ball rather than covering the defender's area in the zone. Defenders need to be aware of this and should move to cover skip passes as the ball is in the air. This allows the zone defender to get to his or her area in time to cover the shooter.

- If the offensive team likes to get the ball to the corner or baseline against a zone defense, the defenders should take this opportunity to double team the baseline player. This will make the offensive team try something different to attack the zone.

- If the offensive team releases a player on the shot in an effort to stop the fast break, this may provide a good fast break opportunity for the defenders if the offensive team does not cover an area for the rebound.

- If the opponent likes to fast break, this will put some pressure on the zone defenders to get back and cover their area to stop the fast break from being successful.

- If the offensive team uses the low-post area effectively, the zone defenders will need to collapse inside to stop the scoring in the lane area. The defenders will need to recover on an inside-out pass to take away the perimeter shots.

- If the offensive team likes to reverse the ball before a shot, the zone defenders should work to keep the ball on the side of the first pass. This makes the defenders' job easier because there will be more defenders on that side of the court.

At a Glance

The following parts of the text offer additional information on playing zone defense:

Defensive Positioning	p. 94
Defensive Rebounds	p. 100
Defending Cuts	p. 103
Defending Screens	p. 105
Defending the Post	p. 108
Applying Pressure	p. 166
Defending the Pass	p. 187

Applying Pressure

Putting pressure on the offense requires a combination of both attitude and aggressiveness by the defenders. The ability, the speed, and the size of defenders are all factors when applying pressure. An effective pressuring defense will not allow offensive movement to take place easily. Defensive pressure can take many forms, such as switching defenses, double teaming defense, quick help defense, or straight man defense. The makeup of your team will determine the type of pressure that your defense can apply to the offensive team.

WATCH OUT!

The following circumstances may distract your athletes:

- Guarding an offensive player who has an advantage in size or speed. This player can disrupt the pressure that the defender is working to apply.

- Facing an opponent with an offensive player who can shoot well against pressure.

- Facing an opponent with an offensive player who can successfully advance the ball against pressure.

READING THE SITUATION

How can your players gain the best advantage when applying pressure? Teach your players to do the following:

- Be continuously aware of the time left in the game and the score. This will dictate the amount of pressure the defense should apply to the offensive team.

- Communicate on screens and cuts. This is important so that switches can be made when necessary and help is available to keep the pressure on the offense.

- Take offensive players out of their comfort zone with and without the ball. For example, defenders should recognize the direction their opponent likes to move with the ball and should work to force the opponent in the direction that he or she is not the most comfortable.

- Apply more pressure to all the offensive players any time the dribbler picks up the ball. The defenders should try to deny the pass and possibly cause a turnover.

ACQUIRING THE APPROPRIATE KNOWLEDGE

To help ensure your team's success in applying pressure, you and your players must know about the following:

Rules

You and your players need to know several main rules related to applying pressure:

- An offensive player who has the ball may not dribble or hold the ball for longer than 5 seconds when being closely guarded. The defenders can force a turnover by applying pressure on the ball and not allowing the offensive player to get rid of the ball within this time limit.

- The offensive team must advance the ball into the front-court within a 10-second time limit. The defense may try to force a 10-second violation by applying pressure in the backcourt.

- An offensive player cannot run into a defender who is stationary or a charge will be called. Defenders can try to draw a charge by getting in the proper position when applying pressure defense.

- When playing pressure defense on a jump shooter, the defender must be careful not to foul the shooter. If the defender is applying pressure on a player who takes a jump shot, an offensive foul can be drawn if the shooter jumps forward on the shot.

REMINDER!

You and your players must understand the team strategy and game plan and must assess applying pressure based on those plans and the situation at hand. Make sure that you and your players consider the questions on page 112.

Strengths and Weaknesses of Opponents

You and your players must account for the opponent's strengths and weaknesses to know how to apply pressure properly. Consider the following about your opponents:

- Is the player with the ball a good ball handler? If an offensive player can dribble the ball quickly, then the defender on the ball may need to give the player more room by staying at least an arm's length away. This will help ensure that the defender does not get beat by the offensive player for an easy drive to the basket.

- How well does the offensive player use the weak hand? If the offensive player cannot easily go in both directions while dribbling the ball, the defender should try to force the player to use the off hand.

- Does the opponent have a size advantage? If the offensive team has a size advantage, the defense may not be able to apply defensive pressure because the bigger offensive players may be resistant to it. If the defense has the size advantage, however, pressure defense can be more effective because the defenders' size will enable them to be more aggressive, control the dribbler more easily, and disrupt passes.

- How strong are the opponent's players? A strong offensive player can back the defender down toward the basket for a good shot. On the other hand, if an offensive player lacks strength, the defender can prevent the player from backing into a good shot and can bump the player away from good position for the shot or pass. The stronger the defensive team's players, the easier it is to wear out the offensive team with pressure. The defenders can make the offensive players work hard on every possession to get a good shot, which will wear out the offensive players.

- How quick and agile are the opponent's players? The defense will apply pressure in different forms based on the quickness of the offensive players. If the offense is quick with the ball, the defense may want to apply pressure with a zone press, which will contain the offensive players to one area and force the offensive team to pass the ball rather than dribble the ball by the defender. Defenders may also choose to double team the offensive player to force a pass.

- Is the player with the ball a good shooter? If the offensive player with the ball is a good close-range or long-range shooter, the defensive team needs to apply the pressure defense at the point where the offensive player can shoot the ball.

(continued)

Self-Knowledge

Besides being aware of your opponent's abilities, you and your players need to know about your own team's strengths and weaknesses. Teach your players to be aware of the following when applying pressure:

- How effective are your players at guarding a dribbler? If defenders can guard the dribbler using steady pressure, this will make the defense much more difficult to score on because the offense must work harder to advance the ball.

- How strong is your bench? If a team has many players who can contribute effectively, then defensive players on the court can work harder to pressure the offense. If the players on the court get tired, the team can easily replace them and keep up the pressure.

- How effective is your weak-side defense? A defensive team will be better at stopping drives to the basket if the team has good weak-side help. More pressure may be applied to the offensive dribbler if the defenders know that they will have weak-side help in stopping the drive if they do get beat by the dribbler.

Decision-Making Guidelines

When deciding how to gain the best advantage when applying pressure, you and your players should consider the previous information as well as the following guidelines:

- If a team is fortunate enough to have a shot blocker, the defenders will be able to pressure the offensive perimeter players without worrying too much about getting beat on the dribble. If an offensive player beats a defender to the basket, the shot blocker will be ready to help.

- When guarding a good dribbler who likes to use the crossover to change directions with the ball, the defender should keep the inside hand down to discourage the crossover dribble. This will allow the defender to apply more pressure on the dribbler.

- To keep the pressure applied as the offensive player dribbles the ball, the defender should focus on the waist of the dribbler so that the defender does not react to fakes made by the offensive player.

- If a defender applies good pressure on the dribbler and forces the dribbler to go toward the sideline, this will give the defensive team a better opportunity to trap the dribbler.

- When the ball is in the frontcourt, the defender should force the dribbler to go baseline, where the help-side defense will be able to help stop the dribbler or trap the dribbler going to the basket.

- If the ball is passed into the post, the defense should be quick to apply pressure by double teaming the post player before he or she can turn and shoot.

Dribble penetration by an offensive player can lead to easy baskets if the defenders off the ball cannot provide help. Help and recover is a defensive technique used by an off-the-ball defender in good position to help stop a dribble penetration or a pass by the offensive player with the ball. The idea behind this technique is that once the defender has helped stop the penetration, the defender must recover to defend his or her own player so this player isn't wide open for a good shot. For example, assume the offensive team has the ball on the wing. An offensive player is also positioned on the baseline on the strong side, with two post players at each block and a player on the weak-side wing. When the ball handler attempts to drive to the basket, the closest help-side defender is guarding the baseline player, who is also a good outside shooter. As the ball handler dribbles toward the basket, the defender guarding the baseline player will slide over to help stop the dribbler, and then recover to the baseline offensive player.

WATCH OUT!

The following circumstances may distract your athletes:

- Guarding an offensive player who is a good shooter. The helping defender may not want to leave the player he or she is guarding if that player is a good shooter.

- Facing an opponent with an offensive player who can score effectively off the dribble. The ability of this player may prevent the helping defenders from recovering back to their offensive player.

READING THE SITUATION

How can your players gain the best advantage when using a help and recover defense? Teach your players to do the following:

- Understand that help should always come from the outside rather than the lane area because this makes for a better recovery. If the on-the-ball defender gets beat by a penetrating offensive player, the closest *outside* off-the-ball defender is in the position to provide help on the dribbler.

- Force the penetrating offensive player to pick up the dribble. When the on-the-ball defender has been beat, the helping defender must slide over to provide help on the dribbler to stop the drive to the basket. The helping defender must work to force the dribbler to pick up the ball before the dribbler can get to the basket and shoot the ball.

- Recover quickly. The dribbler will typically try to pass to the helping defender's offensive player, who is left open. The helping defender will need to recover back to his or her player as soon as the dribbler has picked up the ball in order to disrupt the pass (or the shot if the pass is successful).

ACQUIRING THE APPROPRIATE KNOWLEDGE

To help ensure your team's success in using a help and recover defense, you and your players must know about the following:

(continued)

REMINDER!

You and your players must understand the team strategy and game plan and must assess the help and recover based on those plans and the situation at hand. Make sure that you and your players consider the questions on page 112.

Rules

You and your players need to know several main rules related to using a help and recover defense:

- An offensive player cannot run into a defender who is stationary or a charge will be called. The help defender can try to draw a charge by getting in a good position to stop the dribbler. (When trying to draw a charge, the defender must be sure to be stationary or a block may be called on the defender.)

- If the helping defender does not get to the dribbler soon enough, the defender must be careful not to reach out to stop the dribbler. This could result in a holding, illegal use of the hands or hand checking foul being called

- An offensive player who has the ball may not dribble or hold the ball for longer than five seconds when being closely guarded. If the helping defender can force the dribbler to pick up the ball and can then recover back to his or her offensive player quick enough to prevent the pass, the dribbler may be forced to hold the ball for longer than the allowed five seconds

- An offensive player holding the ball must keep the pivot foot stationary or traveling will be called. This may come into play if the helping defender successfully forces the dribbler to pick up the ball and a pivot is used incorrectly.

Strengths and Weaknesses of Opponents

You and your players must account for the opponent's strengths and weaknesses to know how to execute a help and recover defense properly. Consider the following about your opponents:

- Does the opponent have strong outside shooters? If the offensive player that a defender is guarding can shoot well from the perimeter, the defender may not want to help as quickly and risk leaving that player open for a shot.

- Can the opponent's players pass well? This will determine if the shooter can get the ball in good position for a shot after the defender has helped on the dribbler. Good passers will put more pressure on the helping defender to recover back to his or her offensive player (the shooter). A good pass to the open offensive player can result in a good shot before the defender can recover.

- How tall are the opponent's players? When the helping defender is recovering back to his or her offensive player, the defender must move more quickly if this player is tall and can pull up for the shot.

- Is the player with the ball quick? Quick offensive players may try to split their defender and the off-the-ball defender who is coming to help stop the dribble penetration. To do this, the dribbler beats the on-the-ball defender and gets by the help defender before this defender can get in front of the dribbler and establish position.

Self-Knowledge

Besides being aware of your opponent's abilities, you and your players need to know about your own team's strengths and weaknesses. Teach your players to be aware of the following when executing a help and recover defense:

- How quick are your players? Helping defenders will need to use quickness to get to the dribbler and then get back to their offensive player to stop a pass or a shot.

- Are your post players good shot blockers? If a team's post players are strong shot blockers, perimeter defenders can put more pressure on the dribbler and play closer to the dribbler on defense. They don't need to be as concerned about getting beat to the basket because a shot blocker will be waiting if the dribbler enters the post and pulls up for a shot.

- Are your players physically stronger than the opponents? If so, the helping defenders can use their strength and size to get to the dribbler and recover to their offensive player with greater ease.

Decision-Making Guidelines

When deciding how to gain the best advantage when executing a help and recover defense, you and your players should consider the previous information as well as the following guidelines:

- When the helping defender is recovering, the defender must get the hand up quickly while sliding back to his or her offensive player (the shooter). The defender should run at the shooter as the ball is released in an effort to put pressure on the shooter and create distraction on the shot.

- When the helping defender leaves his or her offensive player to help on the dribbler, the defender must use a sliding motion with the feet and keep the shoulders square to the dribbler. By doing this, the help defender can be in a position to draw a charge on the dribbler, resulting in a turnover.

- If the on-the-ball defender can successfully prevent the dribbler from getting to the basket, the help defender can fake the move to help on the dribbler and stay with his or her offensive player. This fake may cause the dribbler to travel or make a bad pass, resulting in a turnover.

- If the dribbler drives at the helping defender when the defender moves in to stop the dribble, the on-the-ball defender who got beat can work to get into position to slide with the dribbler, creating a good opportunity for the two defenders to trap the dribbler. However, the helping defender may not get back for the recovery if the dribbler can successfully make a pass to the defender's offensive player from the trap.

At a Glance

The following parts of the text offer additional information on help and recover:

Defensive Positioning	p. 94
On-the-Ball Defense	p. 154
Off-the-Ball Defense	p. 157
Playing Man Defense	p. 160
Trapping the Ball	p. 184
Defending the Pass	p. 187

Forcing Shooters Out of Position

A team's defensive strategy should focus on not allowing shooters to catch the ball in a position where they can make a good shot attempt. If the defense can successfully prevent the offensive players from taking good shots by forcing them out of position, this will go a long way toward increasing the defensive team's chances for a victory. A good defender will make sure that the offensive player never gets to his or her "spot" for the shot and will force the player to take a shot from a different angle or position. If the defender knows that an offensive player is a good baseline shooter, then the defender should try to keep that player off the baseline for the shot. When playing against an opponent with good shooters, the defensive team should always be aware of where the shooters are located on the court and should try to force the shooters out of their "comfort" position for the shot.

⚠ WATCH OUT!

The following circumstances may distract your athletes:

- Guarding a shooter who has good physical size and ability. The shooter may be able to shoot over the defender.

- Allowing ball fakes or screens used by the offensive team to result in open shots.

- Focusing on the time left in the game and the score instead of on the shooter that the defender is guarding.

READING THE SITUATION

How can your players gain the best advantage when trying to force shooters out of position? Teach your players to do the following:

- Deny offensive players the ball by having a foot and arm in the passing lane between the ball and the offensive player.

- Anticipate the offensive player's movement and be familiar with his or her strengths and preferences. This will allow the defender to stop the offensive player from catching or shooting the ball where the player is most comfortable and will allow the defender to force the shooter out of position.

- Apply good pressure as the offensive player dribbles. This will make the shot tougher for the offensive player when he or she picks the ball up to adjust for the shot.

- Work together to communicate on defense. For example, defensive players must talk about screens being used by the offense and must have a plan in place to pressure the offensive player coming off the screen for a shot.

- Learn where the offensive player likes to shoot the ball and work to take away this spot or area by beating the player there and denying the pass.

ACQUIRING THE APPROPRIATE KNOWLEDGE

To help ensure your team's success in forcing shooters out of position, you and your players must know about the following:

Rules

You and your players need to know several main rules related to forcing shooters out of position:

○ An offensive player who has the ball may not dribble or hold the ball for longer than five seconds when being closely guarded. This may come into play if the defense can successfully prohibit the shooter from getting the shot in the desired location and the shooter is forced to hold the ball for longer than the allowed five seconds.

○ When denying shots, defenders must be careful not to get too close to the shooter and foul the shooter on the shot. This could result in free throws for the offense. Defenders must also try to avoid fouling the shooter when using double teams to deny the shot.

REMINDER!

You and your players must understand the team strategy and game plan and must assess how to force shooters out of position based on those plans and the situation at hand. Make sure that you and your players consider the questions on page 112.

Strengths and Weaknesses of Opponents

You and your players must account for the opponent's strengths and weaknesses to know how to force shooters out of position properly. Consider the following about your opponents:

○ Do the opponent's players shoot well off of screens? If the offensive team likes to set screens for their shots, communication between defenders is a must. Defensive players must be prepared to defend the shooter as he or she tries to come off the screen in a good position to shoot the ball. The defense can use options such as switches, double teams, or fighting over the top of screens when working to force a shooter out of position. These options can be effective for distracting the shooter and causing the shooter to take a shot out of his or her normal rhythm.

○ What is the shooting range of the offensive player? The farther out a shot is taken, the lower the chance of the shot being successful. When guarding a strong shooter with a range of 15 feet or more, the defender will need to work hard to force the shooter to catch the ball out of this range. If the offense has a player who is a strong shooter in the post, the defense must work to deny passes to this player in the post area by playing in front of the player.

○ Which offensive player is the first option in the offense? This will determine which defenders should provide help and which defenders should stay with their offensive player. When guarding the player who is the offensive team's first option for a score, the defender will need to stay with that player. When guarding an offensive player who is not the first option, the defender can be in a position to provide help, knowing that his or her player is not the offensive team's first look for a score.

○ Does the offensive player have a strong jump shot? When guarding an offensive player who has a strong jump shot, the defender must learn this early and must make sure to guard the player closely long before he or she gets the ball. This will help the defender keep the offensive player away from areas of the floor where the player's shot is strongest.

Self-Knowledge

Besides being aware of your opponent's abilities, you and your players need to know about your own team's strengths and weaknesses. Teach your players to be aware of the following when forcing shooters out of position:

○ Are your players physically stronger than the offensive players they are guarding? If so, this is an advantage because the defenders will have the ability to stop the offensive players from making cuts to areas of the court where they would like to receive passes.

○ Are your players quicker than the offensive players they are guarding? With a quickness advantage, defenders can take the pass away from the offense by getting in the passing

(continued)

lane quickly to deny the pass. This will force the offensive players to go out farther on the court than they would like in order to catch the ball for the shot, thus reducing their opportunities to score.

- Are your players taller than the offensive players they are guarding? If the defenders have a size advantage, this will help them in taking away the shot if their player gets the ball. Defenders should keep the hands up to discourage the shot.

- Does your team have good weak-side defense? If a team has a strong weak-side defense, the defenders should force the offensive player to put the ball on the floor in areas where help is strong. Defenders can do this by making the offensive player go in the direction of the help defenders, using the lead foot to force the player in that direction (the lead foot is the foot positioned higher than the offensive player's foot).

- How well can your team guard offensive players as they come off screens? Defenders need to effectively guard the offensive player for whom the screen is set and prevent the player from coming off the screen in position to catch the ball and take a shot. This requires communication among the defenders, but they must also look to use switching or fighting over the top of screens.

At a Glance

The following parts of the text offer additional information on forcing shooters out of position:

Decision-Making Guidelines

When deciding how to gain the best advantage when forcing shooters out of position, you and your players should consider the previous information as well as the following guidelines:

- When shooters are going to their strong side, defenders must be aware that the shooter will first need to pivot to get the shooting foot around and in a good position for the shot. The defender should not let this pivot take place easily. This is a longer pivot because the shooting foot needs to be in front for a good shot. For example, a right-handed player going to the right must pick up the dribble and pivot on the left foot to bring the right foot into shooting position. The defender can take away this pivot by getting in close to the player off the dribble (as the player tries to turn).

- Shooters may attempt to go to their weak side on the shot (for example, a right-handed shooter will go to his or her left). This is a quicker shot because the shooting foot will already be in front when the player stops, allowing the player to be in good balance to shoot. For a right-handed shooter, then, the defender should stay on the shooter's right shoulder, forcing the shooter to take the shot over the outstretched hands of the defender.

- When an offensive player comes off a screen using the dribble, the defenders should force the player back in the direction the player came from. The defender must play the offensive player close as the player comes off the screen on the dribble (if a switch occurs, the switching defender will play the offensive player close) so that the offensive player must go back in the direction he or she came from in order to shoot the ball. This makes the shot tougher because the player cannot shoot the ball where he or she originally wanted to.

- If the shooter likes to put the ball on the floor and dribble before taking a shot, the defender must recognize this and be ready to slide the feet in the direction the offensive player is dribbling. In this way, the defender can prevent the shooter from dribbling into the area where the shooter wants to shoot.

Protecting the Basket

Protecting the basket is a very important part of the defensive structure. Stopping the ball from getting to the basket will eliminate the offensive players' aggressiveness and force the offensive team to depend more on the perimeter game. When this occurs, the offense must settle for lower-percentage shots instead of taking easier shots closer to the basket. Protecting the basket largely depends on the weak-side defenders being able to provide effective help to stop dribble penetration into the lane. If an offensive player with the ball gets around the on-the-ball defender and gets to the lane area, the weak-side defender must be in a position to help prevent the offensive player from getting to the basket for an easy shot.

WATCH OUT!

The following circumstances may distract your athletes:

- Facing a team that uses a lot of speed in running the court. This can prevent defenders from protecting the basket because their focus will be on slowing down the offense.
- Facing bigger or physically aggressive offensive players, especially when rebounding.
- Letting the communication on offense interfere with the defenders' communication with each other.

ACQUIRING THE APPROPRIATE KNOWLEDGE

To help ensure your team's success in protecting the basket, you and your players must know about the following:

READING THE SITUATION

How can your players gain the best advantage when protecting the basket? Teach your players to do the following:

- Learn to anticipate drives to the basket. To do this, defenders should keep the eyes on the ball and maintain a ball–you–man triangle, which will allow them to see the ball and their offensive player at all times.
- Understand that defensive post players need to be aware of the offensive players driving to the basket and must be ready to help protect the basket. Many times the defensive post player can be in a position to block the shots when the offensive players get to the lane and shoot the ball.

Rules

You and your players need to know several main rules related to protecting the basket:

- An offensive player cannot be in the lane for longer than three seconds. If the defender can effectively slow the offensive player's drive to the basket, this player may be caught in the lane for longer than three seconds, resulting in a turnover.
- An offensive player cannot run into a defender who is stationary or a charge will be called. Defenders can try to draw a charge when they move into position to protect the basket against the drive.
- An offensive player who has the ball may not dribble or hold the ball for longer than five seconds when being closely guarded. This may come into play if the defender forces the offensive player to pick up the ball before getting to the basket and the player cannot pass or shoot the ball within the allowed five seconds.
- When defending a drive to the basket, the defender must be careful not to get out of position and reach for the ball. This could result in a foul being called.

(continued)

REMINDER!

You and your players must understand the team strategy and game plan and must assess how to protect the basket based on those plans and the situation at hand. Make sure that you and your players consider the questions on page 112.

Strengths and Weaknesses of Opponents

You and your players must account for the opponent's strengths and weaknesses to know how to protect the basket properly. Consider the following about your opponents:

- Can the offensive player with the ball drive to the basket well? If so, defenders need to give the dribbler more room and not pressure as much away from the basket. When the defender is off the dribbler, this makes it more difficult for the dribbler to drive around the defender to get to the basket.

- Are the opponent's players physically strong and aggressive? If an offensive player can overpower a defender using strength or aggressiveness, the help- or ball-side defenders must establish a good position to draw the charge when the offensive player drives to the basket.

- Are the opponent's players quick with the ball? If this is the case, the helping defender must be ready to help protect the basket quickly by sliding into position before the driver gets to the lane for a shot.

- How strong are the opponent's post players? If the offensive post players are strong, the post defender may not be able to help stop the driver in order to protect the basket. If the post defender helps on the driver, the offensive post player will get the pass from the driver and score. Instead, the perimeter defenders will need to help stop the driver. They can do this by quickly helping from the weak (or help) side.

- Are the opponent's players tall? If the offensive player is taller than the defender, the help must come quicker in order to make the offensive player shoot the ball farther out, rather than getting a close shot at the basket. A size advantage will allow offensive players to get easy shots if they can get close to the basket.

Self-Knowledge

Besides being aware of your opponent's abilities, you and your players need to know about your own team's strengths and weaknesses. Teach your players to be aware of the following when protecting the basket:

- How big are your post players? Size is an obvious indicator of how well a defensive team can protect the basket. If a team has a big post player who can block shots well, this can be a huge advantage on defense because the post player is in position to help protect the basket. The post defender should be in a help position and should be ready to block the shot when an offensive player drives to the basket and shoots the ball.

- How effective are your weak-side defenders? If the weak-side defenders maintain a proper help position and can provide good help on drives, this will increase the team's ability to protect the basket.

- How well does your team deny the passing lanes? Denying the passing lanes is the best defensive strategy for keeping the ball away from an offensive player who drives hard to the basket.

Decision-Making Guidelines

When deciding how to gain the best advantage when protecting the basket, you and your players should consider the previous information as well as the following guidelines:

- If an offensive player with the ball gets around his or her defender and goes to the basket, help-side defenders should rotate—with the post defender rotating over and the perimeter defenders rotating down—to protect the basket. When the post defender rotates to help on the driver, the help-side perimeter defenders must rotate to guard the area left by the post defender.

- When an offensive player is driving to the basket, a quick double team is a good defensive ploy to use to protect the basket. The off-the-ball defender closest to the on-the-ball defender will move over and help on the dribbler.

- On fast breaks, protecting the basket is essential. Therefore, any defenders who must get back in position to stop the fast break (typically the point guard is the first defender) should sprint down the floor in transition to the basket so that the offensive team cannot go directly to the basket for a score.

- If the offense uses a screen to get the dribbler open for a drive to the basket, the on-the-ball defender guarding the dribbler and the off-the-ball defender guarding the offensive player setting the screen must switch to stop the drive and protect the basket. A switch is the quickest method to stop a drive to the basket because it will allow the off-the-ball defender to stop the dribbler while the on-the-ball defender is being screened.

At a Glance

The following parts of the text offer additional information on protecting the basket:

An offensive charging foul occurs when a defensive player establishes good defensive position and contact is initiated by the offensive player. Typically, a charge happens when a defender is guarding a dribbler going to the basket and the defender is able to get into a position where the dribbler will run into the defender. However, a charge may also be called on an offensive player who does not have the ball. If the defender can get position on his or her offensive player as the player cuts to receive a pass, a charge may result when the offensive player runs into the defender blocking the player's path to the ball. Taking a charge can be a huge momentum builder because it will often prevent the offense from scoring.

 WATCH OUT!

The following circumstances may distract your athletes:

- Watching the pass and not moving quickly enough to get into position for the charge.

- Going for the ball instead of moving into a defensive position to take the charge.

- Being uncertain about how to defend because of the number of offensive players attacking the basket.

READING THE SITUATION

How can your players gain the best advantage when taking a charge? Teach your players to do the following:

- Recognize when the offensive player can be beat to a position on the court. If the offensive player makes contact with a defender who has the feet set and the shoulders squared away to the offensive player, a charge will be called.

- Keep the eyes on the waist of the offensive player when attempting to draw a charge on the player with the ball. This will help the defender avoid reacting inappropriately to a fake by the offensive player and moving out of position.

- Understand that help-side defenders, usually the one closest to the dribbler, must move into position to take a charge as soon as they see the dribbler beat the on-the-ball defender.

ACQUIRING THE APPROPRIATE KNOWLEDGE

To help ensure your team's success in taking a charge, you and your players must know about the following:

Rules

You and your players need to know several main rules related to taking a charge:

- If the dribbler gets around the on-the-ball defender, this defender must be careful not to reach out and hold the dribbler. This could result in a holding foul being called.

- If the defender does not get into position for the charge and attempts to stay with the dribbler, the defender must be careful not to put the hands on the dribbler as the dribbler gets around. This could result in a hand-check foul being called.

Strengths and Weaknesses of Opponents

You and your players must account for the opponent's strengths and weaknesses to know how to take a charge properly. Consider the following about your opponents:

REMINDER!

You and your players must understand the team strategy and game plan and must assess taking a charge based on those plans and the situation at hand. Make sure that you and your players consider the questions on page 112.

- Is the player with the ball quick? If the offensive player with the ball is quicker than the on-the-ball defender, the defender must anticipate the drive to the basket and should move back so that the defender is not pressuring the dribbler as closely. This will help ensure that the defender has time to get the feet set before the drive.

- Is the player with the ball a good passer? If the offensive player with the ball is a good passer, helping defenders may not want to leave their offensive player as quickly to help on the drive. As soon as the dribbler sees the helping defender slide over for an attempt at drawing the charge, the dribbler will most likely pass to the offensive player that the helping defender left.

- Is the opponent a jump-shooting team? If so, taking a charge will be more difficult for the defenders because the offensive team can look to score on a jump shot as opposed to going to the basket, where a charge is more likely to occur.

Self-Knowledge

Besides being aware of your opponent's abilities, you and your players need to know about your own team's strengths and weaknesses. Teach your players to be aware of the following when taking a charge:

- How quick are your players? Quick defenders are more likely to be able to get into position early enough to get the feet set and draw a charge.

- How effective is the on-the-ball defender? If defensive players can defend the dribble well, the help does not need to come as quickly because the defender guarding the dribbler can draw a charge. The help defenders should focus on the offensive player they are guarding and work to stop their player's cuts to the ball.

- Does your team have a strong defender at the post? If so, off-the-ball defenders may not want to draw a charge but rather let the shot blocker move into a position to make the block and start the fast break.

Decision-Making Guidelines

When deciding how to gain the best advantage when taking a charge, you and your players should consider the previous information as well as the following guidelines:

- A defender at the post may be in the best position to draw a charge on hard drives to the basket. This defender will not have to slide as far as the perimeter players to defend the dribbler.

- When an offensive player dribbles full court, an off-the-ball defender should work to take the charge against the sideline when the on-the-ball defender guides the dribbler up the sideline. It is easier to take the charge in this area because the sideline acts as a third defender.

- Baseline drives to the basket are usually the easiest opportunity to draw the charge because the weak-side help is in a good position to slide over and take the charge.

(continued)

○ When a defender recognizes that the offensive player is out of control going to the basket, this is an opportunity to get in position for a charge. In this situation, the offensive player may not be able to make a jump stop to avoid the charge.

Limiting Fast Break Opportunities

When playing defense, limiting fast break opportunities for the offense can have a major impact on the game because successful fast breaks can lead to quick and easy shots. The defensive transition against the fast break should be organized in such a way that all the defenders know what to do to stop the break. Getting back on defense and successfully limiting the offense's opportunities for a fast break require the defenders to sprint back and effectively cover the offensive players running the court.

WATCH OUT!

The following circumstances may distract your athletes:

- Facing an offense whose size and speed may prevent the defenders from getting back on defense as quickly as they need to.

- Facing an offense that can get a shot off quickly if the defense is not prepared and in position to defend the quick shot.

ACQUIRING THE APPROPRIATE KNOWLEDGE

To help ensure your team's success in limiting fast break opportunities, you and your players must know about the following:

Rules

You and your players need to know several main rules related to limiting fast break opportunities:

- The offensive team must advance the ball into the frontcourt within a 10-second time limit. Defenders who pressure the ball after a rebound in an effort to slow the fast break may cause a 10-second backcourt violation, resulting in a turnover.

- An offensive player who has the ball may not dribble or hold the ball for longer than 5 seconds when being closely guarded. The defenders can force a turnover by getting the offensive player to pick up the dribble and not allowing the player to get rid of the ball within this time limit.

READING THE SITUATION

How can your players gain the best advantage when trying to limit fast break opportunities? Teach your players to do the following:

- Understand that the designated guard must sprint back to the half-court line as soon as a shot is released by a player on his or her team. This guard must be the first defender back on defense in order to direct the defensive team on how to stop the break. From here, the guard will direct the defensive transition by communicating who should guard the ball and who should guard the basket area.

- Work hard to get the offensive rebound. A good rebounding team can make it difficult for the opponents to get the fast break started. When the opponent is forced to start the offense by taking the ball out of bounds, the fast break will get started much slower than when the team is able to start the break off a rebound.

- Understand that the post players need to run the court as soon as a defensive rebound is secured by the other team. If the post players can run up the middle of the court and get back to the lane, they have a better opportunity to provide help defense as the offensive post players set up for the fast break.

(continued)

REMINDER!

You and your players must understand the team strategy and game plan and must assess how to limit fast break opportunities based on those plans and the situation at hand. Make sure that you and your players consider the questions on page 112.

- An offensive player cannot run into a defender who is stationary or a charge will be called. Defenders can draw a charge by getting back on the break and establishing position on the dribbler before the dribbler can stop.

- When defending the break, a defender may force a held ball situation (when two players from opposite teams are holding the ball at the same time). When this occurs, the alternate jump ball arrow will determine which team gets possession of the ball.

Strengths and Weaknesses of Opponents

You and your players must account for the opponent's strengths and weaknesses to know how to limit fast break opportunities properly. Consider the following about your opponents:

- How well does the opponent secure rebounds after shots? If the opponent's players do not rebound well, a team may want to send four players to the offensive boards. Getting the offensive rebounds will help limit the opponent's fast break opportunities.

- Does the opponent handle pressure well? If not, the best way to slow the break may be to use defensive pressure on the rebounder as he or she gets the ball. The defense will want to put pressure on the offensive players before they can get the ball across the half-court line.

- How does the opponent start the break? Defenders must learn if the opponent likes to power dribble or make the outlet pass to start the break. The defense can work to eliminate the option that the opponents prefer, forcing them to use the other option.

- Does the opponent have strong outside shooters? If the opponent's players like to spot up on the fast break and go for an immediate shot, the defenders must quickly get out and find the shooters spotting up on the perimeter.

- Does the opponent's post player run the court well? A good offensive post player will run the court on the fast break, looking for the pass and an easy layup. This is one of the best ways to score on a fast break, so the defenders must cover the post player as he or she runs to the basket. The defense must make sure they get a defender back quickly to the lane area to guard the offensive post player on the break.

Self-Knowledge

Besides being aware of your opponent's abilities, you and your players need to know about your own team's strengths and weaknesses. Teach your players to be aware of the following when trying to limit fast break opportunities:

- How well does your team rebound the ball? A good rebounding team should have four players going to the offensive boards and working to get the second shot, which will limit the opponent's fast break opportunities. If a team does not rebound well, the team should be sure to have two defenders back to stop the break instead of having them rebound.

- How quick is your team? More specifically, does your team have the speed to stop the offensive team's point guard on the dribble? If the defense is quick, defenders can pressure the point guard to force this player to pick up the dribble or to slow him or her down. A defense that lacks quickness may need to drop two players back to stop the fast break as soon as the rebound is secured.

- Does your post player run the court well? If the defensive post player can get up the middle and help cover the fast break, this gives the perimeter defenders some help if the offensive team makes a quick drive to the basket.

- Does your team have a size advantage? A size advantage will allow the team to defend the fast break easier if the players get back on defense. Taller defenders can keep the offensive team from driving to the basket and can help limit the offense to one shot.

- Does your team have the advantage at the point guard position? If so, the defensive point guard can control the dribbling and passing of the opponent's point guard, which will slow down the fast break.

Decision-Making Guidelines

When deciding how to gain the best advantage when trying to limit fast breaks, you and your players should consider the previous information as well as the following guidelines:

- If the offensive team prefers to use the outlet pass to start a fast break because their point guard is quick, defenders should first work to take away the pass to the point guard. Defenders should cover the point guard after the rebound is secured so that the point guard cannot cleanly or easily get the outlet pass. If the pass is successful, defenders should then work to force the point guard to go to the sidelines and not straight to the basket on the fast break. This will slow down the break and limit the point guard's options by pressuring him or her to dribble in one direction.

- If the offensive team prefers to use a power dribble to start the break, the defense should double team or pressure the rebounders when they get the ball. This can slow the break by forcing the offensive player to pick up the dribble.

- If the offensive team can shoot jump shots off the fast break, more concentration is needed on defense. Defenders must force the shooters to put the ball on the floor by guarding them closely so that the offensive players cannot just stand and shoot.

- Late in a game, the time and score will determine whether a team should send players back on defense to stop the break. If the team is ahead, they should send everyone back immediately when the opponent gets the defensive rebound so that the opponent cannot get an easy basket. If the team is behind, they should pressure the offensive players quicker to try to cause a turnover.

At a Glance

The following parts of the text offer additional information on limiting fast breaks:

Offensive Rebounds	p. 77
Defensive Positioning	p. 94
Applying Pressure	p. 166
Taking a Charge	p. 178
Defending the Pass	p. 187

Trapping the Ball

Trapping the ball is a defensive tactic where two defensive players double team the offensive player who has the ball in an effort to stop the dribble and force the player to throw a lob or bounce pass. The other defenders on the team then rotate to cover all of the closest passing lanes, looking for the steal. This trap on the ball is designed to cause the ball handler to panic and throw a bad pass that can be intercepted by the defense—and possibly lead to a quick score for the defensive team. Defenders will usually execute a trap in the sideline area because this is a good area to trap a ball handler between a guard and a forward. Another good area for the trap on the ball is the baseline area when the post defender can be a part of the trap. The trap can also be effective when the offensive team sets a screen; in this case, the two defenders will trap the dribbler coming around the screen. If your game strategy is to aggressively attack the offense, setting the trap is a good option that can allow your defenders to create turnovers.

 WATCH OUT!

The following circumstances may distract your athletes:

- Being overpowered because of the physical size and ability of the offensive player being trapped.

- Trying to make a quick steal instead of taking the time to set up a trap and force a bad pass.

- Not communicating or coordinating with the other defender involved in setting the trap.

READING THE SITUATION

How can your players gain the best advantage when trapping the ball? Teach your players to do the following:

- Guide the ball handler into trapping positions at the corner areas of the court or the half-court line. The trap is most effective in these areas of the court because the boundaries can act as a third defender.

- Try to disguise the trap. The off-the-ball defender who is coming to help should move in for the trap when the offensive player dribbles away from him or her so that the offensive player cannot see the trap coming.

- Get into the proper position on the trap. When two defenders set a trap on the offensive player with the ball, the legs of the two defenders should actually touch or overlap each other so that the dribbler cannot split the two defenders in the trap.

- Rotate when teammates trap the ball. When a trap occurs, the other defenders must rotate to the basket area so that an easy basket will not be given up if the pass is made. As the trap occurs on the ball, the nearest help-side defender should rotate to the offensive player who is open because of the defender leaving to trap. After the rotation, the offensive player who is open because of the trap should be the player farthest away from the ball.

ACQUIRING THE APPROPRIATE KNOWLEDGE

To help ensure your team's success in trapping the ball, you and your players must know about the following:

Rules

You and your players need to know several main rules related to trapping the ball:

REMINDER!

You and your players must understand the team strategy and game plan and must assess the trap based on those plans and the situation at hand. Make sure that you and your players consider the questions on page 112.

- An offensive player who has the ball may not dribble or hold the ball for longer than 5 seconds when being closely guarded. The defenders can force a turnover by trapping the ball and not allowing the offensive player to get rid of the ball within this time limit.

- The offensive team may not return the ball to the backcourt after having possession of it in the frontcourt. If a trap is set at the half-court line and the offensive player steps into the backcourt, an over-and-back violation will be called, resulting in a turnover.

- The offensive team must advance the ball into the frontcourt within a 10-second time limit. The defense may try to force a 10-second violation by setting the trap in the backcourt.

- When trapping the ball, the defenders may draw a charge if the offensive player tries to dribble through the trap, resulting in a turnover. (If the defender does not establish proper position, a blocking foul may be called on the defender.)

- When trapping the ball, the defenders must be careful not to reach out and hold the offensive player if the player successfully gets out of the trap and dribbles past the defenders. This could result in a holding foul being called.

Strengths and Weaknesses of Opponents

You and your players must account for the opponent's strengths and weaknesses to know how to trap the ball properly. Consider the following about your opponents:

- How tall is the player with the ball? Taller players are more difficult for defenders to trap because their height advantage enables them to throw over the trap. When trapping a taller player, defenders should set the trap quickly and keep the hands high to try to obstruct the player's view.

- Is the player with the ball a good ball handler? If a strong ball handler has the ball, trapping is a good defensive strategy because it can force the ball out of this player's hands (and into those of a player who may not be as strong a ball handler). However, good ball handlers who also pass well are difficult to trap because they usually keep the head up on the dribble and can pass the ball before the two defenders trap. The defenders will need to trap after the dribble has been picked up to allow the help-side rotation defenders to cover better.

- How quick is the opponent? If the opponents are quick, trapping may be used to neutralize their quickness. Traps will force the offensive players to give up the ball earlier than they would like, and a different offensive player will then need to handle the ball. As a result, a player who may not be used to handling the ball will have to make the offensive plays. Trapping takes the offense out of its flow and may eliminate some of the offense's options.

(continued)

Self-Knowledge

Besides being aware of your opponent's abilities, you and your players need to know about your own team's strengths and weaknesses. Teach your players to be aware of the following when trapping the ball:

- How big are your players? If the defenders setting the trap have a size advantage, the ball handler may have more difficulty passing the ball out of the trap, thus increasing the chance of a turnover or steal. If the defenders are smaller, the pass may be easier because the offensive player can pass over the top of the trapping defenders.
- Does your team have good help-side defenders? The help-side defenders need to anticipate the trap by their teammates and make the proper rotation. If they do this effectively, the pass may be intercepted from the offensive player as he or she tries to make a pass out of the trap.
- Are your players quick? A quick team can make several consecutive traps on the offensive team. A trap may also occur after the offensive player makes a pass out of the trap to a teammate.

At a Glance

The following parts of the text offer additional information on trapping:

Defensive Positioning	p. 94
Defending Screens	p. 105
On-the-Ball Defense	p. 154
Off-the-Ball Defense	p. 157
Applying Pressure	p. 166
Help and Recover	p. 169
Taking a Charge	p. 178

Decision-Making Guidelines

When deciding how to gain the best advantage when trapping the ball, you and your players should consider the previous information as well as the following guidelines:

- A good time to trap is when an offensive player dribbles the ball toward the baseline and the defensive post player can step out and trap the dribbler on the baseline.
- When defenders try to trap in the backcourt (before the ball gets to the frontcourt), they should not run at the offensive player out of control; if they do, the ball handler will simply dribble around the trap. Defenders must stay under control in a good stance to trap the ball.
- When the offensive player dribbles off a screen set by a teammate, the on-the-ball defender and the defender whose offensive player set the screen can set a trap to stop the dribbler from going to the basket and possibly cause a turnover.
- If the offense is holding the ball to try to run out the clock when ahead late in the game—and the defense needs to get the ball—trapping can be effective because it can force a turnover or steal.

Defending the Pass

When defenders can properly defend passes, the flow of the offense is disrupted, because the offensive players must work harder to get the ball in good shooting position. The defender who is one pass away from the offensive player with the ball is the defender who can put the most pressure on the pass. Defenders must get the arm and shoulder in the passing lane—in a direct path between the offensive player they are guarding and the player with the ball—and they must have the palm out with the thumb down to try to hit the pass away. Using this technique to defend the pass can lead to turnovers. It can also force offensive players trying to receive a pass to step out farther away from the basket to catch the ball, taking them out of their shooting range.

 WATCH OUT!

The following circumstances may distract your athletes:

- Watching the ball in the air when it is passed, rather than moving into proper position.
- Facing offensive players whose size and speed make it difficult to defend the pass.
- Facing an offense that effectively uses cuts or screens to get open.
- Listening to the communication of the offensive team instead of focusing on where the ball is located.

ACQUIRING THE APPROPRIATE KNOWLEDGE

To help ensure your team's success in defending the pass, you and your players must know about the following:

Rules

You and your players need to know several main rules related to defending the pass:

- An offensive player who has the ball may not dribble or hold the ball for longer than five seconds when being closely guarded. This may come into play if the defense can successfully deny passes and the offensive player is forced to hold the ball.

READING THE SITUATION

How can your players gain the best advantage when defending the pass? Teach your players to do the following:

- Anticipate how and where the offensive player will move to get open for the pass. Defenders need to learn where the offensive player they are guarding likes to catch the ball. They must immediately recognize when the dribble has been picked up and must work to deny passes to the offensive player in this area.

- When guarding an offensive player without the ball, keep the inside hand up high with the palm out and the thumb down. Most passes will be made as a high pass as opposed to a bounce pass.

- When guarding a player with the ball, work to force the player in a direction away from where he or she wants to pass the ball. This will make the pass longer and more difficult for the player to make.

- When guarding the receiver of a pass, move toward this offensive player as the ball is in the air. This will help ensure that the defender is in a position to defend the pass as soon as it reaches the offensive player.

(continued)

Defending the Pass (continued)

REMINDER!

You and your players must understand the team strategy and game plan and must assess how to defend the pass based on those plans and the situation at hand. Make sure that you and your players consider the questions on page 112.

○ As defenders work to deny passes, the passer may need to pivot in an effort to make a pass to another player, which could, in turn, cause a charge or travel.

○ If the defender is positioned in the path of the player trying to receive a pass, the defender could be charged with blocking if the defender is moving at the time of contact.

○ When defending the pass, defenders should be careful not to hold an offensive player in an effort to prevent the player from receiving a pass. This could result in a holding foul being called.

Strengths and Weaknesses of Opponents

You and your players must account for the opponent's strengths and weaknesses to know how to defend the pass properly. Consider the following about your opponents:

○ Are the opponent's players physically strong? When guarding an offensive player who is physically strong, the defender may need to stay at least one arm's length away from the offensive player. This will help prevent the offensive player from using his or her strength to get the pass and beat the defender for an easy score.

○ Do the opponent's players use effective fakes? If the defender inappropriately reacts to a fake, this will allow the offensive player to catch the ball easily without much pressure on the pass. Defenders must be alert to the opponent's attempts to fake a pass and should not go with the first fake by the offensive player trying to receive the ball. A good strategy for defenders is to make their offensive player try to go backdoor to receive the pass, because this is a much more difficult pass to make.

○ Does the opponent use screens to get players open? Defending the pass will take more effort by the defenders if the offensive players use screens to get the ball. Defenders involved in the screen must communicate and, if necessary, switch to defend the pass.

Self-Knowledge

Besides being aware of your opponent's abilities, you and your players need to know about your own team's strengths and weaknesses. Teach your players to be aware of the following when defending the pass:

○ How quick are your players? If the defenders are quick, the defense will be able to deny and defend the passing lanes better because the defenders will have the ability to beat the offensive players to the spot where they want to catch the ball.

○ How well do your players apply pressure? If the defense puts good pressure on the ball, this will make the pass much more difficult. The defender on the ball and the defender guarding the offensive player whom the pass is intended for must work together to make the pass difficult—one defender applies pressure on the ball, and the other defender denies the pass.

○ How strong is your weak-side defense? If a team has strong weak-side defense, defenders can use more pressure when denying a pass and can force the offensive player to go backdoor, because the defenders know that they have good help available to stop the backdoor cut.

Decision-Making Guidelines

When deciding how to gain the best advantage when defending the pass, you and your players should consider the previous information as well as the following guidelines:

- When a defender works to deny a pass to an offensive player and the player goes backdoor, the defender must open up so that he or she is in a position to see the ball. To do this, the defender drops the top foot back and pivots on the back foot.

- If the offensive player with the ball thinks an off-the-ball defender is helping too much, the offensive player may attempt a skip pass to get the ball to the other side of the floor and away from the defender. When this occurs, the help-side defender guarding the offensive player at the opposite wing must recognize that the skip pass is coming to that player. As the ball is in the air, the defender should move to guard the offensive player who will receive the pass. This will enable the defender to get there quickly to defend the pass and to be in position to guard the ball the moment it reaches the offensive player.

- When the offense executes a screen away from the ball in an effort to get an offensive player open for a pass, the off-the-ball defenders involved should switch in order to defend the pass. If the two defenders immediately go for a switch, this will help them keep pressure on the pass and deny the pass to the offensive player who wants to receive the ball. If they don't switch, the defenders can get caught in the screen and may not be able to defend the pass.

- When the dribbler gets around the on-the-ball defender to go to the basket, the off-the-ball defender guarding the player one pass away should open up to help stop the dribbler. To do this, the defender drops the top foot back so that he or she can see the dribbler coming around the on-the-ball defender. After helping, the defender should quickly slide back to defend the player one pass away in case a pass is made.

At a Glance

The following parts of the text offer additional information on defending the pass:

Defending the Give-and-Go

The give-and-go is executed when a player passes the ball to a teammate and then cuts to the basket, expecting to get a return pass from that teammate for a layup. This is typically used in situations where the defender is closely guarding the offensive player who has just passed the ball, allowing the player to make a quick cut to the basket in front of the defender. The defender on the first pass must play correct position and jump to the ball on the pass in order to take away the cut and lay-up.

 WATCH OUT!

The following circumstances may distract your athletes:

○ Watching the pass rather than effectively guarding the cutter.

○ Failing to communicate who is covering the cutter from the help side, if needed.

○ Focusing on the size or quickness of the player cutting to the basket rather than actually stopping the cut.

ACQUIRING THE APPROPRIATE KNOWLEDGE

To help ensure your team's success in defending the give-and-go, you and your players must know about the following:

READING THE SITUATION

How can your players gain the best advantage when defending the give-and-go? Teach your players to do the following:

- Jump to the ball immediately on the pass and create a ball–you–man triangle position. This will help ensure that the offensive cutter cannot cut in front of the defender to get the ball back for a shot.

- Be ready to move quickly. If a defender is guarding a player who always moves after making a pass, then the defender must be ready to stay on the offensive player and stop the player from getting the ball back on the return pass.

- Understand that help-side defenders will be in the path of the cutter in most cases and must be prepared to help on the cutter and discourage the return pass.

- Pressure the offensive player who receives the first pass. Immediately after the pass, the defender should pressure this player so that the pass to the cutter is not an easy pass.

- Work to prevent the cutter from going directly to the basket because this will be the best path for the cutter to score if the return pass is successful.

- Identify the opponent's best player. The defense should then work hard to keep the ball out of this player's hands.

Rules

You and your players need to know several main rules related to defending the give-and-go:

○ When guarding the cutter on the give-and-go, a defender must be careful not to hold the cutter in an effort to stop the cut after the initial pass. Defenders must also avoid reaching out to prevent the cutter from receiving the return pass if they are slow to cover the cut. These situations could result in a holding foul being called.

o When helping on the cutter in the give-and-go, help-side defenders must avoid being late and failing to get into position. This could result in a blocking foul being called.

o An offensive player cannot run into a defender who is stationary or a charge will be called. Defenders can try to draw a charge by getting into position in the path of the cutter on the give-and-go.

REMINDER!

You and your players must understand the team strategy and game plan and must assess how to defend the give-and-go based on those plans and the situation at hand. Make sure that you and your players consider the questions on page 112.

Strengths and Weaknesses of Opponents

You and your players must account for the opponent's strengths and weaknesses to know how to defend the give-and-go properly. Consider the following about your opponents:

o How tall are the opponent's players? If the offensive players are tall, they may be able to throw over the front denial of the give-and-go to get the ball to the cutter. Off-the-ball defenders should be in position with the hands up high to deflect or intercept a pass to a taller offensive player cutting to the basket. If the cutter is small, the passer cannot easily throw over the defender to get the return pass to the cutter.

o Are the opponent's players quick? If the offensive player is quicker than the defender, the defender must drop to the ball quicker and give the offensive player more room on the cut in order to avoid getting beat on the cut.

Self-Knowledge

Besides being aware of your opponent's abilities, you and your players need to know about your own team's strengths and weaknesses. Teach your players to be aware of the following when defending the give-and-go:

o How quick are your players? Quicker defenders can use their quickness advantage to get position on the offensive cutter and make the cutter go in a different direction. This will help the defense take the best cut away from the offensive player.

o Does your team have a good defender at the post? If so, this will allow defenders to guard the cutter more closely because if the defender gets beat, the post defender will be in a position to block the shot of the offensive player who receives the return pass.

o Are your players strong and physical? If the defenders guarding the give-and-go cut are strong, physical players, they will be able to force the cutter to go a different direction by getting in position to stop the easy cut to the basket.

Decision-Making Guidelines

When deciding how to gain the best advantage when defending the give-and-go, you and your players should consider the previous information as well as the following guidelines:

o Offensive cutters often try to take advantage of situations where they can catch defenders off guard by faking a cut. On the give-and-go, the offensive cutter may try to set up the defender by taking a step away from the pass to get the defender leaning out of position. If successful, this can lead to an easy basket. Therefore, the defender must be sure to jump to the ball and not go with the fake or the step away by the offensive player.

(continued)

At a Glance

The following parts of the text offer additional information on defending the give-and-go:

○ If the defender takes away the give-and-go cut and the offensive player goes behind the defender using a back-door cut, the defender should open up so that he or she can see the ball at all times on the cut.

○ When guarding an offensive player who likes to use a give-and-go to get the ball in better position, the defender should not play as close when the player has the ball. Because the defender is not playing close, the offensive player will likely choose not to cut to the basket on the give-and-go. The offensive player will stay on the perimeter to get the pass.

Defending the Backdoor Cut

A backdoor cut is used by an offensive player when the defender is overplaying the pass—that is, when the defender has a hand and foot in the passing lane to prevent the offensive player from receiving a pass. The offensive player sees this overplay by the defender and cuts hard to the basket, looking for a pass (typically a bounce pass) and an easy score. When an offensive player goes backdoor on a cut to get open for a pass, the defender may lose sight of the player. Therefore, defenders must learn how to stay with the offensive player on a backdoor cut and how to keep the ball in sight by opening to the ball as the offensive player goes back door.

WATCH OUT!

The following circumstances may distract your athletes:

- Failing to communicate on defense. This prevents the defenders from helping each other on a backdoor cut.
- Trying to defend a backdoor cutter whose size allows the ball to be easily thrown over the defenders.
- Listening to the communication of the offensive players instead of focusing on defending the backdoor cut.
- Trying to defend a backdoor cutter whose quickness can prevent the defender from opening up to guard the pass to the cutter.

ACQUIRING THE APPROPRIATE KNOWLEDGE

To help ensure your team's success in defending the backdoor cut, you and your players must know about the following:

READING THE SITUATION

How can your players gain the best advantage when defending the backdoor cut? Teach your players to do the following:

- Anticipate when an offensive player may attempt a backdoor cut. Also, defenders should recognize when their offensive player plants the top foot, the one closest to the centerline, because this can tip off the beginning of a backdoor cut to the basket.
- Keep the palm out and the thumb down on the deny hand when guarding an offensive player making a backdoor cut. This hand position will enable the defender to knock the ball away on the pass.
- Be ready to help on a backdoor cutter. A help defender must be in proper help position to stop a shot by the cutter after an offensive player gets by a defender on the backdoor cut and receives the pass.
- Understand that the post defender must be in a good off-the-ball position and must be able to slide over to help on the backdoor cut. The post defender should be ready to block the shot after the pass has been made to the backdoor cutter.

Rules

You and your players need to know several main rules related to defending the backdoor cut:

- When trying to stop the backdoor cut, defenders must be careful not to hold the cutter, or a holding foul may be called.
- When weak-side defenders come to help on a backdoor cut, the defenders must avoid being late to help and causing the cutter to run into them. This can result in a blocking foul being called.

(continued)

Defending the Backdoor Cut (continued)

REMINDER!

You and your players must understand the team strategy and game plan and must assess how to defend the backdoor cut based on those plans and the situation at hand. Make sure that you and your players consider the questions on page 112.

○ When trying to stop the backdoor cut, defenders must be careful not to use the hands to push the offensive player during the cut. This can result in a tagging foul (holding, hand-checking, or illegal use of hands) being called.

Strengths and Weaknesses of Opponents

You and your players must account for the opponent's strengths and weaknesses to know how to defend the backdoor cut properly. Consider the following about your opponents:

○ How big is the player with the ball? If the offensive player with the ball is tall and can pass over the defender, defenders who are guarding an offensive player one pass away from the ball will need to play closer to the opponent to stop the high pass. As the backdoor cut is made, the defender should guard the cutter more closely because the size of the passer will allow a high pass to be completed. Playing closely will enable the defender to try to get to the pass.

○ Is the opponent a strong passing team? When playing a poor passing team, defenders can play much tighter defense than normal. It takes a very good pass to complete the backdoor pass; therefore, if the offensive team is not a good passing team, they may not have a good chance of completing the backdoor pass. As a result, the defender will able to overplay the passing lanes without worrying about the backdoor cut.

○ Are the opponent's players slow? If the offensive players are slow, especially with their cuts, the defense can apply more pressure and can play a more aggressive denial defense at the wing. The defender will have an advantage against a slower offensive player trying to make the backdoor cut.

○ How well does the opponent shoot the ball? If the opponent is not a very good perimeter shooting team, the defense may not want to deny the pass to the wing; rather, the defense can let the offensive players catch the ball at the wing. This would result in the offensive team being open for the outside jump shot and not open for the backdoor cut.

Self-Knowledge

Besides being aware of your opponent's abilities, you and your players need to know about your own team's strengths and weaknesses. Teach your players to be aware of the following when defending the backdoor cut:

○ Does your team have strong help defense? If so, defenders may be able to put more pressure on the offensive player that is one pass away from the ball. The defenders will know that they have some help if the offensive player goes backdoor.

○ How big are your team's post players? If a defense has a big post defender in the lane area who can block shots, the defense may encourage the offensive team to use backdoor cuts. Again, defenders guarding an offensive player one pass away from the ball can apply good pressure, knowing that a post defender will be ready to block the shot in the lane if they get beat on a backdoor cut.

○ Are your perimeter players quick? Perimeter defenders with good quickness can apply pressure to deny passes at the wings and still be able to cover backdoor cuts. Good quickness enables the defender to deny the perimeter pass to the offensive player and then defend the backdoor pass by opening up quickly as the pass is made to the offensive player on the cut.

Decision-Making Guidelines

When deciding how to gain the best advantage when defending the backdoor cut, you and your players should consider the previous information as well as the following guidelines:

- If an off-the-ball defender who is guarding a player one pass away from the ball must deny a pass to that player, the defender will open up to the passer in order to see the ball. When doing so, the defender may lose sight of the offensive player he or she is guarding, which will provide an opportunity for the offensive player to go backdoor. The defender must be prepared to defend the backdoor appropriately in this situation.

- If the passer fakes a pass to an offensive player and that player's defender goes with the fake, this will open up an opportunity for the backdoor cut. Therefore, the defender must stay in the open denial position and not go for the fake on the pass.

- When the pass is made to the backdoor cutter, the defender on the help side should try to take a charge by quickly establishing position with the feet and getting the shoulders squared to the backdoor cutter.

- If the ball is on the baseline and the backdoor cut comes from the offensive player at the wing position, the defender guarding the wing player must drop to the lane immediately to stop the backdoor cut and pass.

- Rotation must occur as the backdoor cut is made to the basket. The off-the-ball defender on the help side should be the first defender sliding to the strong side to take away the pass or to guard the backdoor cutter. The top guard must then drop down to cover the offensive player that the help-side defender just left open to guard the backdoor cutter.

At a Glance

The following parts of the text offer additional information on defending the backdoor cut:

Defensive Positioning	p. 94
Skip Pass	p. 126
Penetrate and Pass	p. 132
Backdoor Cut	p. 140
Off-the-Ball Defense	p. 157
Help and Recover	p. 169

Defending the Flash Cut

The flash cut is a cut made by a weak-side offensive player to the ball side of the court, most often across the lane, in order to receive a pass and get a quick score. If the defender "goes to sleep" on defense and does not get in the path of the flash cutter, this cut can allow the offense to get a good shot off in the middle of the lane. Defenders must be prepared to make a flash cut when the offensive team makes a skip pass in order to properly set up the cut and get into position.

WATCH OUT!

The following circumstances may distract your athletes:

- Focusing only on the offensive player with the ball instead of effectively guarding the cutter.
- Guarding a bigger or stronger offensive player who is making the flash cut.
- Guarding a cutter whose quickness forces the defender to focus only on the cutter rather than the cutter *and* the ball.

ACQUIRING THE APPROPRIATE KNOWLEDGE

To help ensure your team's success in defending the flash cut, you and your players must know about the following:

Rules

You and your players need to know several main rules related to defending the flash cut:

- When defending the flash cut, the defender must be careful not to use the hands in an attempt to stop the cut (rather than getting into a good position to stop the cut). This can result in a holding foul being called.

READING THE SITUATION

How can your players gain the best advantage when defending the flash cut? Teach your players to do the following:

- Anticipate the offensive player's cut by knowing all of the player's options when the ball is on the opposite side of the floor. Defenders should recognize that if the player they are guarding is opposite the ball, chances are the player will be making a cut to the ball to receive a pass, because this is typically the offensive player's best option.

- Maintain the ball–you–man positioning when defending an offensive player without the ball. This enables defenders to see both the ball and the player they are guarding. Defenders must also remain in the basic defensive stance at all times so that they will be ready to move if their offensive player starts to make a flash cut.

- Understand that the defender should not follow the offensive player as the player cuts to the ball but instead should "lead" the player across to the ball by denying the cutting lane and passing lane.

- Try to be in a position to make the offensive cutter go high (usually to the high post) to receive the ball rather than allowing the player to go low for the ball. The higher the offensive player must go to receive the pass, the more difficult the shot will be because of the distance from the basket.

- An offensive player cannot run into a defender who is stationary or a charge will be called. Defenders can try to draw a charge by getting into a good position to stop the flash cut.

- An offensive player who has the ball may not dribble or hold the ball for longer than five seconds when being closely guarded. This may come into play if the defender does not allow the flash cut to be completed and the passer holds onto the ball for longer than the allowed five seconds.

REMINDER!

You and your players must understand the team strategy and game plan and must assess how to defend the flash cut based on those plans and the situation at hand. Make sure that you and your players consider the questions on page 112.

- An offensive player cannot be in the lane for longer than three seconds. If the defender can make it difficult for the flash cutter to get the pass, this player may be caught in the lane for longer than three seconds, resulting in a turnover.

Strengths and Weaknesses of Opponents

You and your players must account for the opponent's strengths and weaknesses to know how to defend the flash cut properly. Consider the following about your opponents:

- How quick is the opponent? If the offensive player making the flash cut is quick, the defender must give the offensive player more room and maintain the proper ball–you–man positioning in order to better defend the cut to the ball. If the defenders leave some space (at least an arm's length) between themselves and their offensive player making a cut, the defenders can make up for the quickness of the offensive player.

- How big is the opponent? If a defender is guarding a taller offensive player, the defender will need to get a hand high in the passing lane to stop a high pass if the offensive player makes a flash cut.

- Is the opponent physically aggressive? When guarding a more physical offensive player on a flash cut, defenders should make sure that the arm bar (the forearm is held at a 45-degree angle in front of the chest) is high and that they are in a solid defensive stance for good balance.

- Does the opponent have an effective inside scorer? If so, the defense should focus on preventing this player from getting the ball in the lane on a flash cut.

Self-Knowledge

Besides being aware of your opponent's abilities, you and your players need to know about your own team's strengths and weaknesses. Teach your players to be aware of the following when defending the flash cut:

- How quick are your players? If the defender is quicker than the offensive player making the flash cut, the defender will be able to beat the cutter to the spot where the offensive player wants to catch the pass. This will make it much more difficult for the offensive player to catch the ball.

- Does your team play good pressure defense on the ball? If the defense puts good pressure on the offensive player with the ball, this will make it much more difficult for the player to complete the pass to the flash cutter.

- Does your team have good help defense? If so, defenders should funnel the flash cutter to the area where they may have more help, such as the high-post area.

(continued)

Defending the Flash Cut (continued)

Decision-Making Guidelines

When deciding how to gain the best advantage when defending the flash cut, you and your players should consider the previous information as well as the following guidelines:

- Defenders should not let the cutter get to the low-post area and establish position for a shot. Instead, they should try to get the cutter to flash to the high post, where they may have more help from the guards.

- To stop the cutter from getting into the lane area, the defender should use the forearm, called an *arm bar*, to restrict the offensive player's movement and keep the player from going where he or she wants to go.

- Defenders guarding a cutter should communicate the flash cut to their teammates by yelling, "Cutter." This will alert teammates about the cut, and the defender will have help ready, if needed.

- Defenders should never turn their back to the ball when attempting to stop the flash cut. If the flash cutter goes to the basket using a backdoor cut, the defender should turn and open up to the ball.

Switching on a Screen

Switching on a screen is a defensive tactic where two defenders switch defensive assignments in an effort to prevent the offense from gaining an advantage on the screen. When an offensive player sets a screen, the defender guarding the screener will call out, "Switch," which cues the defender being screened to switch defensive assignments and pick up the teammate's player (i.e., the screener). The defender who was guarding the screener picks up the offensive player coming off the screen. Switching on screens will give the offensive players very little space to execute a shot or a pass. The defender who is guarding the screener needs to switch to the offensive player coming off the screen immediately. This will limit the time for the shot if the offensive player is dribbling off the screen or will deny the pass if the offensive player coming off the screen does not have the ball.

 WATCH OUT!

The following circumstances may distract your athletes:

- ○ Not communicating when making the switch.

- ○ Turning the head away from the ball and losing sight of the ball.

- ○ Guarding offensive players on the switch who have a size advantage.

- ○ Facing an offensive player whose quickness coming off of screens puts pressure on the switch.

- ○ Facing offensive players who are good shooters coming off the screen. This may force the defender to concentrate on the shooter rather than the screen.

READING THE SITUATION

How can your players gain the best advantage when switching on a screen? Teach your players to do the following:

- • Be alert to the size and ability of the screener and the player using the screen. The defenders may switch when the offensive players are the same size or of unequal size, but defenders must be prepared to handle the mismatch or disadvantage that may ensue. The switch must come early and aggressively to neutralize any advantage that the offensive players may have on the defenders.

- • Communicate with teammates. Communication between the defenders is critical in switching because the defender guarding the offensive player using the screen may not see the screener coming. This needs to be communicated by the defender whose offensive player is setting the screen so that the switch can take place with proper timing.

ACQUIRING THE APPROPRIATE KNOWLEDGE

To help ensure your team's success in switching on screens, you and your players must know about the following:

Rules

You and your players need to know several main rules related to switching on a screen:

- ○ When switching on a screen, defenders must be careful not to hold the dribbler as he or she tries to use the screen. This could result in a holding foul being called.

(continued)

REMINDER!

You and your players must understand the team strategy and game plan and must assess switching on screens based on those plans and the situation at hand. Make sure that you and your players consider the questions on page 112.

○ An offensive player cannot run into a defender who is stationary or a charge will be called. The defenders may be able to draw a charge if they can switch quickly and one of the defenders steps out to guard the dribbler. If the defender is too late in getting position to draw the charge, a blocking foul could be called on the defender.

○ An offensive player who has the ball may not dribble or hold the ball for longer than five seconds when being closely guarded. This may come into play if the defenders force the dribbler to keep the ball after the switch for longer than the allowed five seconds.

○ An offensive player cannot be in the lane for longer than three seconds. A lane violation could be called if the switch takes place in the lane and an offensive player stays in the lane for longer than the allowed three seconds.

Strengths and Weaknesses of Opponents

You and your players must account for the opponent's strengths and weaknesses to know how to switch on a screen properly. Consider the following about your opponents:

○ How big are the opponent's players? If the offensive players are bigger, this can cause some problems for switching defenses because a small defender may switch to a taller offensive player. If this happens, the defenders must be very aggressive to neutralize the size advantage of the offensive players. The defenders should also make sure the switch is very quick, which is dependent on the communication of the defenders.

○ Is the player with the ball a strong shooter? If the offensive player for whom the screen was set is a good shooter, the defenders must switch quickly to stop the player from shooting the ball behind the screen. The defenders must switch as the offensive player dribbles over or off the screen so that the player cannot get an open shot.

○ Does the screener roll to the basket or step back for a jump shot? If the screener rolls to the basket after the screen, the defender who switches onto the screener must get in front of this player to discourage the pass. If the screener steps back after the dribbler uses the screen, the defender must get a hand up to discourage the jump shot if the screener receives a pass.

○ Does the offensive player using the screen have good quickness? If so, as the offensive player comes off the screen using the dribble, the defender who is switching onto this player should get in a position to prevent the player from taking a direct path to the basket around the screen.

Self-Knowledge

Besides being aware of your opponent's abilities, you and your players need to know about your own team's strengths and weaknesses. Teach your players to be aware of the following when switching on a screen:

○ How quick are your players? If the defender who switches onto the offensive player using the screen is quicker than that offensive player, this will help make the switch more successful. The defender will be able to get in front of the player using the screen and prevent the player from going to the basket.

○ How physically strong are your players? If the switching defenders are physically strong, this will help when there is a mismatch or difference in size between the defenders and the offensive players after the switch takes place. The defender who switched onto the screener will be able to stop the screener from going to the basket on the roll.

- How big are your players? If the defenders are all about the same size, switching will be much easier because the defenders will not be in a mismatch situation when the switch occurs.

Decision-Making Guidelines

When deciding how to gain the best advantage when switching on a screen, you and your players should consider the previous information as well as the following guidelines:

- If the opponent typically uses a pick-and-roll and the screener rolls off the screen and to the basket, the defender who switches to guarding the screener must work to get in front of the screener on the roll. This will help the defender prevent a pass to the screener as the screener rolls to the basket.

- If the offensive player who is going to set a screen sees the switch coming, this player may attempt a backdoor cut before setting the screen. If this occurs, the help-side defenders must be prepared to cover this cut as the offensive player goes to the basket for a pass.

- The screener may have a screen set for him or her by another player in the offense—in other words, "screening the screener" may take place in the offense. In this situation, two switches may be executed by the defense.

- A screen will often be set when a dribbler is trying to get the ball from the backcourt into the frontcourt against good defensive pressure. When the defenders switch on this screen, a big defender may end up guarding the smaller dribbler on the switch. If this occurs, the defender must make sure to keep proper spacing so the dribbler cannot go by the bigger, and probably slower, defender.

At a Glance

The following parts of the text offer additional information on switching on a screen:

Fighting Over the Top of a Screen

Fighting over the top of a screen can be a difficult defensive move to make, but defenders must learn this move in order to be able to stay with their offensive player. Fighting over the screen eliminates the mismatch that may occur when a switch takes place. Defenders should also fight over the screen when they are guarding an exceptionally good shooter; in this situation, the defender needs to stay with the shooter so that the shooter cannot stop behind the screen and shoot. When an opponent sets a screen, the screener's defender should communicate "screen right" or "screen left," and the defender being screened fights over the screen by taking a big step on the top side of the screener. The screener's defender must step out in that direction to delay the cutter getting through. Communication is of the utmost importance so that the defender being screened can adjust to the screen before it is set and can get over the top of the screen in plenty of time. Defenders can also fight over the top of an off-the-ball screen—for example, the weak-side defender may fight over a screen off the ball so that the offensive player does not have an open path to the ball on the strong side of the court.

READING THE SITUATION

How can your players gain the best advantage when fighting over the top of a screen? Teach your players to do the following:

- Recognize when the offense doesn't set up their screens well or when they can't successfully cut off their screens. In these cases, the defender who is being screened should try to fight over the top of the screen by getting a foot over the top foot of the screener.

- Remember that communication is essential when screens are involved and that screens must be called out before they take place. The defender guarding an offensive player who is looking to set a screen must call out the screen so the teammate guarding the offensive player who will use the screen knows the screen is coming.

- Recognize when offensive players are within their shooting range and that sliding through on a screen would leave them open in this range. When a screen is set for an offensive player in an area where the player can get off a good shot, the defender must get the front foot over the top of the screener to get over the screen and defend the shooter.

 WATCH OUT!

The following circumstances may distract your athletes:

- Not hearing the screener's defender call out the screen because of communication by other players.
- Being unable to fight over the screen because of the size of the screener.
- Guarding an offensive player who is good at shooting over the top of the screen.

ACQUIRING THE APPROPRIATE KNOWLEDGE

To help ensure your team's success in fighting over the top of screens, you and your players must know about the following:

Rules

You and your players need to know two main rules related to fighting over the top of a screen:

○ When fighting over the top of a screen, defenders must be careful not to push or hold the offensive player who is using the screen, especially if the defender is slow in getting over the screen. This could result in a tagging foul (holding, hand-checking, or illegal use of the hands) foul being called.

○ When fighting over the top of a screen and trying to get in front of the offensive player using the screen (in order to stop the player or to draw a charge), a blocking foul may be called if the defender is late in getting into proper position.

REMINDER!

You and your players must understand the team strategy and game plan and must assess fighting over the top of screens based on those plans and the situation at hand. Make sure that you and your players consider the questions on page 112.

Strengths and Weaknesses of Opponents

You and your players must account for the opponent's strengths and weaknesses to know how to fight over the top of screens properly. Consider the following about your opponents:

○ Does the opponent's best player have the ability to drive effectively off a ball screen? If so, the defense may want to use a double team (with the defender who is guarding the ball and the defender who is guarding the screener) or a quick switch when this player dribbles off the screen in order to prevent the drive to the basket.

○ Is the player with the ball quick off the dribble? If the offensive player using the screen is quick off the dribble, the defender guarding the screener must hedge, or step out, to control the dribbler until the defender who is guarding the dribbler can get over the screen.

○ Is the player with the ball slow on the dribble? If so, the defender should try to get the offensive player to change directions on the dribble before getting to the screen. This will help prevent the drive to the basket.

○ Is the player with the ball a strong shooter? When guarding a good shooter, defenders must know that they need to get over a screen or the offensive player will be open for a shot. When the defender hears a teammate call out "Screen," the defender should be in position to get over the top of the screen so that a switch does not take place.

Self-Knowledge

Besides being aware of your opponent's abilities, you and your players need to know about your own team's strengths and weaknesses. Teach your players to be aware of the following when fighting over the top of a screen:

○ How quick are your players? Defenders with a quickness advantage will be able to force the offensive player away from the screen. Any time a defender can make the dribbler go opposite the screen, this will make the defender's job easier because the defender will not have to fight over screens that are set to free up the dribbler. Quickness will also help the defender get over a screen more easily, because the defender will be able to beat the dribbler to the screen and get the foot on top of the screen to stay with the dribbler.

○ Are your players physically strong? If the defender guarding the dribbler is strong, the defender should try to take away the angle of the dribbler so the dribbler cannot use the screen. Being somewhat physical with the dribbler will push the angle of the dribbler away from the screen. In this case, the defender guarding the dribbler will easily get over the top of the screen.

(continued)

○ Does your team communicate well on defense? Good communication makes getting over the top of the screens much easier because the defenders know when the screen is coming.

○ How big are your players? If the defender has a size advantage, the defender will be able to block the vision of the offensive player by keeping the hands up and out as the defender gets over the screen.

Decision-Making Guidelines

When deciding how to gain the best advantage when fighting over the top of a screen, you and your players should consider the previous information as well as the following guidelines:

○ When defenders know the screen is being set for the player they are guarding, they should try to force the offensive player to go away from the screen so the player will not be able to use the screen to get open. Fighting over the screen is a difficult defensive maneuver to perform on a regular basis, so if the defender can push the dribbler away from the screen, this will make it easier for the defender to stay with the dribbler.

○ Offensive players may set screens away from the ball (the screen is set for a player who does not have the ball) to get a teammate open for a pass cutting to the ball. To make it easier to get over the top of an off-the-ball screen, defenders should maintain good help-side defensive position. If the defender who is getting screened is in a good ball–you–man triangle position, this will allow the defender to get over the top of the screen and take away the pass to the offensive player using the screen.

○ When fighting over the top of the screen, the defender must get the foot on the top side of the screen as the offensive player uses the screen to free up. This will allow the defender to keep sliding with the offensive player he or she is guarding.

○ When screens are set for the player with the ball, the defender guarding the screener should communicate about the screen and then step out from behind the screen, forcing the dribbler to move and creating some space between the screener and the dribbler. This space will allow the defender on the ball to get over the top of the screen and stay with the dribbler.

Double Teaming the Post

When the offense successfully moves the ball into the post—the area close to the basket where the offense has the highest probability of making a shot—the defensive post player may have a difficult time preventing the offense from scoring without the help of another defender. The primary purpose of double teaming the post is to use the pressure of two defenders to force the post player with the ball to pass back out to the perimeter, thus preventing a shot close to the basket. But the double team can also result in a steal if performed correctly.

The double team will usually come from the defender on the perimeter player who just passed the ball to the post player. However, the offensive team may have a strong inside-out attack in which a two-person game is created between the post and the perimeter player on the same side of the court. If the wing player passes into the post and the wing defender leaves to double team, the post player can pass back out for the jumper. Therefore, the double team on the post player may need to come from other defenders, such as a second post defender or the point guard defender from the top of the key.

WATCH OUT!

The following circumstances may distract your athletes:

- Facing an offensive post player with good physical size and ability.
- Being unsure about double teaming because of the score and time left in the game. Defenders may question whether they should double team and leave the perimeter open.

ACQUIRING THE APPROPRIATE KNOWLEDGE

To help ensure your team's success in double teaming the post, you and your players must know about the following:

Rules

You and your players need to know several main rules related to double teaming the post:

(continued)

READING THE SITUATION

How can your players gain the best advantage when double teaming the post? Teach your players to do the following:

- Know where the double team should come from. The perimeter defender closest to the post player will be the most likely player to go into the post when the double team is needed to force a pass back out. However, if the offensive post player catches a pass in the middle of the lane, the defenders can come from any direction, such as either wing area, to double team.

- Rotate defensively when a teammate moves in for a double team. The other defenders need to help guard the open offensive player and prevent an open jump shot. The rotation will come from the defender who is closest to the offensive player who passed the ball into the post. For example, if the offensive wing player passes the ball into the post, the defender guarding the passer may leave to double team. The defender from the top (usually the defender guarding the point guard) will rotate to cover the offensive player at the wing who just passed the ball.

- When double teaming, the two defenders should try to strip the ball away from the post player before the player can get the ball up to shooting position, because the offensive post player is usually taller than the double teaming defenders.

Double Teaming the Post (continued)

REMINDER!

You and your players must understand the team strategy and game plan and must assess the double team on the post based on those plans and the situation at hand. Make sure that you and your players consider the questions on page 112.

○ When double teaming the post, the defenders may draw a charge if the offensive post player turns to the basket for a drive and runs into a defender who has established correct position.

○ When double teaming the post to deny the shot, defenders must be careful not to foul the post player on the shot. This could result in free throws for the offense.

○ If the double team can come quick enough, the defender may be able to force a held ball situation (when two players from opposite teams are holding the ball at the same time). When this occurs, the alternate jump ball arrow will determine which team gets possession of the ball.

○ An offensive player cannot be in the lane for longer than three seconds. If the double team is in place to stop the shot when the offensive post player gets in the lane with the ball, the player may get caught in the lane for longer than the allowed three seconds, resulting in a turnover.

○ When a defense double teams the post, the offensive post player may commit a traveling violation when trying to make a quick move to shoot before the double team arrives, resulting in a turnover for the defensive team.

Strengths and Weaknesses of Opponents

You and your players must account for the opponent's strengths and weaknesses to know how to double team the post properly. Consider the following about your opponents:

○ Are the opponent's players good passers? When guarding an offensive player on the perimeter who is a good passer into the post, the defender may need to use more aggressiveness and closely guard the offensive player to make the pass more difficult.

○ Does the opponent have a strong inside-out attack? If so, the offensive wing player will often pass into the post, and when the wing defender leaves to double team, the post player will pass the ball back out for a jumper. The perimeter defender who double teams the post must be able to get back to the shooter and anticipate this in order to stop the outside shot.

○ Are the opponent's players strong outside shooters? If the offensive player making the pass into the post is a good shooter, the defender needs to pay attention to this player because the player will be able to score if the defender goes to double the post. This is when the double team may need to come from another defender, such as the point guard defender or the help-side defender.

○ How big are the opponent's players? If the offensive post player is taller than the post defender, the perimeter double team must come quickly before the offensive player can turn and shoot over the post defender. The perimeter defender who is double teaming must start the move to double team as the ball is being passed. This will enable the defender to get there for the double team as the ball is caught by the post player. Whenever the offensive post player is taller and can shoot over the post defender, the best way to stop the post player from scoring is to bring a perimeter player on the double team.

Self-Knowledge

Besides being aware of your opponent's abilities, you and your players need to know about your own team's strengths and weaknesses. Teach your players to be aware of the following when double teaming the post:

- How quick are your players? This will determine the effectiveness of the double team on the post player. If the defender is quick, the double team will come quick enough to stop the post player as the player turns to shoot the ball. If the defender is slow to double team, the offensive post player can get the shot off before the double team is set.

- How big are your players? If the defender guarding the post is small, a double team will be necessary to help stop the offensive post player from scoring. If the offensive post player can turn and shoot over the defensive post player, the perimeter defender must double to stop the shot.

- Does your team have good help-side defense? If the defenders on the help side are in proper position, the defensive post player may be able to play in front of the offensive post player. The help-side defender can be in a position to play behind the offensive post player on the double team.

- Can your defense recognize different offensive players in the post and double team with different defenders? An offense can have any player post up, including the guards or the forwards. The defenders must recognize the offensive player in the post area, and the double team should come from the appropriate defender. This will sometimes be a defender who may not be used to double teaming. For example, the offensive post player may go out to the baseline and receive a pass from the wing, and the wing player may then go to the post position and receive a pass from the post player. In this situation, the double team would come from the defensive post player, who is not the normal defender to double in the post.

Decision-Making Guidelines

When deciding how to gain the best advantage when double teaming the post, you and your players should consider the previous information as well as the following guidelines:

- The off-the-ball defender who is guarding the help-side offensive player may be a good option for double teaming the offensive post player. The advantage to having this defender double team is that the offensive post player cannot see the double team approaching from behind.

- If the defensive game plan is to make the post player pass the ball back out when it enters the post area, the defender must move quickly to double team as soon as the pass is made into the post. If there is a delay on the double team, the post player will likely use this opportunity to shoot the ball before the double team can help.

- If the offensive post player is quick, the double team can be most effective coming from the help side. If the double team comes from the defender who is guarding the passer, the offensive post player can make a quick move to the basket before the double team arrives. The help-side defender is in a better position to double team quickly as the offensive post player makes a move to go around the post defender.

- Defenders can fake the double team occasionally to create indecision on the part of the offensive post player. For example, when the offensive post player receives a pass into the post from the wing, the wing defender can fake the double team by coming partway. This will make the post player think the double team is coming. As a result, the post player may try to pass the ball back out to the perimeter, and the defender who faked the double team is in position to intercept this pass.

At a Glance

The following parts of the text offer additional information on double teaming the post:

Defensive Positioning	p. 94
Defending the Post	p. 108
Skip Pass	p. 126
Inside-Out Pass	p. 129
Flash Cut	p. 143
Help and Recover	p. 169
Defending the Pass	p. 187

Planning for Teaching

Part IV helps you apply what you learned in the previous chapters to developing a plan for the upcoming season. By having a good season plan that outlines your practices for the year and then creating specific practice plans based on your season plan, you will be ready to coach and get the most out of your season.

In chapter 7, we explain how to create a season plan, which is a framework for the practices that make up a season. In addition to describing the six essential steps to developing the season plan, this chapter provides a sample season plan based on the games approach.

After you have a season plan, you must create what is called a *practice plan*, which outlines how you will approach each practice. Chapter 8 helps you do this by explaining the important components of a good practice plan and then providing you with samples of the first eight practices of a season based on the sample season plan provided in chapter 7.

Season Plans

John Wooden, the great UCLA basketball coach, followed a simple coaching philosophy that emphasized execution over winning. He felt that if his Bruins concentrated on executing the basics, winning would follow. In that regard, his well-planned practice sessions created a foundation for 10 national titles in a 12-year span in the 1960s and 1970s. As Wooden said, "Failure to prepare is preparing to fail." Before the first practice of the season, you should review your coaching philosophy and reflect on the upcoming year. By doing so, you can avoid the pitfalls of previous years and set goals for the one to come. No matter what the sport, a good coach makes plans.

Planning begins with formulating a sound coaching philosophy. Do you press end line to end line? Do you believe in man-to-man or zone defense? Do you get the ball into the post, or do you shoot the three whenever you're open? These and myriad other considerations go into the building of a coaching philosophy.

How do you form a philosophy? First, you should always go with your gut feelings. You shouldn't try to adopt a viewpoint that goes against your personal beliefs. You will have difficulty selling something to players that you don't believe in yourself. That being said, you shouldn't be afraid to borrow from successful approaches that have worked for others. Pay close attention to schools or teams that win often. What makes those teams successful? You shouldn't be afraid to ask other coaches how they prepare for a season, run practices, or discipline players. A good coach will be flattered and more than willing to share information.

But as you know, gathering information from other coaches or from books provides only the raw material for an aspiring coach. The next step is to process this information and organize it into a useful plan. Good coaches are good teachers. Just as a teacher wouldn't think about walking into a classroom without a lesson plan, a coach shouldn't begin a season without a plan. You need to organize information into a working whole, or a season plan, by skillfully analyzing, observing, and prioritizing.

The Six Steps to Instructional Planning

Chapter 1 of Rainer Martens' *Successful Coaching, Third Edition* provides a framework for creating and implementing coaching values. You may want to read that chapter and begin to refine your coaching philosophy.

After you have articulated your philosophy, you can begin planning for the season ahead by following a simple six-step procedure called the "Six Steps to Instructional Planning":*

Step 1: Identify the skills that your athletes need.

Step 2: Know your athletes.

Step 3: Analyze your situation.

Step 4: Establish your priorities.

Step 5: Select your methods for teaching.

Step 6: Plan your practices.

Step 1: Identify the Skills That Your Athletes Need

To help athletes become excellent basketball players, you must know what skills are necessary for playing the game. Some of these skills may not be within the reach of most high school players, so you must filter this all-encompassing list. First, you need to isolate the skills that your players need to be successful (as shown in column 1 of figure 7.1).

Figure 7.1 provides an overview of the basic to intermediate skills needed in basketball. These include skills mentioned in chapters 3 through 6 of this book as well as communication, physical, mental, and character skills discussed in Rainer Martens' *Successful Coaching, Third Edition*. At this stage, you should examine the list of skills and add others if desired. Step 4 of the planning process will further explain how you can put this list to work for your team.

Step 2: Know Your Athletes

Before going into a season, you should be familiar with your athletes. If you coached the team the year before, you can just review the list of returning players and evaluate them—their strengths, their weaknesses, how much they still have to learn, and so on. If you are a new coach with no knowledge of the skill level of the team, the process is more difficult. You should review the guidelines for evaluation discussed in chapter 2 before attempting this process.

*Adapted, by permission, from R. Martens, 2004, *Successful coaching*, 3rd ed. (Champaign, IL: Human Kinetics), 237.

Figure 7.1 Identifying and Evaluating Skills

STEP 1	STEP 4							
	Teaching Priorities			Readiness to Learn		Priority Rating		
Skills Identified	Must	Should	Could	Yes	No	A	B	C
Offensive technical skills								
Offensive footwork	M	S	C	Yes	No	A	B	C
Triple-threat position	M	S	C	Yes	No	A	B	C
Dribbling basics	M	S	C	Yes	No	A	B	C
Speed dribble	M	S	C	Yes	No	A	B	C
Control dribble	M	S	C	Yes	No	A	B	C
Reverse dribble	M	S	C	Yes	No	A	B	C
Crossover dribble	M	S	C	Yes	No	A	B	C
Change of pace dribble	M	S	C	Yes	No	A	B	C
Passing basics	M	S	C	Yes	No	A	B	C
Chest pass	M	S	C	Yes	No	A	B	C
Bounce pass	M	S	C	Yes	No	A	B	C
Baseball pass	M	S	C	Yes	No	A	B	C
Overhead pass	M	S	C	Yes	No	A	B	C
Sidearm pass	M	S	C	Yes	No	A	B	C
Behind-the-back pass	M	S	C	Yes	No	A	B	C
Catching	M	S	C	Yes	No	A	B	C
Shooting basics	M	S	C	Yes	No	A	B	C
Set shot	M	S	C	Yes	No	A	B	C
Jump shot	M	S	C	Yes	No	A	B	C
Layup	M	S	C	Yes	No	A	B	C
Offensive rebounds	M	S	C	Yes	No	A	B	C
Cuts	M	S	C	Yes	No	A	B	C
Screens	M	S	C	Yes	No	A	B	C
Playing the post	M	S	C	Yes	No	A	B	C
Defensive technical skills								
Defensive positioning	M	S	C	Yes	No	A	B	C
Blocking shots	M	S	C	Yes	No	A	B	C
Defensive rebounds	M	S	C	Yes	No	A	B	C
Defending cuts	M	S	C	Yes	No	A	B	C
Defending screens	M	S	C	Yes	No	A	B	C
Defending the post	M	S	C	Yes	No	A	B	C
Offensive tactical skills								
Playing against man defense	M	S	C	Yes	No	A	B	C
Playing against zone defense	M	S	C	Yes	No	A	B	C
Moving without the ball	M	S	C	Yes	No	A	B	C
Running inbounds plays	M	S	C	Yes	No	A	B	C
Skip pass	M	S	C	Yes	No	A	B	C
Inside-out pass	M	S	C	Yes	No	A	B	C

(continued)

Figure 7.1 *(continued)*

STEP 1	STEP 4							
	Teaching Priorities			Readiness to Learn		Priority Rating		
Skills Identified	Must	Should	Could	Yes	No	A	B	C
Offensive tactical skills, continued								
Penetrate and pass	M	S	C	Yes	No	A	B	C
Give-and-go	M	S	C	Yes	No	A	B	C
Fast break	M	S	C	Yes	No	A	B	C
Backdoor cut	M	S	C	Yes	No	A	B	C
Flash cut	M	S	C	Yes	No	A	B	C
Pick-and-roll	M	S	C	Yes	No	A	B	C
Cross screen	M	S	C	Yes	No	A	B	C
Defensive tactical skills								
On-the-ball defense	M	S	C	Yes	No	A	B	C
Off-the-ball defense	M	S	C	Yes	No	A	B	C
Playing man defense	M	S	C	Yes	No	A	B	C
Playing zone defense	M	S	C	Yes	No	A	B	C
Applying pressure	M	S	C	Yes	No	A	B	C
Help and recover	M	S	C	Yes	No	A	B	C
Forcing shooters out of position	M	S	C	Yes	No	A	B	C
Protecting the basket	M	S	C	Yes	No	A	B	C
Taking a charge	M	S	C	Yes	No	A	B	C
Limiting fast break opportunities	M	S	C	Yes	No	A	B	C
Trapping the ball	M	S	C	Yes	No	A	B	C
Defending the pass	M	S	C	Yes	No	A	B	C
Defending the give-and-go	M	S	C	Yes	No	A	B	C
Defending the backdoor cut	M	S	C	Yes	No	A	B	C
Defending the flash cut	M	S	C	Yes	No	A	B	C
Switching on a screen	M	S	C	Yes	No	A	B	C
Fighting over the top of a screen	M	S	C	Yes	No	A	B	C
Double teaming the post	M	S	C	Yes	No	A	B	C
Physical skills								
Strength	M	S	C	Yes	No	A	B	C
Speed	M	S	C	Yes	No	A	B	C
Power	M	S	C	Yes	No	A	B	C
Endurance	M	S	C	Yes	No	A	B	C
Flexibility	M	S	C	Yes	No	A	B	C
Quickness	M	S	C	Yes	No	A	B	C
Balance	M	S	C	Yes	No	A	B	C
Agility	M	S	C	Yes	No	A	B	C
Mental skills								
Emotional control—anxiety	M	S	C	Yes	No	A	B	C
Emotional control—anger	M	S	C	Yes	No	A	B	C
Self-confidence	M	S	C	Yes	No	A	B	C

STEP 1	STEP 4							
	Teaching Priorities			Readiness to Learn		Priority Rating		
Skills Identified	Must	Should	Could	Yes	No	A	B	C
Mental skills, continued								
Motivation to achieve	M	S	C	Yes	No	A	B	C
Ability to concentrate	M	S	C	Yes	No	A	B	C
Communication skills								
Sends positive messages	M	S	C	Yes	No	A	B	C
Sends accurate messages	M	S	C	Yes	No	A	B	C
Listens to messages	M	S	C	Yes	No	A	B	C
Understands messages	M	S	C	Yes	No	A	B	C
Receives constructive criticism	M	S	C	Yes	No	A	B	C
Receives praise and recognition	M	S	C	Yes	No	A	B	C
Credibility with teammates	M	S	C	Yes	No	A	B	C
Credibility with coaches	M	S	C	Yes	No	A	B	C
Character skills								
Trustworthiness	M	S	C	Yes	No	A	B	C
Respect	M	S	C	Yes	No	A	B	C
Responsibility	M	S	C	Yes	No	A	B	C
Fairness	M	S	C	Yes	No	A	B	C
Caring	M	S	C	Yes	No	A	B	C
Citizenship	M	S	C	Yes	No	A	B	C

From ASEP, 2007, *Coaching Basketball Technical and Tactical Skills*, (Champaign, IL: Human Kinetics). Adapted, by permission, from R. Martens, 2004, *Successful coaching*, 3rd ed. (Champaign, IL: Human Kinetics), 250-251.

You may want to conduct a tryout camp on the first day of practice or before the season (if the rules allow). During this tryout process, players could be tested on the technical and tactical skills of basketball in addition to the physical and nonphysical skills as discussed in chapter 2. Completing forms such as the Bounce Pass Evaluation and Switching on a Screen Evaluation forms on page 16 would give you a good idea of a player's skill and potential ability. Armed with this knowledge, you could then reevaluate the skills identified in step 1 to ensure that they are the appropriate skills for the team.

Step 3: Analyze Your Situation

You also need to analyze your situation in preparing for a season. Before embarking on grandiose schemes such as buying new uniforms or traveling great distances to play games, you need to consider the amount of help that you will get from the community, including parents and school and civic officials. You must be aware of budgetary concerns and have clear goals regarding fund-raising if any is needed. The availability of the practice facility is also a concern. A program self-evaluation form can help you with this process (see figure 7.2).

You must remember to consider many factors other than technical and tactical skills when planning for a season. Note that as the season progresses, the time available for practice diminishes; therefore, you must be sure to teach all the basics early. During the first 2 weeks of the season, practice will normally be held five times a week. But during the following 10 to 12 weeks, the team will likely have games twice a week, so only three days will be open for practice.

Figure 7.2 Evaluating Your Team Situation

How many practices will you have over the entire season? How long will practices be?

How many games will you have over the entire season?

What special events (team meetings, parent orientation sessions, banquets, tournaments) will you have and when?

How many athletes will you be coaching? How many assistants will you have? What is the ratio of athletes to coaches?

What equipment will be available for practice?

How much money will you have for travel and other expenses?

What instructional resources (videos, books, charts, CDs) will you need?

What other support personnel will be available?

What other factors may affect your instructional plan?

From ASEP, 2007, *Coaching Basketball Technical and Tactical Skills,* (Champaign, IL: Human Kinetics). Reprinted, by permission, from R. Martens, 2004, *Successful coaching*, 3rd ed. (Champaign, IL: Human Kinetics), 247-248.

Step 4: Establish Your Priorities

You must institute a set of priorities before a season. Given the limited practice time available to most high school teams, you cannot cover everything within the game of basketball. You should also consider the abilities of the athletes before establishing priorities. Refer to figure 7.1, paying special attention to the column under "Step 4." Here you examine the list of essential skills and evaluate them to establish practice priorities for the season. First, you must give each skill a priority according to its importance. Ask yourself, Is this a skill that I *must*, *should*, or *could* teach? You should then ask, Are my athletes ready to learn this skill? The results from step 2 may help you with this phase. Finally, based on those two factors—the teaching priority and the athletes' readiness to learn—you can give each skill a priority rating in column 4. The A-rated skills would be those that you feel are essential to teach, so you should cover them early and often. Likewise, you should teach as many B-rated skills as possible. Finally, depending on the ability and rate of progression of the players, you could teach C-rated skills.

Although most of the skills have been tabbed as must-teach skills, circumstances may arise that make teaching some skills impractical at various times during the season. For various reasons, your team may not be ready or able to learn the complicated assignments necessary to successfully execute a particular tactical skill. Some players may have difficulty reading the play and picking up on the cues to execute it properly. Some may be easily distracted or have trouble acquiring the necessary knowledge. Maybe the players at key positions lack the physical abilities to effectively execute the play. In this case, the coach might come up with a conservative approach to these tactical skills and delay teaching more complicated responses entirely.

Step 5: Select Your Methods for Teaching

Next, you should choose the methods that you want to use in daily practices to teach the skills that you have decided are necessary. Take care in implementing this important step. The traditional approach to practice involves using daily drills to teach skills, interspersed with half- and full-court scrimmages. This approach emphasizes technical skill development; it is based on the belief that the more a player drills the individual skills, the better the player will become at performing them in games.

This traditional method might cover the techniques of basketball adequately—and even approximate most of the tactical situations that a team will face during games—but it does have several shortcomings. First, traditional practice sessions overemphasize techniques at the expense of tactics. Second, too much direct instruction occurs. Typically, a coach would explain a skill, show how to perform it, and then set up situations in which players could learn the skill.

Recent educational research has shown, however, that students who learn a skill in one setting, say the library, have difficulty performing it in another setting, such as the classroom. Compare this finding to the common belief among coaches that young players today don't have the basketball sense—that is, the basic knowledge of the game—that players used to have. For years, coaches have been bemoaning the fact that players don't react as well to game situations as they used to, blaming everything from video games to the increasing popularity of other sports. But external forces may not be entirely to blame for the decline in basketball logic. Bookstores offer dozens of drill books to help coaches teach the technical skills of basketball, and teams around the country practice those drills ad infinitum. If drills are so specific, numerous, and clever, why aren't players developing that elusive basketball sense? Perhaps just learning basketball techniques and performing drill after drill do not lead to expertise, but only to the ability to do drills.

An alternative way to teach basketball skills is the games approach. As outlined in chapter 1, the games approach allows players to take responsibility for learning skills. A good analogy is to compare the games approach in sports to the holistic method of teaching writing. Traditional approaches to teaching students to write included doing sentence-writing exercises, identifying parts of speech, and working with different types of paragraphs. After drilling students in these techniques, teachers assigned topics to write about. Teachers used this method of teaching for years. When graduating students could not write a competent essay or work application, educators began questioning the method and began to use a new approach, the holistic method. In the holistic method of teaching writing, students wrote compositions without learning parts of speech or sentence types or even ways to organize paragraphs. Teachers looked at the whole piece of writing and made suggestions for improvement from there, not worrying about spelling, grammar, or punctuation unless it was germane. This method emphasized seeing the forest instead of the trees.

This forest versus trees approach is applicable to teaching basketball skills as well. Instead of breaking down skills into their component parts and then having the athletes put the pieces back together, you can impart the whole skill and then let the athletes discover how the parts relate. This method resembles what actually occurs in a game, and learning occurs at game speed. These latter two concepts are crucial to understanding the games approach.

This method does not take you, the coach, out of the equation; in fact, you must take a more active and creative role. You must shape the play of the athletes to get the desired results, focus the attention of the athletes on the important techniques, and enhance the skill involved by attaching various challenges to the games played.

You can use the games approach to teach almost any area of the game. Instead of having two or three players shooting and rebounding at a basket and simply charting their progress, coaches could create games around the shooting workout and encourage competition. Instead of just having players do a rebounding drill, coaches could devise a way to make the drill more gamelike by shaping, focusing, and enhancing the drill. Working on a double team might be more effective if the players are put into a gamelike situation.

Step 6: Plan Your Practices

At this stage of the planning process, you should sketch a brief overview of what you want to accomplish during each practice of the season. Using the information compiled in the previous five steps, you can sketch an outline for an entire season, both practices and games. This outline is referred to as a *season plan*. Figure 7.3 shows a sample season plan based on the games approach, using a 12-week season that includes a 3-week period for postseason playoffs. (For a sample season plan based on the traditional approach, please refer to the *Coaching Basketball Technical and Tactical Skills* online course.)

This sample plan presumes that the first two weeks of the season will be devoted primarily to tryouts, with practices beginning in the third week. The early practices are more detailed and complete. After games begin, practice plans become more open ended so that you can focus on problems that may have occurred in past games and can develop practices according to the game plan (see chapter 9). The game plan should include a review of the previous game, scouting reports, and the team's overall strategy. Approaching practices in this manner helps you fine-tune practices to prepare for upcoming games. At this point in the season, the main objective of practices is to focus on the game plan, but when time permits, you should revisit key skills so that the learning process continues all season long.

Figure 7.3 Games Approach Season Plan

		Purpose	New skills to introduce
WEEK 1 (PRESEASON)	**Practice 1**	Review team expectations and evaluate players for team selection; review basic offensive and defensive technical and tactical skills.	Offensive footwork • Triple-threat position • Dribbling basics • Passing basics • Catching • Shooting basics • Layup • Defensive positioning • Defensive rebounds • Moving without the ball • On-the-ball defense • Off-the-ball defense
	Practice 2	Review the offensive technical skills of dribbling, shooting, passing, and catching; build on these skills by introducing more advanced technical and tactical skills.	Speed dribble • Control dribble • Change of pace dribble • Chest pass • Set shot • Offensive rebounds • Cuts • Screens • Defending cuts • Defending screens • Applying pressure • Forcing shooters out of position • Protecting the basket • Trapping the ball • Defending the give-and-go • Defending the backdoor cut • Fighting over the top of a screen
	Practice 3	Expand on the offensive technical skills of dribbling, shooting, and passing by introducing more advanced skills; also introduce post skills, the fast break, and the give-and-go. Build on skills related to screens.	Reverse dribble • Crossover dribble • Overhead pass • Jump shot • Playing the post • Skip pass • Give-and-go • Fast break • Backdoor cut • Limiting fast break opportunities • Trapping the ball • Defending the pass • Defending the give-and-go • Defending the backdoor cut • Switching on a screen
	Practice 4	Build on passing skills by introducing additional types of passes; introduce the pick-and-roll and expand on skills related to screens and cuts. Also, introduce man defense and how to play against a man defense.	Sidearm pass • Behind-the-back pass • Defending the post • Playing against man defense • Flash cut • Pick-and-roll • Cross screen • Playing man defense • Help and recover • Taking a charge • Defending the flash cut
	Practice 5	Expand on basic technical and tactical skills by teaching players how to penetrate and pass, how to use the inside-out pass, how to trap the ball, and how to double team the post. Introduce zone defense and how to play against a zone.	Playing against zone defense • Inside-out pass • Penetrate and pass • Playing zone defense • Trapping the ball • Double teaming the post
WEEK 2 (PRESEASON)	**Practice 6**	Help players refine previously taught skills; introduce blocking shots and running inbounds plays.	Blocking shots • Running inbounds plays
	Practice 7	Hold a scrimmage.	
	Practice 8	Skill work will depend on the outcome of the previous scrimmage. Take time in this practice to refine skills that need work and to prepare players for the next day's scrimmage.	Review skills as necessary.
	Practice 9	Hold a scrimmage.	
	Practice 10	Skill work will depend on the outcome of the previous scrimmage. Take time in this practice to refine skills that need work.	Review skills as necessary.

(continued)

Figure 7.3 *(continued)*

		Purpose	New skills to introduce
WEEK 3 (IN-SEASON)	**Practice 11**	Prepare for game 1.	Review skills as identified in the game plan.
	[Game 1]		
	Practice 12	Review game 1. Discuss the next opponent and view video of that opponent; work on offensive and defensive technical skills.	Review skills as necessary.
	Practice 13	Prepare for game 2. Work on offensive and defensive technical skills; review tactical skills based on game situations; and review both man and zone defenses.	Review skills as necessary.
	[Game 2]		
WEEK 4 (IN-SEASON)	**Practice 14**	Review game 2. Prepare for game 3; fine-tune offensive and defensive technical and tactical skills.	Review skills as necessary.
	[Game 3]		
	Practice 15	Review game 3. Work on offensive and defensive technical skills that need improvement.	Review skills as necessary.
	Practice 16	Prepare for game 4. Work on offensive and defensive technical skills; review tactical skills based on game situations.	Review skills as necessary.
	[Game 4]		
WEEK 5 (IN-SEASON)	**Practice 17**	Review game 4. Refine offensive and defensive technical and tactical skills; prepare for game 5.	Review skills as necessary.
	[Game 5]		
	Practice 18	Review game 5.	Review skills as necessary.
	Practice 19	Prepare for game 6.	Review skills as necessary.
	[Game 6]		
WEEK 6 (IN-SEASON)	**Practice 20**	Review game 6; prepare for game 7.	Review skills as necessary.
	[Game 7]		
	Practice 21	Review game 7.	Review skills as necessary.
	Practice 22	Prepare for game 8.	Review skills as necessary.
	[Game 8]		
WEEK 7 (IN-SEASON)	**Practice 23**	Review game 8; prepare for game 9.	Review skills as necessary.
	[Game 9]		
	Practice 24	Review game 9.	Review skills as necessary.
	Practice 25	Prepare for game 10.	Review skills as necessary.
	[Game 10]		

	Purpose	New skills to introduce
WEEK 8 (IN-SEASON)		
Practice 26	Review game 10; prepare for game 11.	Review skills as necessary.
[Game 11]		
Practice 27	Review game 11.	Review skills as necessary.
Practice 28	Prepare for game 12.	Review skills as necessary.
[Game 12]		
WEEK 9 (IN-SEASON)		
Practice 29	Review game 12; prepare for game 13.	Review skills as necessary.
[Game 13]		
Practice 30	Review game 13.	Review skills as necessary.
Practice 31	Prepare for game 14.	Review skills as necessary.
[Game 14]		
WEEK 10 (IN-SEASON)		
Practice 32	Review game 14; prepare for game 15.	Review skills as necessary.
[Game 15]		
Practice 33	Review game 15.	Review skills as necessary.
Practice 34	Prepare for game 16.	Review skills as necessary.
[Game 16]		
WEEK 11 (IN-SEASON)		
Practice 35	Review game 16; prepare for game 17.	Review skills as necessary.
[Game 17]		
Practice 36	Review game 17.	Review skills as necessary.
Practice 37	Prepare for game 18.	Review skills as necessary.
[Game 18]		
WEEK 12 (IN-SEASON)		
Practice 38	Review game 18; prepare for game 19.	Review skills as necessary.
[Game 19]		
Practice 39	Review game 19.	Review skills as necessary.
Practice 40	Prepare for game 20.	Review skills as necessary.
[Game 20]		
WEEK 13 (POSTSEASON)		
Playoffs		

Although the plan in figure 7.3 is shown in isolation, you can employ both approaches in your season plan. You may feel more comfortable teaching shooting by using the traditional approach but may find that the games approach works better for you when teaching screens. Remember to work through the six steps yourself to create a season plan that is best suited for your team.

After completing the season plan, you can further refine step 6 of the process by adding specifics about the individual practices. The next chapter helps you in this procedure by showing the components of a good practice session and providing a sample of the games approach to practices.

chapter 8

Practice Plans

To get the most out of your practice sessions, you must plan every practice. Completing the season plan (as described in the previous chapter) helps you do this. But you have to take that season plan a step further and specify in detail what you will be doing at every practice.

As described in *Successful Coaching, Third Edition*, every practice plan should include the following:

- Date, start time, and length of the practice session
- Objective of the practice
- Equipment needed
- Warm-up
- Practice of previously taught skills
- Teaching and practicing of new skills
- Cool-down
- Coaches' comments
- Evaluation of the practice

Using those elements, we have developed eight sample practice plans based on the season plan in chapter 7 (see figure 7.3 on page 219). These practice plans provide an example of the games approach to practices. The early practices focus on basketball as a whole, including the essential tactical skills. Then, as players need to refine technical skills, those skills are brought into the practices. Focused games are used to work on specific skills in the practice sessions. When athletes play focused games early in the season, they quickly discover their weaknesses and become more motivated to improve their skills so that they can perform better in game situations.

PRACTICE 1

Date

Monday, November 14

Practice Start Time

3:20 p.m.

Length of Practice

2 hours, 10 minutes

Practice Objectives

- Work on team conditioning (include a proper warm-up and cool-down).
- Evaluate players for varsity squad selection.
- Review basic offensive and defensive technical skills.
- Review basic offensive and defensive tactical skills.

Time	Name of activity	Description	Key teaching points
3:20–3:30	Prepractice meeting and team building	Explain the evaluation procedures to be used for selecting players for the team and assigning players to various squads (e.g., varsity, JV); review expectations for players.	• Teamwork • Dedication
3:30–3:50	Warm-up	Players jump rope, do push-ups and sit-ups, and play a running and dribbling game against the clock. The team then stretches for flexibility.	• Offensive footwork • Dribbling basics
3:50–3:55	Station time	Set up 8 stations throughout the gym. Players are at each station for 45 seconds, with 15 seconds to transition between stations.	• Offensive footwork • Dribbling basics • Passing basics • Catching • Shooting basics • Defensive rebounds
3:55–4:00	Water break		
4:00–4:10	Passing and Fast Break game	Players play a full-court passing game in which 3 offensive players use proper spacing while trying to gain an advantage over 2 defenders. The player who scores goes back on defense, and the 2 defenders begin a 2-on-1 situation against that player.	• Offensive footwork • Triple-threat position • Dribbling basics • Shooting basics • Defensive positioning • Moving without the ball
4:10–4:25	Shooting drills	Players perform various drills at 6 baskets to work on shooting.	• Triple-threat position • Shooting basics • Layup
4:25–4:30	Water break		

Time	Name of activity	Description	Key teaching points
4:30–4:40	Defensive Rebounding game	Three defenders are positioned 8 to 10 feet from the basket (at the wing areas and the middle of the key), and the remaining players form 3 equal lines directly behind these 3 players. The coach shoots a missed shot, which initiates the game. All 3 defenders box out the first person in their line, who is also trying to get the ball. After rebounding the ball, the defender makes an outlet pass to the next player in line. Three consecutive rebounds and successful outlets must be made before rotating.	• Defensive positioning • Defensive rebounds • Off-the-ball defense
4:40–4:50	5-Player Passing drill	Players perform a 5-player weaving drill with a layup as the end goal.	• Offensive footwork • Passing basics • Catching • Layup
4:50–5:05	3-Lane Passing game	Separate the team into 3 equal lines at the baseline. Players play a 3-on-3 game where 3 offensive players try to advance the ball up the court against 3 defenders. Remind the players that they must stay in their lanes, they cannot dribble, and they must always pass back to the middle lane.	• Offensive footwork • Triple-threat position • Passing basics • Catching • Moving without the ball • On-the-ball defense • Off-the-ball defense
5:05–5:10	5-Minute Layup game (right)	Divide the team into 2 equal groups at opposite baselines. When the clock starts (counting down from 5 minutes), the first person in each line throws a ball up into the right lane and sprints after it. Then, they speed dribble into a right-handed layup. The next person grabs the rebound and repeats the process. A team goal can be set for the number of layups made within the 5-minute period (e.g., 80 layups).	• Dribbling basics • Layup
5:10–5:25	Cool-down and stretching	Light jog followed by static stretching.	
5:25–5:30	Coach's comments	Communicate any reminders or end-of-practice comments; discuss criteria for making the teams.	• General comments and feedback • Importance of teamwork and effort
5:30–5:45	Coaches' meeting	Meet in the coach's office to assess the day's practice and discuss the next practice; also discuss player evaluations.	

PRACTICE 2

Date

Tuesday, November 15

Practice Start Time

3:20 p.m.

Length of Practice

2 hours, 10 minutes

Practice Objectives

- Work on team conditioning (include a proper warm-up and cool-down).
- Review the offensive technical skills of dribbling, shooting, passing, and catching.
- Introduce advanced technical and tactical skills such as cuts, screens, protecting the basket and forcing shooters out of position, and trapping the ball.

Time	Name of activity	Description	Key teaching points
3:20–3:30	Prepractice meeting and team building	Review the procedures to be used for selecting players for the team and assigning players to various squads (e.g., varsity, JV). Go over expectations for players.	• Teamwork • Dedication
3:30–3:50	Warm-up	Players jump rope, do push-ups and sit-ups, and play a running and dribbling game against the clock. The team then stretches for flexibility.	• Offensive footwork • Dribbling basics • Speed dribble • Control dribble • Change of pace dribble • Chest pass • Bounce pass
3:50–3:55	Station time	Set up 6 to 8 stations throughout the gym to practice footwork, dribbling, passing, catching, shooting, and rebounding skills. Players are at each station for 45 seconds, with 15 seconds to transition between stations.	• Offensive footwork • Dribbling basics • Passing basics • Catching • Shooting basics • Defensive rebounds
3:55–4:00	Water break		
4:00–4:05	Passing and Fast Break game	Players play a full-court passing game in which 3 offensive players use proper spacing while trying to gain an advantage over 2 defenders. The player who scores goes back on defense, and the 2 defenders begin a 2-on-1 situation against that player.	• Offensive footwork • Triple-threat position • Dribbling basics • Shooting basics • Defensive positioning • Moving without the ball
4:05–4:20	Shooting drills (at 6 baskets)	Players perform various drills to work on shooting the set shot and the layup.	• Shooting basics • Set shot • Layup
4:20–4:25	Water break		

Time	Name of activity	Description	Key teaching points
4:25–4:35	Offensive Rebounding game	Three defenders are positioned 8 to 10 feet from the basket (at the wing areas and the middle of the key), and the remaining players form 3 equal lines directly behind these 3 players. The coach shoots a missed shot, which initiates the game. All 3 defensive players box out the first person in their line, and the offensive players make a move to gain position for an offensive rebound and put back. Three consecutive offensive rebounds and successful shots must be made before rotating.	• Offensive rebounds • Defensive positioning • Defensive rebounds • Off-the-ball defense
4:35–5:00	4-on-4-on-4 Full-Court game	Four players are on offense at one end against the defensive team. The offense will run a 2-2 set and will screen and cut after every pass. When the defense gets the ball, they will fast break to the other end against 4 other players who will be waiting. The offense that lost possession will play defense against the breaking team until they get to half court. Remind players that no switches on screens are allowed.	• Cuts • Screens • Defending cuts • Defending screens • Forcing shooters out of position • Protecting the basket • Fighting over the top of a screen
5:00–5:05	Water break		
5:05–5:15	3-Lane Passing game	Separate the team into 3 equal lines at the baseline. Players play a 3-on-3 game where 3 offensive players try to advance the ball up the court against 3 defenders. Remind the players that they must stay in their lanes, they cannot dribble, and they must always pass back to the middle lane.	• Offensive footwork • Triple-threat position • Passing basics • Catching • Moving without the ball • On-the-ball defense • Off-the-ball defense
5:15–5:20	5-Minute Layup game (left)	Divide the team into 2 equal groups at opposite baselines. When the clock starts (counting down from 5 minutes), the first person in each line throws a ball up into the left lane and sprints after it. Then, they speed dribble into a left-handed layup. The next person grabs the rebound and repeats the process. A team goal can be set for the number of layups made within the 5-minute period (e.g., 80 layups).	• Dribbling basics • Layup
5:20–5:25	Cool-down and stretching	Light jog followed by static stretching.	
5:25–5:30	Coach's comments	Communicate any reminders or end-of-practice comments.	• General comments and feedback • Importance of teamwork and effort
5:30–5:45	Coaches' meeting	Meet in the coach's office to assess the day's practice and discuss the next practice.	

PRACTICE 3

Date

Wednesday, November 16

Practice Start Time

3:20 p.m.

Length of Practice

2 hours, 10 minutes

Practice Objectives

- Work on team conditioning (include a proper warm-up and cool-down).
- Expand on the offensive technical skills of dribbling, shooting, and passing by reviewing more advanced skills.
- Introduce post skills, the fast break, and the give-and-go.
- Expand on skills related to screens.

Time	Name of activity	Description	Key teaching points
3:20–3:30	Prepractice meeting and team building	Discuss motivational goals for the day; review expectations for players.	• Teamwork • Dedication
3:30–3:50	Warm-up	Players jump rope, do push-ups and sit-ups, and play a running and dribbling game against the clock. The team then stretches for flexibility.	• Offensive footwork • Dribbling basics • Speed dribble • Control dribble • Reverse dribble • Crossover dribble • Change of pace dribble
3:50–3:55	Station time	Set up 6 to 8 stations throughout the gym to practice footwork, dribbling, passing, catching, shooting, and rebounding skills. Players are at each station for 45 seconds, with 15 seconds to transition between stations.	• Offensive footwork • Dribbling basics • Passing basics • Catching • Shooting basics • Offensive rebounds • Defensive rebounds
3:55–4:00	Water break		
4:00–4:10	The Breaking game	Players perform a full-court 5-player weave where the players focus on the fast break after completing their layup. Emphasize proper spacing and ball movement on the fast break.	• Offensive footwork • Passing basics • Chest pass • Baseball pass • Catching • Moving without the ball • Skip pass • Give-and-go • Backdoor cut
4:10–4:25	Shooting drills (at 6 baskets)	Players perform various drills to work on shooting the jump shot and other basic shooting skills.	• Triple-threat position • Shooting basics • Set shot • Jump shot • Layup • Playing the post

Time	Name of activity	Description	Key teaching points
4:25–4:30	Water break		
4:30–4:40	Defensive Shell game	Separate the team into 3 equal groups—1 team on offense, 1 team on defense, and 1 team under the basket. The players play a 4-on-4 game where the 4 offensive players use the give-and-go and the backdoor cut to gain an advantage over their defenders. After the offensive team scores 3 baskets, it goes to defense, the defensive team goes out, and a new team comes in on offense.	• Give-and-go • Backdoor cut • Defending the pass • Defending the give-and-go • Defending the backdoor cut
4:40–4:50	Switching Screens game	Players play a 4-on-4-on-4 full-court game where 4 players are on offense at one end against the defensive team. The offense will run a 2-2 set and will screen and cut after every pass. When the defense gets the ball, they will fast break to the other end against 4 other players who will be waiting. The offense that lost possession will play defense against the breaking team until they get to half court. Switching on screens is encouraged in this game.	• Give-and-go • Fast break • Backdoor cut • Defending the give-and-go • Defending the backdoor cut • Switching on a screen
4:50–5:05	Catching Up game	Players play a game in which 4 offensive players attack 2 defenders, while 2 other defenders who start behind the offensive players sprint to catch up and stop the break (making it a 4-on-4 situation).	• Fast break • Applying pressure • Limiting fast break opportunities
5:05–5:10	5-Minute Layup game (right)	Divide the team into 2 equal groups at opposite baselines. When the clock starts (counting down from 5 minutes), the first person in each line throws a ball up into the right lane and sprints after it. Then, they speed dribble into a right-handed layup. The next person grabs the rebound and repeats the process. A team goal can be set for the number of layups made within the 5-minute period (e.g., 80 layups).	• Dribbling basics • Layup
5:10–5:25	Cool-down and stretching	Light jog followed by static stretching.	
5:25–5:30	Coach's comments	Communicate any reminders or end-of-practice comments.	• General comments and feedback • Importance of teamwork and effort
5:30–5:45	Coaches' meeting	Meet in the coach's office to assess the day's practice and discuss the next practice.	

PRACTICE 4

Date

Thursday, November 17

Practice Start Time

3:20 p.m.

Length of Practice

2 hours, 10 minutes

Practice Objectives

- Work on team conditioning (include a proper warm-up and cool-down).
- Expand on passing skills by introducing additional types of passes.
- Introduce the pick-and-roll.
- Expand on skills related to screens and cuts.
- Introduce man defense and how to play against a man defense.

Time	Name of activity	Description	Key teaching points
3:20–3:30	Prepractice meeting and team building	Take time to review academic expectations, as well as to build up the team for the upcoming practice.	• Teamwork • Dedication
3:30–3:50	Warm-up	Players jump rope, do push-ups and sit-ups, and play a running and dribbling game against the clock. The team then stretches for flexibility.	• Offensive footwork • Dribbling basics
3:50–3:55	Station time	Set up 6 to 8 stations throughout the gym to practice footwork, dribbling, passing, catching, shooting, and rebounding skills. Players are at each station for 45 seconds, with 15 seconds to transition between stations.	• Offensive footwork • Dribbling basics • Sidearm pass • Behind-the-back pass • Catching • Shooting basics • Defensive rebounds
3:55–4:00	Water break		
4:00–4:10	Breaking Off the Missed Shot game	Players play a full-court game where the coach's missed shot initiates the game. Five defensive players get in good rebounding position and start the break after the shot.	• Overhead pass • Defensive rebounds • Moving without the ball • Fast break • Flash cut
4:10–4:25	Shooting drills	Players perform various drills at 6 baskets to work on shooting.	• Triple-threat position • Shooting basics • Set shot • Jump shot • Playing the post
4:25–4:30	Water break		

Time	Name of activity	Description	Key teaching points
4:30–4:40	The Cut and Screen game	Separate the team into 3 equal groups—1 team on offense, 1 team on defense, and 1 team under the basket. Players play a 4-on-4 game where the 4 offensive players use the flash cut, pick-and-roll, and cross screen to gain an advantage over their defenders. After the offensive team scores 3 baskets, the offensive team goes to defense, the defensive team goes out, and a new team comes in on offense.	• Flash cut • Pick-and-roll • Cross screen • Help and recover • Defending the flash cut
4:40–4:50	In the Pit game	Two players play a 1-on-1 post game, with 3 other offensive players on the perimeter to make passes into the post. The offensive post player uses his or her post moves to gain an advantage over the defender. Remind players that no lob passes are allowed in this game.	• Chest pass • Bounce pass • Overhead pass • Sidearm pass • Playing the post • Defending the post • Flash cut • Defending the flash cut
4:50–5:05	Man-to-Man game	Separate the team into 3 equal groups—1 team on offense, 1 team on defense, and 1 team under the basket. Players play a 4-on-4 game where the 4 defensive players work on man defense principles. After the defensive team stops 3 attempts, the defensive team goes out, the offensive team goes to defense, and a new team comes in on offense.	• Playing the post • Defensive positioning • Defending the post • Playing against man defense • Flash cut • Pick-and-roll • Cross screen • Help and recover • Taking a charge • Defending the flash cut
5:05–5:10	5-Minute Layup game (left)	Divide the team into 2 equal groups at opposite baselines. When the clock starts (counting down from 5 minutes), the first person in each line throws a ball up into the left lane and sprints after it. Then, they speed dribble into a left-handed layup. The next person grabs the rebound and repeats the process. A team goal can be set for the number of layups made within the 5-minute period (e.g., 80 layups).	• Dribbling basics • Layup
5:10–5:25	Cool-down and stretching	Light jog followed by static stretching.	
5:25–5:30	Coach's comments	Communicate any reminders or end-of-practice comments.	• General comments and feedback • Importance of teamwork and effort
5:30–5:45	Coaches' meeting	Meet in the coach's office to assess the day's practice and discuss the next practice.	

PRACTICE 5

Date

Friday, November 18

Practice Start Time

3:20 p.m.

Length of Practice

2 hours, 10 minutes

Practice Objectives

- Work on team conditioning (include a proper warm-up and cool-down).
- Expand on basic technical and tactical skills by teaching players how to penetrate and pass, how to use the inside-out pass, how to trap the ball, and how to double team the post.
- Introduce zone defense and how to play against a zone.

Time	Name of activity	Description	Key teaching points
3:20–3:30	Prepractice meeting and team building	Review the evaluation procedures to be used for selecting players for the team and assigning players to various squads (e.g., varsity, JV). Discuss expectations for players.	• Teamwork • Dedication
3:30–3:50	Warm-up	Players jump rope, do push-ups and sit-ups, and play a running and dribbling game against the clock. The team then stretches for flexibility.	• Offensive footwork • Dribbling basics
3:50–3:55	Station time	Set up 6 to 8 stations throughout the gym to practice footwork, dribbling, passing, catching, shooting, and rebounding skills. Players are at each station for 45 seconds, with 15 seconds to transition between stations.	• Offensive footwork • Dribbling basics • Passing basics • Catching • Jump shot • Defensive rebounds
3:55–4:00	Water break		
4:00–4:10	The Breaking game	Players perform a full-court 5-player weave where the players focus on the fast break after completing their layup. Emphasize proper spacing and ball movement on the fast break.	• Offensive footwork • Passing basics • Chest pass • Baseball pass • Catching • Moving without the ball • Skip pass • Give-and-go • Backdoor cut
4:10–4:25	Shooting drills (at 6 baskets)	Players perform various drills to work on shooting the jump shot, the free throw, and the 3-point shot.	• Triple-threat position • Shooting basics • Jump shot • Playing the post
4:25–4:30	Water break		

Time	Name of activity	Description	Key teaching points
4:30–4:40	Double In the Pit game	Four players play a 2-on-2 post game, with 3 other offensive players on the perimeter to make passes into the post. The offensive post players use their post moves to gain an advantage over their defenders. Remind players that no lob passes are allowed in this game.	• Chest pass • Bounce pass • Overhead pass • Playing the post • Inside-out pass • Flash cut • Defending the flash cut • Double teaming the post
4:40–4:50	5-Player Passing drill	Players perform a 5-player weaving drill with a layup as the end goal.	• Offensive footwork • Passing basics • Catching • Layup
4:50–5:05	The Zone game	Players play a 5-on-5 full-court game where the 5 defensive players work on zone defense principles. After the defensive team stops 3 attempts, the defensive and offensive teams switch. Take time to work on the full-court press.	• Playing against zone defense • Inside-out pass • Penetrate and pass • Playing zone defense • Trapping the ball • Double teaming the post
5:05–5:10	5-Minute Layup game (right)	Divide the team into 2 equal groups at opposite baselines. When the clock starts (counting down from 5 minutes), the first person in each line throws a ball up into the right lane and sprints after it. Then, they speed dribble into a right-handed layup. The next person grabs the rebound and repeats the process. A team goal can be set for the number of layups made within the 5-minute period (e.g., 80 layups).	• Dribbling basics • Layup
5:10–5:25	Cool-down and stretching	Light jog followed by static stretching.	
5:25–5:30	Coach's comments	Communicate any reminders or end-of-practice comments.	• General comments and feedback • Importance of teamwork and effort
5:30–5:45	Coaches' meeting	Meet in the coach's office to assess the day's practice and discuss the next practice.	

PRACTICE 6

Date

Monday, November 21

Practice Start Time

3:20 p.m.

Length of Practice

2 hours, 10 minutes

Practice Objectives

- Work on team conditioning (include a proper warm-up and cool-down).
- Help players refine previously taught skills.
- Introduce blocking shots and running inbounds plays.

Time	Name of activity	Description	Key teaching points
3:20–3:30	Prepractice meeting and team building	Discuss team goals.	• Teamwork • Dedication
3:30–3:50	Warm-up	Players jump rope, do push-ups and sit-ups, and play a running and dribbling game against the clock. The team then stretches for flexibility.	• Offensive footwork • Dribbling basics
3:50–3:55	Station time	Set up 8 stations throughout the gym. Players are at each station for 45 seconds, with 15 seconds to transition between stations.	• Offensive footwork • Dribbling basics • Passing basics • Catching • Shooting basics • Defensive rebounds
3:55–4:00	Water break		
4:00–4:10	Passing and Fast Break game	Players play a full-court passing game in which 3 offensive players use proper spacing while trying to gain an advantage over 2 defenders. The player who scores goes back on defense, and the 2 defenders begin a 2-on-1 situation against that player.	• Offensive footwork • Triple-threat position • Dribbling basics • Shooting basics • Defensive positioning • Moving without the ball
4:10–4:25	Shooting drills (at 6 baskets)	Players perform various drills to work on shooting the jump shot, the free throw, and the 3-point shot.	• Triple-threat position • Shooting basics • Jump shot • Playing the post
4:25–4:30	Water break		

Time	Name of activity	Description	Key teaching points
4:30–4:45	Man-to-Man game	Separate the team into 3 equal groups—1 team on offense, 1 team on defense, and 1 team under the basket. Players play a 5-on-5 full-court game where the 5 defensive players work on man defense principles. After the defensive team stops 3 attempts, the defensive team goes out, the offensive team goes to defense, and a new team comes in on offense. Take time to work on the full-court press.	• Offensive rebounds • Playing the post • Defensive positioning • Defensive rebounds • Defending the post • Playing against man defense • Flash cut • Pick-and-roll • Cross screen • Help and recover • Taking a charge • Defending the flash cut
4:45–4:55	Shot-blocking drills	Players perform drills to work on blocking shots.	• Defensive positioning • Blocking shots
4:55–5:10	The Zone game	Players play a 5-on-5 half-court game where the 5 defensive players work on zone defense principles. After the defensive team stops 3 attempts, the defense and offense switch.	• Playing against zone defense • Inside-out pass • Penetrate and pass • Playing zone defense • Trapping the ball • Double teaming the post
5:10–5:20	Inbounds plays	Work on team inbounds plays.	• Cuts • Screens • Moving without the ball • Running inbounds plays
5:20–5:25	Cool-down and stretching	Light jog followed by static stretching.	
5:25–5:30	Coach's comments	Communicate any reminders or end-of-practice comments.	• General comments and feedback • Importance of teamwork and effort
5:30–5:45	Coaches' meeting	Meet in the coach's office to assess the day's practice and discuss the next practice.	

PRACTICE 7

Date

Tuesday, November 22

Practice Start Time

3:20 p.m.

Length of Practice

3 hours

Practice Objectives

- Work on team conditioning (include a proper warm-up and cool-down).
- Allow players to practice and refine skills in a competitive environment.

Time	Name of activity	Description	Key teaching points
3:20–3:30	Prescrimmage meeting and team building	Discuss the game plan.	• Teamwork • Dedication
3:30–3:50	Warm-up	Players perform layup drills and then stretch for flexibility.	• Passing basics • Shooting basics • Layup
3:50–6:00	Scrimmage		
6:00–6:10	Cool-down and stretching	Light jog followed by static stretching.	
6:10–6:20	Coach's comments	Use this time to evaluate the scrimmage.	• Focus on being positive. • Emphasize areas to improve
6:20–6:30	Coaches' meeting	Meet in the coach's office to assess the day's scrimmage. Focus on skills to refine in the next practice.	

Date

Wednesday, November 23

Practice Start Time

3:20 p.m.

Length of Practice

2 hours, 10 minutes

Practice Objectives

- Work on team conditioning (include a proper warm-up and cool-down).
- Review skills based on the outcome of the previous day's scrimmage, and help players refine skills that need further work.
- Prepare the team for the next practice's scrimmage.

Time	Name of activity	Description	Key teaching points
3:20–3:30	Prepractice meeting and team building	Touch on the previous day's scrimmage, again emphasizing positive elements while focusing on areas that need improvement.	• Teamwork • Dedication
3:30–3:50	Warm-up	Players jump rope, do push-ups and sit-ups, and play a running and dribbling game against the clock. The team then stretches for flexibility.	• Offensive footwork • Dribbling basics
3:50–3:55	Station time	Set up 8 stations throughout the gym. Players are at each station for 45 seconds, with 15 seconds to transition between stations.	• Offensive footwork • Dribbling basics • Passing basics • Catching • Shooting basics • Defensive rebounds
3:55–4:00	Water break		
4:00–4:10	Game TBD	Use this period to focus on one of the areas that need improvement based on the players' performance in the scrimmage.	• Refining skills that need improvement based on the scrimmage
4:10–4:25	Shooting drills (at 6 baskets)	Players perform various drills to work on shooting.	• Triple-threat position • Shooting basics • Jump shot • Layup • Playing the post
4:25–4:30	Water break		
4:30–4:40	Game TBD	Use this period to focus on one of the areas that need improvement based on the players' performance in the scrimmage.	• Refining skills that need improvement based on the scrimmage

Time	Name of activity	Description	Key teaching points
4:40–4:50	The Zone game	Players play a 5-on-5 half-court game where the 5 defensive players work on zone defense principles. After the defensive team stops 3 attempts, the defense and offense switch.	• Playing against zone defense • Inside-out pass • Penetrate and pass • Playing zone defense • Trapping the ball • Double teaming the post
4:50–5:05	Man-to-Man game	Separate the team into 3 equal groups—1 team on offense, 1 team on defense, and 1 team under the basket. Players play a 4-on-4 half-court game where the 4 defensive players work on man defense principles. After the defensive team stops 3 attempts, the defensive team goes out, the offensive team goes to defense, and a new team comes in on offense.	• Offensive rebounds • Playing the post • Defensive positioning • Defensive rebounds • Defending the post • Playing against man defense • Flash cut • Pick-and-roll • Cross screen • Help and recover • Taking a charge • Defending the flash cut
5:05–5:10	5-Minute Layup game (right)	Divide the team into 2 equal groups at opposite baselines. When the clock starts (counting down from 5 minutes), the first person in each line throws a ball up into the right lane and sprints after it. Then, they speed dribble into a right-handed layup. The next person grabs the rebound and repeats the process. A team goal can be set for the number of layups made within the 5-minute period (e.g., 80 layups).	• Dribbling basics • Layup
5:10–5:25	Cool-down and stretching	Light jog followed by static stretching.	
5:25–5:30	Coach's comments	Communicate any reminders or end-of-practice comments.	• General comments and feedback • Importance of teamwork and effort
5:30–5:45	Coaches' meeting	Meet in the coach's office to assess the day's practice and discuss the next practice.	

Game Coaching

You can plan and you can practice all day long. But if your team does not perform to the best of its ability during your games, what has all that planning and practicing done for you? Part V will help you prepare for game situations.

In chapter 9, we describe how you can begin to prepare long before the first game, covering issues such as communication, scouting the opponent, and creating a game plan. Chapter 10 focuses on how to be ready to make decisions during and after the game. We include information on making substitutions, calling time-outs, talking with the press, and speaking with your players after the game.

After all the time and effort you have put into preparation, game day is when it really becomes exciting, especially if you and your team are ready for the challenge.

chapter 9

Preparing for Games

The performance of a basketball team on game day reflects its preparation. A well-prepared team will be fundamentally sound, organized, and efficient, opening the game with a strong attack and handling crucial situations effectively because the players have rehearsed those situations. In the following sections, we discuss the areas that you should consider when preparing yourself and your team for a game.

Communication

As a coach, you must communicate well at many levels—with players, team captains, coaching staff, school and community officials, parents, game officials, and the media. You must be aware of your nonverbal communication because it can be just as loud as what you say verbally.

Players

When you communicate well, you engage your players in the learning process. When players become partners and have a stake in their own development, you become a facilitator, not merely a teacher. The players' participation in the learning process is the key to the games approach and what makes it such a valuable approach to coaching. Although shaping, focusing, and enhancing play is difficult, it is ultimately more rewarding because it allows players to take ownership of their development.

As part of the communication process, you should assemble a team manual that contains notes on the season plan, information on basic technical skills, and a summarized review of the tactical skills that will be covered. Distribute this resource to players several weeks before the first day of practice. The manual should not be too long, because the longer it is, the less apt the athletes are to read it. Meet with players often and encourage them to study the manual thoroughly.

Before the beginning of a season, you should prepare a list of expectations that outlines the policies that you expect players to follow. The term *expectations* is preferable to the term *rules*, which conveys a sense of rigidity. The term *expectations* also communicates to players that they are responsible for living up to them. The coaching staff must reinforce expectations daily so that they become second nature to the team. Any breaches of discipline that arise should be handled immediately and evenhandedly. You must treat all players alike, starters no differently than subs. Finally, you should make sure that your list of expectations covers any exigency that may occur in your local situation.

You may decide to have the team elect captains, who can then assist you in communicating to the team. Emphasize to captains that their main role is to help make their teammates better players, not to order them around. Show captains the many ways to accomplish that—by encouraging teammates, by helping them work on their skills, by supporting them, and by modeling good practice habits.

Parents

Before the season begins, you should schedule a preseason meeting with the parents of all basketball candidates, separate from the meeting that most schools already sponsor during each sport season. A few weeks before the season begins, you should mail a letter to the homes of players to invite the parents to this meeting (with an RSVP enclosed). This personal touch will pique the interest of parents and make them feel valuable to the program. A special invitation letter should go to the superintendent, the principal, and the athletic director, who should be present to explain school policies, athletic codes, and general school issues.

Prepare a simple agenda for this meeting and follow it to keep the meeting on track and to convey to parents a sense of your organizational ability. Besides setting an agenda, you should prepare and distribute a list that outlines the roles of parents, players, and coaches. Parents want to be involved in their child's progress, so stating the method of communication between parent and coach is important.

Coaching Staff

Coaches need to communicate well with their assistants. Each season, you should hold a formal preseason meeting with your coaching staff to outline expectations.

Discuss your coaching philosophy and specific techniques that you will emphasize, especially if changes have occurred from the previous year or if new members have joined the staff. You should spell out (or even write out) the roles and responsibilities of assistants or volunteer coaches, including how to deal with parents, who should be referred to you. Assistants should be firm and fast in noting breaches of discipline and bringing them to your attention.

Game Officials

Coaches must also communicate well with officials. You should treat officials as the professionals that they are, even when they are wrong. When questioning a ruling, you should approach the official slowly and respectfully. Be aware that your players will model their behavior with officials on your behavior. Because most states and leagues provide outlets for evaluations of officials, you can address shortcomings and commendations of officials through that process.

Community and Media

Involvement with the community and the media demands that you be a good communicator. You should be accommodating to the press and should instruct players on tactics for talking to the media. Players need to understand that the role of the media may come in conflict with the goals and expectations of the team. Players should respectfully answer questions that deal with games, but they should defer questions about philosophy or game management to the coaching staff. Players must be careful not to say anything derogatory about an opponent that might find its way onto an opponent's locker room bulletin board.

Scouting an Opponent

An essential step in preparing for games is to scout the opponent thoroughly and eliminate the element of surprise from the game equation. Good scouting can make practices more engaging if the players are made aware of the reasons why certain offensive or defensive plays might be successful against an upcoming opponent. Following are a few ways to help make the job of scouting easier and ultimately help players better understand how you will prepare for a particular opponent.

Video

Videotaping an opponent before your game is perhaps the best means of scouting, and sometimes you may be able to film two important opponents playing each other, thus saving you time and money. By reviewing tapes, you can develop more accurate scouting reports than you can by watching games in person, allowing you to prepare your team better for competition.

When reviewing video, you should also evaluate matchups, trying to determine how your players will compare in size, strength, and speed (or quickness) to the players whom they will be facing on the opposing team. In matchups that do not favor your player, you might consider double teaming a particular post player or trapping a very quick guard on the baseline. Conversely, with favorable matchups, you should make sure that your game plan features those advantages.

Shot Chart

Another important tool to use when scouting an opponent is a shot chart (see figure 9.1). A shot chart is used to keep track of the entire team's shot selection and accuracy for a quarter. This will help you identify both team and individual tendencies when shooting so that you can make the necessary adjustments. Shots can be charted using copies of blank court templates, which you may already have on hand for demonstrating plays or drills to your team.

When a player attempts a shot, you will write the player's number on the shot chart to designate the area on the court where the player shot the ball from. If the player makes the shot, you should circle the number, and if the player misses the shot, you should leave the number uncircled. In addition, you can note if the shot was taken off the dribble, pass, or screen by adding the letter *d*, *p*, or *s* to the shot location. The information recorded on the shot chart will tell you, for example, if a player always shoots off the dribble. You will then be able to make adjustments, such as having the defender play off the player a little until the dribble. Understanding where an individual player shoots most successfully as well as the tendencies of how the player gets open for the shot will help your players better defend this individual. In effect, your players will feel more confident when they are knowledgeable about an opponent, and their play will reflect this confidence.

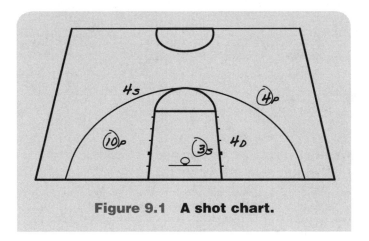

Figure 9.1　A shot chart.

Checklists

A scouting checklist will help ensure that you have adequately covered all aspects of the opponent's game. This tool is very important when watching an opponent play, and even when you have an opponent on film, you should use a checklist to help analyze the opponent.

Figures 9.2, *a* through *c*, are sample offensive, defensive, and individual checklists that can be used when scouting an opponent. These checklists will be helpful in determining how to maximize your team's strengths and capitalize on the opponent's weaknesses.

Figure 9.2a   Offensive Scouting Checklist

OFFENSIVE SET

- Does the opponent use a one- or two-guard front?
- What is the overall setup (e.g., 1-2-2, 1-3-1)?
- Does the opponent use one or two post players?
- Is the opponent playing against zone or man-to-man defense? If zone, what kind?
- What offensive pattern is the opponent using?

OFFENSIVE TENDENCIES

- Are most of the opponent's screens used on or off the ball?
- How does the opponent execute ball reversal? Is it back through the point guard, through the high post, or via the skip pass?
- From what area of the court does the opponent execute post entry passes? Is it from the wing, baseline, high-post, or point areas of the court?
- How does the post player call for the ball?
- What moves do the post players execute after receiving the pass?
- Which player or players are the playmakers?
- Do certain players look for certain teammates on the court?
- Who are the best offensive rebounders and how do they pursue the rebound?
- Who are the best free throw shooters?
- Does the opponent run a fast break? If so, is it a sideline fast break and is a secondary break executed?

OFFENSIVE PRESS BREAK

- Does the opponent clear against man-to-man defense?
- Does the opponent try to break the press with the dribble or the pass?
- Does the opponent use ball reversal?
- Does the opponent try to break the press up the sideline or up the middle?

SPECIAL SITUATIONS—OFFENSE

- Are inbounds plays made under the basket or on the sideline?
- Does the opponent attempt to fast break off the jump ball?

From ASEP, 2007, *Coaching Basketball Technical and Tactical Skills,* (Champaign, IL: Human Kinetics).

Figure 9.2b Defensive Scouting Checklist

MAN-TO-MAN DEFENSE
- Does the opponent pressure the passing lane?
- How does the opponent defend on the help side?
- How does the opponent defend the post (i.e., front or play behind)?
- How does the opponent defend the screen (i.e., fight over the top, slide through, or switch)?
- How does the opponent defend the give-and-go and backdoor cuts?
- How does the opponent defend dribble penetration? Do they push the dribbler to the side or to the middle?
- Where does help defense come from?

ZONE DEFENSE
- What kind of zone defense does the opponent run (e.g., 2-3, 1-3-1)?
- Does the opponent match up on the ball side?
- How does the opponent defend on the weak or help side?
- How does the opponent rotate on ball reversal?
- How does the opponent defend the post (i.e., front or play behind)?
- How does the opponent defend the flash cutter?
- How does the opponent defend the offensive overload?
- How does the opponent defend the high post?
- Does the opponent move on the pass?
- How does the opponent defend the dribble penetration?
- How does the opponent defend the pass penetration?
- Where is the weakest area of the zone?

DEFENSIVE PRESS
- What type of press does the opponent use?
- What is the opponent's court alignment?
- Does the opponent defend the player inbounding the ball?
- Where on the court does the opponent trap?
- Does the opponent trap before the dribble or after the dribble?
- What areas are open against the press?
- How does the press respond to ball reversal?
- Does the opponent execute any kind of run and jump?
- How does the opponent respond to ball fakes?

FAST BREAK DEFENSE
- Does the opponent get back on defense?
- Does the opponent pressure the outlet pass?
- Does the opponent defend the secondary break?

SPECIAL SITUATIONS—DEFENSE
- How does the opponent defend an inbounds play under the basket?
- How does the opponent defend a sideline inbounds play?
- How does the opponent defend the jump ball?

From ASEP, 2007, *Coaching Basketball Technical and Tactical Skills*, (Champaign, IL: Human Kinetics).

Figure 9.2c Individual Player Scouting Checklist

- Which hand is dominant when shooting, dribbling, and passing?
- Does the player use one particular move when going to the basket?
- Does the player follow his or her shot for the rebound?
- Does the player tend to shoot off the dribble, pass, or screen?
- Is this a "go to" player?
- Does the player screen for other players? If so, does the player roll to the basket from the screen?
- How does the player respond to a trap?
- How does the player move off the ball?

From ASEP, 2007, *Coaching Basketball Technical and Tactical Skills*, (Champaign, IL: Human Kinetics).

Developing the Game Plan

Although the methods you use to scout your opponent are extremely important, how you relate the information to your team is even more so. Thus, after completing and analyzing the scouting report, the coaching staff must begin the process of developing a game plan for the opponent. The game plan, simply put, identifies the particular strategies that you have chosen to give your team the best chance for success against the schemes that the opponent uses. You formulate a game plan by carefully considering the scouting report, your overall strategy, and your team's offensive and defensive capabilities. Your game plan should be specific to the opponent being played and should be based on the overall strategy that you have established for the season. The actual game plan should be clear and simple, often a one-page listing of three or four plays for the offense, one to four important defensive tactics, and any special situations that are apt to arise in the game and how you will play them.

At practice the day before the game, you should simulate your opponent's offense and defense in gamelike situations, so your team knows your game plan. Reviewing film the day before the game is also effective as long as the film is broken down into the various areas you want to emphasize.

Team Building and Motivation

Basketball is a team game. A malfunction by any of the parts of the whole can destroy the rhythm of the team. You should therefore spend quality time each day motivating players to behave as a team.

One method is to include some fun elements during practice sessions. For example, after practice one day of the first week, you can conduct a nonbasketball activity such as going to a movie or out to dinner as a team. You can make practices fun by incorporating games to stimulate players, or you can allow players to plan a Parent's Day and activities. You may also want to think about pairing returning letter winners with new players during the first week of practice; this will help the rookies learn the drills and the routine more easily and will help them gain confidence. Instilling a sense of pride in the players and making them feel a part of the process give them self-esteem. Rewarding the whole team every once in a while can be effective, especially after a difficult week of practice. These special things help build camaraderie. You should also use daily practices to motivate players. Don't wait until the pregame pep talk to do your motivating. Rah-rah talks and "Win one for the Gipper" speeches are rarely effective.

Another area in which you should play a direct role is setting individual and team goals. Tell players in advance that you expect them to write out their personal and team goals before the end of the first week of practice. To give players a concrete focus for their goals, you should create and distribute a simple fill-in-the-blanks form with space to list individual and team goals. But you cannot expect players to formulate realistic goals without assistance. You should spend a few minutes explaining the characteristics of goals—that they should provide direction, be specific, aim high but be achievable, and be written down. After players submit their goals, you should discuss them individually with the players.

To make certain that the team is always emphasized above the individual, you need to expend a lot of effort. You must never single out players or hold them above others. Doing so can lead to animosity and destroy team unity. You should try to make team members feel that they have ownership and that their opinion counts.

Controlling a Team's Performance

In preparing a game plan, you need to remind players that they can manage only their own play and have no control over the officials, the fans, and the way the other team plays. But as the coach, you can control other things in the performance arena, particularly the game routine. Established routines for pregame meetings and warm-ups help players feel relaxed.

Pregame Meeting

The pregame meeting, which should take place in either the locker room or a classroom (depending on the facility at an away game) before the warm-up, is used to embed the players' focus for the day. This meeting should emphasize the points worked on in practice and meaningful items from the scouting report.

Pregame Warm-Up

The pregame warm-up should incorporate the skills needed in a game and should be accomplished easily in less than 15 minutes. As a coach, you should work with your team before the first game and establish a set routine for the warm-up. In this warm-up routine, every player should have an opportunity to perform skills that the player will use during the game. Following is a list of some of the skills that you should be sure to include in the warm-up:

- Layups
- Three-player weave
- Three on two play
- Partner drills
- Free throws
- Open shooting

By following the preceding approaches, you can create an atmosphere of organization and certainty around your program. Through effective scouting, developing a sound game plan, and working on controlling your team's performance, you are taking steps in the direction of success.

chapter 10

During and After the Game

Coaches make dozens of tactical decisions during a game. For example, suppose that your game plan calls for pushing the ball up the court and running a fast break after every rebound. The game has reached the last two minutes of the fourth quarter, and the score is tied at 61. The opponent is getting back on defense and taking away the break. Here you should be willing to discard the game plan and take time off the clock. The ability to adjust and read the game as it develops is a critical application of the tactical triangle.

The three-step tactical triangle approach to analyzing a game situation (detailed earlier in this book) creates a blueprint for you and your players to follow in making decisions during a game. While the game is in progress, you must accurately read the cues presented, apply technical and tactical knowledge on the spot, adjust the game plan accordingly, and make decisions immediately. The logical format of the triangle helps you slow the speed of the game and apply organized, logical thinking to any situation. The following sections show how to apply the tactical triangle to several key situations that commonly occur in games.

Substitutions

Substitutions are used for a variety of reasons, and you must be prepared to substitute players during a game. The most common reasons for substitutions are as follows:

- A player on the court needs a break.
- A player on the court is in foul trouble.
- A player on the court is not performing as expected.
- There is a mismatch in personnel on the court.
- The coach wants to make a change in strategy.
- The coach may want to give another player an opportunity.
- The score of the game is lopsided—starters should be out of the game at that time.

If you lay the groundwork daily in practice and communicate the idea that players must play roles, then substitution will not cause an ego crisis. Substitution problems can be eliminated if all players learn a second position. Players should practice this second position often during the week. Doing this creates the belief that other players can play every position and that the team will not suffer when the "normal" defense is not in place. By working hard in word and action to make each player feel valuable, you can overcome the "me" attitude prevalent in sport today. You will know that you have been successful when the player taken out of the game becomes the biggest cheerleader for the sub. Working to make every player adept at a second position creates team depth and versatility and contributes to the team-building process.

When planning substitutions and alternative positions, however, you must bear in mind the talents of each player. Do you need someone to rebound on the defensive end? Do you need someone to attack the press better? Once again, the game plan comes into play. How is the team carrying out the game plan? Is the game plan working? Do you need to make adjustments? Do those adjustments need to be made with different players? Remember that even the most carefully laid plans for substitutions must remain flexible so that you can make adjustments based on the game. Make players aware that fluctuating game situations may force you to alter the game plan on the fly, adversely affecting their playing time. Again, open communication can help soothe feelings.

You should teach players that they must communicate with each other when entering and leaving the game on a substitution. Both players should make eye contact and physical contact, and the player leaving the game should verbally indicate the player whom he or she was guarding. The player leaving the game should then take a seat next to the head coach for instructions.

Time-Outs

Time-outs, when used efficiently, can offer valuable time for coaches to communicate with their team. The NFHS (National Federation of State High School Associations) rules specify that each team is allowed five time-outs—three 60-second time-outs and two 30-second time-outs. In addition to this, there is a 1-minute time-out after the first and third quarter and a 10-minute halftime intermission.

During any type of time-out, you must be organized and prepared to discuss strategy and other game concerns. For example, assume an opponent is trapping your point guard as he or she crosses the half-court line and has successfully caused a turnover the last two times down the court. You must make adjustments to create ball reversal with a pass before the guard crosses the centerline. You can help your players better understand the adjustments you want to make by diagramming them on a clipboard, clearly illustrating when you want the players to make the pass, where you want the receiver to be, and how players will move on the pass. When communicating with your team during a time-out, you must be clear, concise, positive, and calm. You should keep your agenda simple, because too much information can be overwhelming. Your players must understand that they are expected to focus on the coach during the time-out and not be distracted by outside influences.

Halftime

The halftime break can also be used to communicate with your players about the game. The NFHS allows 10 minutes for halftime, so your time must be very well organized. During the first few minutes, the players should catch their breath and go to the bathroom if needed. During that time, the coaching staff should meet outside the locker room to discuss adjustments that need to be made for the second half. You need to examine the stat sheet and be aware of foul situations for both teams. After this, several minutes should be spent communicating to the team about the one or two most important adjustments to make on offense and defense. Use a chalkboard for clarity and be very specific. To wrap things up, you will want to conclude on a positive note before the players go back out onto the court.

Overtime

If the score is tied at the final buzzer, the game will go into overtime. An overtime period, according to the NFHS, is an additional four-minute period to be played after regulation time expires. The teams will play as many overtime periods as necessary until one team wins the game. The teams report to the bench for a one-minute time-out after regulation before the overtime period begins. Each team is also given an additional time-out for this overtime period. Any time-out not yet used by a team will carry over to the overtime period.

Regardless of the reason a game goes into overtime, you must be positive with your team. If your opponent made a comeback and tied it at the buzzer, you should convince your team that they must regain the momentum, and you should identify the strategies you will incorporate to establish that momentum. If, on the other hand, your team has the momentum with a late comeback, you must work at continuing that momentum into the overtime. In either situation, you must be very clear and concise with the plan for the overtime period.

In the time-out before the overtime, you should take the first 15 to 20 seconds to meet with your assistants and make sure you are all on the same page. Then, clearly communicate to your players the strategy you want them to use in the next 4 minutes. You should always know how many time-outs you have left and if anyone on your team or the opponent's team is in foul trouble. If your team gets a lead in overtime, using the clock is very important. If your team gets behind and needs to stop the clock (and get the ball back), you should know which player you want them to foul.

Postgame

Although postgame activities should follow a familiar routine, your management job is not over. The time immediately after the game offers the best opportunity to teach your team good sporting behavior. This task will not be difficult if you have instructed your players all season long about what makes good character: trustworthiness, respect, responsibility, fairness, and caring. Win or lose, you and the captains should thank the officials for their work. If the officials have not done an effective job, a simple thank-you without elaboration is all that is necessary. You can evaluate the officials later. Nothing positive ever comes from an angry postgame encounter.

After the final buzzer, players should line up to shake hands with the opposing team, and coaches should shake hands with the opposing coaches. Even after an emotional game, you should remain calm and say a kind word to the opposing coach, win or lose. If a problem occurred during the game, you can handle it later with a meeting.

Immediately after shaking hands, players should leave the floor and head to the locker room for a postgame meeting. Holding this meeting in the locker room helps avoid the distraction of fans or parents. Before meeting with the team, you and your staff should confer about what you will say about the game. A good rule is to keep all comments positive, even after a loss. You can address the negative points in the prepractice meeting the following day.

After the postgame talk, you should make plans for the treatment of any injury. If a player should be taken to a doctor for a checkup, you must inform the player's parents. If a trainer is on-site, injured players should report to the trainer or make an appointment to see the trainer before practice the next day. You should never play a player who is injured unless the player has been released by a trainer or doctor.

Only after all the preceding items are covered should you allow the media to talk to the players. Letting the media interview players before the completion of postgame rituals detracts from the team-first atmosphere that should prevail.

index

Note: The italicized *f* and *t* following page numbers refer to figures and tables, respectively.

about asep

Coaching Basketball Technical and Tactical Skills was written by the American Sport Education Program (ASEP) with the assistance of Kathy McGee, the winningest high school girls' basketball coach in the state of Michigan.

As the nation's leading sport education provider, ASEP works with national, state, and local sport organizations to develop educational programs for coaches, officials, administrators, and parents. These programs incorporate ASEP's philosophy of "athletes first, winning second."

ASEP has been developing and delivering coaching education courses and resources since 1981. *Coaching Basketball Technical and Tactical Skills* serves as a resource for the "Coaching Basketball Technical and Tactical Skills" online course, a part of ASEP's Bronze Level Professional Coaches Education Program.

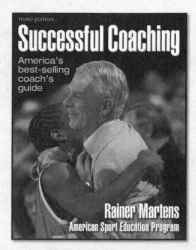 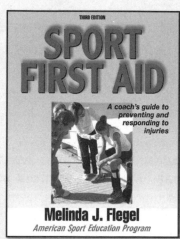 

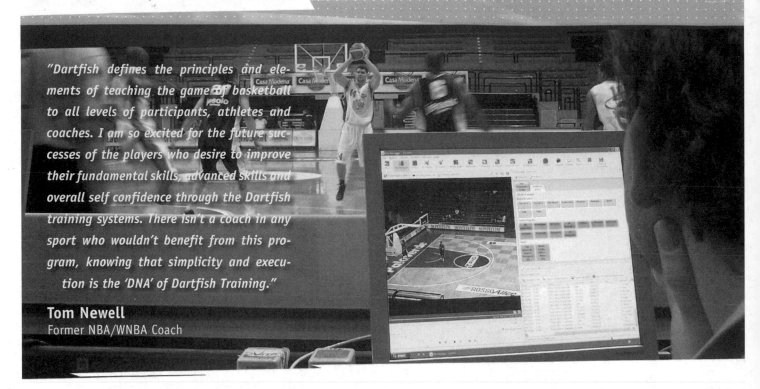